COOKING WITH JACK LIRIO

COOKING
WITH
JACK LIRIO

BY

JACK LIRIO

Photographs by Allan Rosenberg

WILLIAM MORROW AND COMPANY, INC. • NEW YORK
1982

Library of Congress Cataloging in Publication Data

Lirio, Jack.
  Cooking with Jack Lirio.

  Includes index.
  1. Cookery.   I. Title.
TX715.L763   .   641.5   81-22521
ISBN 0-688-00989-1   AACR2

Printed in the United States of America

First Edition

1 2 3 4 5 6 7 8 9 10

BOOK DESIGN BY HELENE BERINSKY

To Dorothy Alvord Lirio

PREFACE

Here is my book. I hope you will find it interesting, useful, and amusing. I have tried very hard to create some dishes that are a little bit different, but are honest, taste good, and look good. Note that taste is placed before looks, as it must be in cooking. Taste has to be the first concern of anyone interested in fine cuisine. If you are artistic, you can add another dimension to food by giving a little thought to the visual aspects of it. The consideration of colors and textures, neatness in presentation, little garnishes, serving dishes—all these things add excitement to food and make it even better than it would otherwise be.

This is a very special cookbook. Many books are written that contain 1,000 recipes with variations and choices galore. I have a number of such books, admire them greatly, and use them often for ideas and for reference. There is another kind of book, however, for which an author has tried 1,000 recipes, has selected some personal favorites, and then describes down to the last detail how to re-create those he loves so much. That is what I have done in this book.

ACKNOWLEDGMENTS

To three women who had a great deal to do with making this book what it is:

Maria Guarnaschelli, senior editor at Morrow, whose taste and judgment influenced every aspect of the work

Marjorie Ray Piper, my pre-editor, who cleaned up the prose, found mistakes and fixed them, and added some excellent information

Susan Lescher, the first person who had faith in the book and helped it on its way

Also, to some wonderful students and friends who helped me when I was getting started and who have supported me over the years: to Dolly, Lloyd, Darlene, Jackie, Barbara, Vera, Valentina, Lily, Mary, Marcie, Pat, Sally, Robin, Paige, Gere, Jane, Doris, Betty, Jane, Cal, Colleen, Carmella, Stanley, Jim, Jana, Carrole, Pat, Terry, Barbara, Ernie, Catherine, Bob, Loretta, Sergio, Karen, Phyllis, Debbie, Nancy, Eva, Hugh, Ethel, Jim, Audrey, Dee, Pat, Bette, Perry, Mark, Jim, Dick, Vivian, Libby, Mercedes, Nikta, Eileen, Mary, Marie, Joe, Gay, Kay, Monie, Fran, Mary Margaret, Marge, Ruth, Gordon, Chris, Stephene, Oona, Dagmar, Shirley, Marlene, Christina, Barbara, Leslie, Muffie, Gretchen, Betsy, Pat, Jean, Joanne, Donna, Clemmie, Nancy, Felice, Cathe, Fenja, Doris, Julie, Charles, Marinette, Kelly, Jan, Helene, Marian, Marion, Shirley, Belle, Martha, Jean, Charlotte, Lou, Dottie, Peggy, Gert, Sue, Pam, Diane, Alice, Berta, Theresa, Ruth, Ruby, Geri, Trish, Virginia, Tatwina, Sheryl, Karen, all the Presidio ladies, Heather, Lynette, Walter, Alice, Alice, Carolee, Florence, Bonita, Max, Paula, Naomi, Roz, Marilyn, Toni, Julie, Laurine, Norma, Jane, Susie, John, Sandy, Libby, Carolyn, Al, Allyse, Roseanne, Polly, Gene, Liz, Elaine, Shellagh, Bernice, Roy, Meckie, Flo, Martha O', Jerry, and to Bobby Little in memoriam; to all the above and to all the others whose names I would like to list,

I am deeply grateful,

Jack

Contents

COOKING WITH JACK LIRIO

SOME "DO" AND "DON'T DO" ADVICE, THOUGHTS, AND OBSERVATIONS

PREPARE AHEAD

When preparing meals for guests, get as much done as you possibly can days or weeks ahead. Most pastries and desserts can be made ahead at least to some stage. Many can be done completely ahead and frozen. In nearly every recipe I indicate what you can do and how far ahead you can do it. Start early and get the work done so that you can feel confident you and your guests will enjoy the dinner.

SHOPPING

Take the trouble to find the best-quality shops in your town or city, then do the shopping yourself. If you live in a larger city, investigate the food shops in the foreign sections. The food there is frequently fresher and more varied. Our Chinese section in San Francisco has an incredible variety of seafood, fresh-killed ducks, live chickens, frogs, turtles, and such. In another section where a pocket of people from Louisiana live, markets sometimes have barrels of wiggling crayfish. Ferret these places out and use them. Find your best produce market and your best butcher shop. Patronize them and get to know the people who work there. If you are friendly and nice, they may respond by helping you with information and advice.

CERTAIN FRESH VEGETABLES AND SEAFOOD SHOULD BE BOUGHT THE DAY OF THE DINNER

Some vegetables such as peas, corn, and string beans lose flavor, sweetness, and food value with the passing hours. They should be bought the day of the dinner. It's a lot easier to get all the shopping done the day before, but if you care, you will plan your time so that you have a minute to dash to the store for those few things that need to be bought at the last possible moment. As for seafood, find out when shipments arrive at your fish market and buy as close as possible to that time.

STICK TO THE SEASONS

Fruits and vegetables at the height of their seasons are wonderful and delicious and frequently cheaper than at any other time. In this book I have tried to indicate the proper seasons for the different foods, but in different areas of the country the time of availability can vary. Check with your produce seller. Take his advice and be flexible enough so that you can change your meal depending on what you find in the market. Occasionally you will find an exception to the rule of the seasons. Sometimes a good produce man will surprise you with something special. He may come up with good Florida strawberries in mid-December when the book says that May is the right month. You may find fresh sweet ears of corn from Mexico in mid-January when your book tells you that the summer months are the best for corn. Be ready to scrap your plans and switch to something really fine but out of season if it is good and *if* you can afford it.

PRE-DINNER DRINKING

Restrict drinking to one hour before serving at a dinner party. Serve whatever you like or whatever you think your guests might like. The nicest thing is to make up a pleasant, mild *apéritif* that everyone can drink and enjoy. There are many combinations of white wine, fruit liqueur, and soda that are very pleasant and will start the meal on a little more creative note than by simply having an open bar. You alone know whether you can get away with this or not. Try it. You might be surprised.

HEAT YOUR PLATES

It is a crime and the supreme negligence not to heat your plates when serving hot food. The plates don't have to be blisteringly hot, but at least the chill should be off them. There are devices you can buy to plug in that heat plates. Many dishwashers have plate-warming cycles. You can use your oven set to 170°F/77°C if it is not already occupied, or as a last resort, you can run the plates under hot water, then dry them well. I know, that's all you need, one more thing to do. But do it!

DON'T OVERSEASON

Fine French food is subtle in flavoring. It has been my experience that high-quality food preparations in the different cuisines of all the countries of mild climates have this in common. The foods are not heavy in herbs, spices, and seasonings. This "don't" is aimed particularly at people who oversalt. You must flavor and season enough, but please do not throw salt in by the handfuls and ruin the taste of good food.

USE A FOOD PROCESSOR

If you do not already own a food processor, I strongly suggest you buy one. For anyone interested in cooking the kinds of meals in this book, I believe that having one is a necessity. I don't mean to be hustling appliances, but this is truly one that I think you should have.

Many of the dishes in this book would be impossibly laborious without the food processor. More than half the recipes call for its use whether it be for vegetable purees, *mousselines*, doughs, cakes, sauces, or ices. Many recipes use it twice. In some cases, perhaps another machine such as a blender or ice cream maker or electric mixer or your own hands or a combination of these could do the job, but generally, using the processor will save you time and work. In many cases the finished product will be better.

Get one, please. It's one of the "unnecessary necessities" like Kleenex and Scotch tape. Once you get used to using a processor, you will wonder how you ever got along without one.

BE ADVENTUROUS WITH YOUR MENUS

Do things you haven't done before. Try different vegetables and different fish. Try *beurre blanc*, puff paste, and cakes without baking powder. With the many good cooking schools and good cookbooks around these days, you should be able to learn the techniques you need. As for the rest, all it takes is to learn how to rescue food that has met with disaster and occasionally, when even that fails, to learn how to deal with failure.

PRACTICE ON YOUR GUESTS

This is controversial, but I say do it. I always have and generally have gotten away with it. If you don't take a chance and try new foods with guests, you will probably never get around to making many dishes. For example, baking a large piece of salmon with a fish mousse in a pastry crust is a dish that could take five or six hours and a fair amount of money to do. Not many people will practice making this for a Monday night supper for two. If you don't schedule this type of dish for the first time at a major dinner, you will surely never do it.

If you can practice small versions or parts of things conveniently at midweek suppers, then do. But if not, take a chance with something new at a big dinner. Even if it doesn't look like the picture in the book, it will probably be edible and you may be the only one who knows it isn't just right.

LEARN TO KEEP YOUR MOUTH SHUT WHEN THINGS GO WRONG

I have trouble with this one. When things go wrong or don't go exactly as they are supposed to, smile and keep on eating. Don't talk about it. There is nothing worse than a cook sitting at the table and apologizing for perfectly good food just because some small or even medium-sized detail was not realized. You ruin your guests' enjoyment of the food. You make them feel stupid for liking the food. Don't do it.

DON'T UPSET PEOPLE'S STOMACHS

Many people have sensitive digestive tracts. I am one of them. It is very sad and disappointing to have a lovely meal at someone's home or at a really fine restaurant, then afterward to spend half the night wide awake burping, belching, and feeling generally miserable. If you know the rules and follow them, this will not happen after your meals. The main culprit is the overheating of fat. Heating fats at high temperatures changes them chemically into something unfit for human consumption. If you are going to sauté anything in butter, do not do it over high heat. Let the pan sing but not screech. And afterward, discard the old butter and use new to make your sauce. When you brown meats in very hot fat, drain off and discard the fat or skim it off later after you have added liquid.

Here's another good rule. When putting hot things in the refrigerator, do not cover them until they are completely chilled through. A cover permits food to retain heat, and a long period of warmth permits bacteria to grow faster than is safe.

Fish and shellfish can be trouble. Buy them at the last minute and make sure they are impeccably fresh.

BE ORGANIZED

I make a schedule and a countdown for every major meal I serve. Here is an example of a menu and the type of schedule that I would make for it.

THE MENU
Oysters on saffron bean threads
Roast filet of beef, minced mushroom sauce
Fresh chestnut puree
Cauliflower with watercress sauce
Lettuce salad, sauce vinaigrette
Spiced apple and pear cobbler

THE SCHEDULE
A week ahead
Buy bean threads and chestnuts (may be hard to find).
Order filet from butcher.
Two days ahead
Shop (except for last-minute things).
Make minced mushroom sauce.
Trim and tie roast.
The day before
Wash lettuce.
Make vinaigrette.
Make cobbler.
Make chestnut puree.
Make watercress sauce.
The day of the party
Final shopping (oysters, cauliflower, cilantro).
Clean house.
Prepare cauliflower.
Soak bean threads; prepare cooking liquid.

FINAL COUNTDOWN (Guests arrive at 7:30; sit down to eat at 8:30.)
5:00 Put white wine to chill.
6:00 Remove from refrigerator to come to room temperature: roast, vinaigrette, cobbler, lettuce, cauliflower.

7:00	If opening oysters yourself, do it now.
7:45	Preheat oven to 450° F/230° C.
8:00	Put beef in to roast.
8:20	Put water on for cauliflower.
	Prepare oyster dish.
8:30	Seat guests at table.
	Serve oysters.
	Remove roast and let rest; oven to 350° F/180° C for cobbler.
8:45	Cook cauliflower.
	Heat watercress sauce, chestnut puree, mushroom sauce.
8:50	Slice roast and assemble plates (get help).
	Serve main course.
9:10	Put cobbler in to heat.
9:15	Toss salad and serve.
9:30	Remove cobbler and let rest.
9:40	Serve cobbler.

Here's a final "don't" of a sort.

DON'T BE DISAPPOINTED IF YOU DON'T GET INVITED OUT TO DINNER VERY MUCH
If you enjoy cooking and work very hard to put out lovely meals, you may find that people do not invite you out to dinner very often. Unfortunately, for many people there is some kind of human competitive factor operating that releases them from any obligation to return your invitation because they are scared they can't cook as well. You must think of this as a reverse compliment. Relax, enjoy it, and take it as a tribute to your cooking. I am afraid that many of us who experience this tend to be picky, introverted snits who might not get invited out to dinners anyway.

A FINAL WORD
This is a good book. You will enjoy it. One of the best things about it is that the recipes work. They are carefully written and well tested. I have done them all many times, and others are variations of dishes I have been cooking and teaching for years. Teaching is my real concern and your success is what will make me happy. I have given you all the hints, clues, tricks, and pitfall warnings that I know. I wish you good luck with these foods and much success and happy cooking.

Jack Lirio

IMPORTANT CONDITIONS

ALL THE RECIPES IN THIS BOOK WILL SERVE 6 UNLESS OTHERWISE NOTED.

ALL THE EGGS CALLED FOR IN THE BOOK ARE U.S. GRADE A LARGE.

ALL THE BUTTER USED IN THE RECIPES SHOULD BE UNSALTED.

In dessert recipes, unsalted butter should always be used. In any other recipes, you may generally substitute salted butter, but if you do, be sure to reduce the amount of salt called for. If a preparation should call for a large amount of butter, a *beurre blanc*, for example, do not substitute salted butter or the dish will be oversalted and not fit to eat.

LITTLE
FIRST COURSES

Asparagus, Beurre Blanc, with Green Pineapple

Summer Squash with Sour Cherry Hollandaise

Oysters on Saffron Bean Threads

*Zucchini Alfredo

Green Onion Appetizer Cake

*Fried Squab Breasts and Legs
and
Fresh White Figs with Squab Livers

*Special quick dishes

I recall reading somewhere, once upon a time, that first courses are supposed to surprise and delight. If that is truly the case, then the dishes in this section are right on the mark. There is a surprise in every one of these little first courses, and each one of them, as far as taste and looks are concerned, is a delight. They are some of my favorite things in this book.

If you are used to serving American style—offering simply a main course, perhaps a side salad, and a dessert—try to break this nasty habit and start your dinners with small first courses. They are charming additions to meals and serve to make dining more varied and enjoyable. People love little first courses, which often become scene stealers, the most memorable moments of a meal. How often have I heard—after having worked very hard on an elaborate dinner including first course, main course, vegetables, salad, and at least one complicated dessert—the parting guests exclaim, almost in unison, "What a marvelous dinner. The meal was superb. Everything was delicious, but that asparagus with the *beurre blanc* was *fabulous!*"

ASPARAGUS, BEURRE BLANC, WITH GREEN PINEAPPLE

6 Servings

To food lovers, asparagus is spring. The first dinners in March and April are the exciting announcements of asparagus's return. This asparagus dish is a wonderful one, with the pineapple in the beurre blanc *as an intriguing surprise. I taught the preparation of this dish in fifteen cities in the spring of 1981, and it was incredibly well liked by everyone. What may strike you initially as a gimmick turns out to be completely delightful and delicious. This* beurre blanc *is every bit as exciting as the classic one, with a little extra something added that really works.*

Beurre blanc, or white butter sauce, is a relative newcomer among French sauces, dating back only one hundred years or so. For many years, conservative French cooking being what it was, one did not dare to serve it with anything except fish and, even then, only with certain fish. In the fifties and early sixties, it seemed almost the exclusive property of a woman named Mère Michelle, a hard-working, simple normande *who had a small restaurant in Paris near the Parc Monceau. People came from all over for Mère Michelle's* beurre blanc. *I don't know why it stayed virtually her property for so many years. The sauce, essentially flavored butter mysteriously suspended in a state between liquid and solid, is a sort of white wine–vinegar Hollandaise, without the egg yolk. It was adopted by the early* nouvelle cuisine *chefs and has become one of the basic sauces of that movement.*

The flavor tang in the traditional beurre blanc *comes from the combination of vinegar and white wine. Some of us have experimented with other acids in place of the wine, trying such things as tomatoes, lemons, tart apples, sour cherries, and even rhubarb. The pineapple* beurre blanc *is intriguing with its slight hint of sweetness. It is not as strange or as obvious as you might think. Most people, on tasting it without seeing the pineapple garnish, cannot identify the pineapple at all.*

Fresh asparagus, enough for six proper servings

1 pineapple, 2 to 3 lbs. (900 to 1350 grams)

1 lb. unsalted butter (450 grams)

4 Tbs. shallots or green onions

¼ cup white (or cider) vinegar (½ dL)

½ cup pineapple juice (1 dL)

¾ tsp. salt

2 Tbs. salt

THE ASPARAGUS Buy:

Fresh asparagus, enough for 6 proper servings
If there is a choice between fat or thin stalks, I would pick the thin; however, I have eaten large asparagus that has been perfectly tender and delicious, so you will have to make up your own mind. Peel the stalks or not, as you like. I suggest you cook one stalk, then eat it and decide. Trim the stalks into uniform lengths that will fit on the plates you have chosen for serving. Reserve and cook right before serving time. Save the odd stem ends to put into a salad the next day.

ON DOING THE BEURRE BLANC AHEAD If you have a Thermos (a wide-mouthed one is preferable, but not necessary), you can make the *beurre blanc* about 5 hours before it is to be eaten. Otherwise, it should be made at the last minute. While you are preparing the sauce, preheat the Thermos by filling it with water as hot as will come from the tap. If you are making only half this recipe, do not heat the Thermos this much or the sauce may melt.

THE PINEAPPLE Have:

1 pineapple, 2 to 3 lbs. (900 to 1350 grams), green as you can find, but a ripe pineapple will do

You need only enough pulp to get ½ cup (1dL) pineapple juice, which 1 pound (450 grams) of pineapple should produce with no trouble. Remove the top and bottom from the pineapple, then cut off the skin. Cut off about two-thirds of the pineapple from the top, or more acid area, reserving the bottom third to be used as a garnish. Chop the larger piece into chunks (coring is not necessary), then place the chunks in the bowl of a food processor fitted with the steel blade. Process 1 or 2 minutes or until well pulverized. Strain until you have ½ cup juice. Reserve this. Keep pulp and any extra juice for another use.

THE PINEAPPLE GARNISH Cut the reserved bottom third of the pineapple in half from top to bottom. One of these halves will be ample for the garnish, so set aside one-half for another use. Remove the core half of the piece that you are using, then slice the pineapple across into ⅛-inch (½-cm)-thick wedge shapes. Cut these wedges into smaller wedges so that you end up with pieces roughly 1 inch (2½ cm) long and measuring ⅛ inch at one end and about ¼ inch (¾ cm) at the other. Toss these pieces into a dry sauté pan and cook over high heat for 3 or 4 minutes, stirring occasionally, until the excess juices are evaporated and some slight browning just starts to take place. Remove and reserve until serving time.

THE BEURRE BLANC Use a large, heavy saucepan that is not of uncoated aluminum. I use a 4½-quart (4-L) size because the sauce tends to splash up on the sides of the pan, but a smaller one will do. Have ready:

> 1 lb. unsalted butter (450 grams), cut into
>   tablespoon-size pieces and chilled

Into the saucepan put:

> 4 Tbs. shallots or green onions, minced fine
> ¼ cup white (or cider) vinegar (½ dL)
> ½ cup pineapple juice (1 dL)
> ¾ tsp. salt

Cook over high heat until the liquid has reduced to about 2 tablespoons. *Be careful not to reduce this any further or the sauce will not work.* Reduce the heat to medium and right away add to the pan all the butter. Whisk it around in the pan. It will gradually soften, liquefy, and turn a very yellowish-white color, but it will not actually melt and turn oily yellow unless you overheat it. Keep whisking constantly and, as the pieces dissolve, check the temperature of the sauce by putting your finger in it. It should be the temperature of warm bathtub water. If it is too cold, increase the heat; if too hot, remove the pan from the heat for a while. When there are only five or six small, solid pieces of butter left, check the temperature again and, if it is still nice and warm, remove from the heat and whisk until completely smooth. Strain the sauce. (This is optional; you can leave the shallots in if you like, but I don't like.) Pour the hot water out of the Thermos, then pour the *beurre blanc* in. Cover with the lids and reserve until serving time.

TO SERVE Have warmed plates on which to serve the asparagus. If the plates are cold, the *beurre blanc* can congeal around the edges, and allowing that to happen would be very gauche. Have a large pot (8-quart size or larger) of boiling water. Add:

2 Tbs. salt

Add the asparagus and boil 5 or 6 minutes or until crisp/tender. Heat the reserved pineapple garnish until warm, but not too hot. Add it to the *beurre blanc*. Stir to mix. When done, drain the asparagus and then line up the individual portions on a cutting board, with all the stalks going in the same direction. Cut the pieces almost in half, keeping the tip sections a little longer. Place the stalk halves in neat rows or clumps on individual serving plates. Place the top halves on top at right angles. Give the sauce a final stir, then pour over the asparagus piles. Make sure at the end that each serving gets a fair amount of the pineapple garnish. Serve. Even dignified people lap up this sauce with spoons.

SUMMER SQUASH WITH SOUR CHERRY HOLLANDAISE

6 servings

I am not a particular fan of crookneck squash, but this squash combined with Bing cherries and a special Hollandaise sauce variation is so subtly exciting and refined that it has become one of my favorite dishes in this book.

Whole yellow squash are boiled, sliced thin, fanned open, and arranged in a puddle of peach-colored Hollandaise made tart with juice extracted from sour red cherries instead of the traditional lemon juice. Rows of fresh Bing cherries that have been sautéed briefly in butter with salt and pepper are placed on either side of the squash.

The result is very elegant, an appetizer guaranteed to evoke quizzical smiles from your guests followed by exclamations of delight. The best thing about the dish is that it tastes so good. Try it when fresh Bing cherries are in season, anywhere from late spring through the end of summer. You could, in a pinch, make this dish out of season (the "summer" squash is available these days almost all year long) by using canned cherries; however, they don't look as pretty; the texture is not as nice; and you lose points.

1 can (16 oz. or 450 grams) pitted sour red cherries packed in water

½ lb. butter (225 grams)

3 egg yolks

⅓ cup reduced cherry juice (¾ dL), previously prepared

½ tsp. salt

2 to 3 Tbs. sour cherry juice

6 small yellow crookneck squash (well shaped and of uniform size)

60 to 70 fresh, barely ripe Bing cherries

3 or 4 quarts water (2¾ or 3¾ L)

1 Tbs. salt

2 Tbs. butter

Salt and pepper

1 to 2 Tbs. boiling water

THE SOUR CHERRY JUICE I would love to make this with tart red cherries right off the tree, but I haven't seen any fresh "pie" cherries on a tree or in a market since I was a kid. Have:

> 1 can (16 oz. or 450 grams) pitted sour red cherries packed in water

Drain the cherries and discard the water (this is not the juice you use to make the sauce.) Place the cherries in a strainer and mash to extract the juice. You will get approximately ¾ cup juice (1¾ dL). Pour this in a saucepan, bring to a boil, and cook until reduced to about ½ cup (1 dL). Reserve.

ABOUT HOLLANDAISE SAUCE Making this sauce generally is considered to be a last-minute affair because it is sensitive to heat—too much makes it separate; reheating is difficult.

Thanks to a suggestion a student gave me years ago, I prepare Hollandaise 4 to 5 hours ahead and keep it warm in a wide-mouthed Thermos. The trick is to move along speedily as you make the sauce so it will be as hot as possible when you put it in the Thermos. Memorize the recipe so you can do it without hesitation. Have everything heated and don't let yourself be interrupted during those 5 to 10 minutes from the time you start cooking the egg yolks until the sauce is in the jug.

THE SAUCE Fill a wide-mouthed Thermos with water as hot as will come from the tap. Put a food processor bowl with the metal blade in place in the sink and fill with very hot water, to heat the bowl. Into a saucepan put:

> ½ lb. butter (225 grams)

Heat until melted, then allow to cool just a bit. Into a small, heavy saucepan (not uncoated aluminum or the sauce can turn gray) put:

> 3 egg yolks
> ⅓ cup reduced cherry juice (¾ dL), previously prepared
> ½ tsp. salt

Place over low heat, then whisk continuously until the sauce shows signs of thickening, about 2 to 4 minutes. It will get so frothy that you will hardly be able to see the thickening, but if you tilt the pan, you'll notice that the sauce is coating the bottom as steam rises all about. If you stick in your finger, the sauce will feel hot.

If anything seems to be going wrong, remove

the pan from the heat and beat the sauce vigorously. You will probably smooth it out. Be careful to stop the cooking just as the sauce begins to thicken or it can develop specks and flecks that may not dissolve.

Moving quickly, cover the saucepan to keep the sauce warm. Dump the hot water from the food processor container (don't bother to wipe it out) and set it up on the machine. Right away dump the frothy sauce into it. Check the temperature of the melted butter. It should still be hot, but not blisteringly so. Turn on the machine, then pour spoonfuls of butter down the feed tube, one after the other, at a fairly good clip. Add all the butter. Right away dump the hot water from the Thermos (do not wipe out) and scoop the sauce from the food processor into the hot Thermos. Quickly add as much of the remaining:

2 to 3 Tbs. sour cherry juice

As you like. I usually add all but the last tablespoon. Cover the Thermos. The sauce will stay warm 4 to 5 hours.

THE SQUASH Have:

6 small yellow crookneck squash (well shaped and of uniform size)

Ideally they should be about 5 inches (13 cm) long and 1½ inches (4 cm) in diameter at the fat part of the bulb. (If you can't find any that small, then use the nicest small ones available, cook a little longer, and trim down a little to fit on the plates.) Cut off the green stem tips and the hard little nubs on the fat ends. Refrigerate, but bring out to the room 1 or 2 hours before cooking.

THE BING CHERRIES Buy:

60 to 70 fresh Bing cherries, ripe but just barely

Up to a day ahead, remove the stems and pits. (You can buy cherry pitters that do this very fast and efficiently.) Refrigerate, but bring out to the room 1 or 2 hours before cooking.

TO COOK AND SERVE At serving time warm six 8-inch (20-cm) salad or dessert plates. Pour into a saucepan and bring to a boil:

3 or 4 quarts water (2¾ or 3¾ L)

Add:

1 Tbs. salt

Stir, add the squash, and cook for 6 to 7 minutes or until just barely tender when poked with a fork.

Drain. Into a saucepan over medium heat put:
    2 Tbs. butter
Melt, then add the pitted Bing cherries. Sauté for 1 minute, stirring or flipping now and then until the cherries are heated through and glistening. Sprinkle over:
    Salt and pepper
Give the Hollandaise a stir in the Thermos. If it seems too thick, you can add:
    1 to 2 Tbs. boiling water
Spoon 2 to 3 tablespoons of sauce in the center of each warmed plate. Cut the bulb part only of each squash into slices a scant ⅛ inch (½ cm) thick, without cutting all the way through. (That is, leave the squash in one piece, with the slices still attached at the skinny neck end.) Flatten each squash to fan the slices out, then put each in a puddle of sauce. Arrange five cherries in a row on each side of each squash at the edge of the plate. Serve while still warm.

OYSTERS ON SAFFRON BEAN THREADS

6 servings

This first-course dish is unusual, beautiful, and delicious. It begins with a bed of Chinese bean-thread noodles simmered in clam juice and saffron until they become transparent, golden strands. The bean threads are topped with slightly warmed oysters tossed briefly in lemon juice, salt, and pepper. The result is a lovely, refined dish. If you want to add even more class, you could make a rich fish broth to use instead of the bottled or canned clam juice the recipe calls for.

Dried bean threads, a Chinese product, are sold in clumps in cellophane packages (usually two, four, or six clumps wrapped in nets). They are so thin, they look like long coconut shreds or nylon fishing line. They are made of a paste of mung peas or beans (the same beans used for bean sprouts) and water. Although they have little or no flavor themselves, they absorb the flavors of the juices in which they are cooked and are a perfect garnish for soups or dishes with flavorful, thin sauces. They are also known as Chinese vermicelli, cellophane noodles, or glass noodles. A Chinese symbol of long life, they are traditionally eaten at birthdays.

8 oz. bean threads (230 grams)
½ tsp. saffron threads
¼ tsp. sugar

TO SOAK AND CUT BEAN THREADS Have:
    8 oz. bean threads (230 grams)
These are very tough and difficult to cut until they have been soaked. Place in a bowl and add cold

2 bottles or cans of clam juice (8 oz. or 225 grams each) or 2 cups good fish broth (½ L)

2 cups chicken broth (½ L) or water

24 medium to small oysters (about 2 inches or 5 cm long)

½ stick butter (2 oz. or 60 grams), cut into pieces, at room temperature

Salt and pepper

1 Tbs. lemon juice

6 to 12 lemon slices (optional)

A few leaves or branches of fresh cilantro (optional)

water to a depth of 2 or 3 inches (5 to 8 cm) above the bean threads. Let soak for 1½ to 2 hours. While they are soaking, avoid the temptation to swirl them around in the water; do not touch them at all. After they have softened and finished soaking, you are going to cut them, and if they stay more or less in their original bundle, it will be a lot easier to lay them on a board and cut them into three or four 8-inch (20-cm) clumps than if they are all mixed up and tangled. Place softened, cut bean threads in a bowl. Cover with plastic, then refrigerate until serving time. This can be done a day ahead.

TO PREPARE THE COOKING LIQUID If you have a small mortar and pestle, use them. If not, place into a cup:

> ½ tsp. saffron threads
> ¼ tsp. sugar

Using the handle of a wooden spoon or anything you can crush with, press down and work the saffron and sugar together until the saffron is ground to a powder. The sugar is used just for its abrasive qualities. Into a saucepan put:

> 2 bottles or cans clam juice (8 oz. or 225 grams each) or 2 cups good fish broth (½ L)
> 2 cups chicken stock (½ L) or water

I use a brand called Doxsee, which comes from Baltimore, Maryland. It is very pleasant and mild, so I use it undiluted. Make sure to taste the clam broth you are using. If it is very strong and salty, you may prefer to thin it with a little water.

Bring the clam juice to a boil with the chicken stock. Add the saffron-sugar mixture and stir well. Let the mixture cool, refrigerate uncovered until chilled, then cover. This can be done a day ahead. If doing this just before using, let the saffron steep in clam juice for 5 minutes before proceeding with the recipe.

THE OYSTERS Buy:

> 24 medium to small oysters (about 2 inches or 5 cm long)

Ideally, you would buy live ones in the shell and get someone at home to open them just before serving. If that is impractical, have the oyster man open them for you, giving you the oysters plus the juices but discarding the shells, which are not needed for this dish. I serve this dish on 8-inch (20-cm) salad plates with 5-inch (13-cm) beds of noodles in the center of each. If possible, select oysters of a size so that three or four of them will fit nicely on the beds of noodles. If you have no choice and the oysters available are big, use larger plates, but you may need to double the recipe for the bean threads.

TO COOK THE NOODLES AND ASSEMBLE THE DISH
Five minutes before serving, bring the saffron clam broth to a boil. Add the softened, cut bean threads. Reurn to the boil. Cover, then remove from heat. Let sit for 1 or 2 minutes. Add:

> ½ stick butter (2 oz. or 60 grams), cut into pieces, at room temperature

Mix in, using a fork and lifting up the noodles.
Taste for seasoning and, if necessary, add:

> Salt

Place the oysters and their juices in a saucepan. Cover and heat, stirring occasionally until they are just nicely warmed, but do not heat them too much or cook them too long—they can toughen. Add to the oysters:

> 1 Tbs. lemon juice (or more to taste)
> Salt and pepper

Arrange beds of bean threads in the centers of six serving plates. Fish out the oysters and place three or four on top of each thread bed. You could place on each plate:

> 1 or 2 attractive, thin slices of lemon (optional)
> A few leaves or branches of fresh cilantro (coriander) (optional)

Serve.

ZUCCHINI ALFREDO

6 servings

This is a variation on the great pasta dish Fettucine Alfredo. Long, very thin strips of zucchini take the place of the pasta. They are cooked briefly just as you would cook spaghetti, then sauced in the Alfredo manner, which is with Parmesan cheese, heavy cream, and butter.

Everything is simple and easy to do. The only time-consuming part is cutting the zucchini. But you should be able to slice all of it in 10 to 15 minutes if you have a good device for making thin slices, as well as a long, sharp knife.

2 lbs. zucchini (900 grams)
4 oz. grated Parmesan cheese (about 1¼ cups or 115 grams)
½ cup whipping cream (1 dL)
Pepper
Nutmeg (easy!)
2 oz. grated Parmesan cheese (about ⅔ cup or 60 grams)
1 stick butter (4 oz. or 115 grams) at room temperature
1 Tbs. salt

THE ZUCCHINI Buy:

2 lbs. zucchini (900 grams)

I pick the smaller ones, about six to the pound, but longer ones might be fun—your "pasta" can be longer. Cut both ends off each zucchini. You need some kind of slicer for the next step. A food processor will not do. A mandoline would be perfect or an inexpensive small tool called a Feemster. If your Feemster is new, attack the job with gloves on because these tools also are great for slicing thumbs and fingers.

With whatever tool you select, slice the zucchini *lengthwise* in ⅛-inch (½-cm) or less slices. Stack four slices at a time and with a long-bladed knife cut the stack into long, spaghetti-like strands a little less than ⅛ inch (½ cm) wide.

Cover with plastic and refrigerate. Bring out to the room and uncover 1 or 2 hours before cooking.

THE SAUCE: If you have a cheese grater, buy a chunk of cheese and grate your own. If you're really rushed, buy cheese already grated, but be warned that you lose a frightful number of points for doing so. You need:

4 oz. grated Parmesan cheese (about 1¼ cups or 115 grams)

Place in a saucepan along with:

½ cup whipping cream (1 dL)
Pepper
Nutmeg (easy!)

Bring to a boil and cook, whisking all the time, for about 1 minute or just until cheese melts and the mixture combines into a sauce. Set aside until serving time.

TO COOK AND SERVE Put on the table for passing around:

2 oz. grated Parmesan cheese (about ⅔ cup or 60 grams)

For the cooking, have ready:

1 stick butter (4 oz. or 115 grams) at room temperature

Heat six plates; 8-inch (20-cm) salad plates are a good size. Put a colander in the sink for draining the zucchini.

Right before serving, bring 8 to 10 quarts (liters) water to a boil in a large pot. Add:

1 Tbs. salt

While the water is heating, put the sauce in a 10-inch (25-cm) sauté pan or whatever is large enough to hold the zucchini after it is cooked. Heat the sauce to bubbling, but remove from the heat while you cook the vegetable. When the water is bubbling vigorously, stir to dissolve the salt and toss in the zucchini in two or three additions. Allow 5 to 10 seconds between additions so the water does not cool off too much. Start timing as soon as all the zucchini is in. Cook for 2 minutes (or slightly less or more), just until barely crisp/tender. Do not overcook.

Dump right away into the colander. Shake and stir a bit to get rid of excess water. Drain for a few seconds while you finish the sauce.

Return the sauce to a boil, then remove from the heat. Add a stick of room-temperature butter and whisk in well. Then add the hot, drained zucchini, stirring to coat the strands with the sauce. Quickly spoon onto the warmed serving plates. Rush to the table and pass around the extra cheese for sprinkling on.

GREEN ONION APPETIZER CAKE

8 servings

Are you ready for an adventure? This first-course dish is quite literally a green onion cake, excitingly delicious and not quite like anything else. If you have friends you would like to impress, perhaps the tired and jaded kind who think they have tried everything in the world there is to eat, this is just the dish to delight them.

This Green Onion Cake is an egg concoction that is related to a soufflé and to a souffléed omelet but is neither. It contains just enough flour to make it a cake, a very, very light and nonsweet cake that somewhat resembles an angel food in texture. I was amazed that the recipe worked, and so well at that. Green onion and salt are the only flavors and all the cake needs.

The presentation transforms this cake into a first-course appetizer. The cake is heated and sliced; then the slices are dipped into melted butter and laid on plates in a small puddle of chicken broth. This is a fascinating dish.

**2 bunches green
  onions (scallions)**
**8 eggs still in their
  shells**
**1½ cups sifted cake
  flour (150 grams)**
**¼ cup plus 2 Tbs.
  warm water (¾ dL)**
1 Tbs. sugar
2½ tsp. salt
**1 stick butter (4 oz. or
  115 grams), melted
  and warm**
**1 cup chicken broth or
  other good broth,
  heated**

THE GREEN ONIONS Buy:
   2 bunches green onions (scallions)
Wash, trim off the hairy roots, and slice across into rounds ¹⁄₁₆ inch (¼ cm) thick or slightly wider. Slice the white part, the pale green part, and as much of the deep green part as needed to produce a total of 1 cup (¼ L) sliced onion. Reserve.

THE CAKE Preheat the oven to 350°F/180°C and arrange a shelf so the cake will bake in the center of the oven. Use a removable-bottom 10-inch (25-cm) pan with a center tube (angel-food pan). Do not butter. *This is important.* The cake must be hung upside down as it cools and must stick to the tin, not fall out. Select a bottle to insert in the top of the center tube to hold the tin up and upside down for this cooling process. Some people use a Coke bottle, but I prefer a Grand Marnier bottle. I think the difference tells.

   In a bowl place:
   8 eggs still in their shells
Presumably these are cold, right from the refrigerator. Cover with water as hot as it will come from the tap and let sit for 5 minutes. Warm another bowl by filling with hot water. Measure:
   1½ cups sifted cake flour (150 grams)
Put the flour back into the sifter and set aside. Separate the eggs, placing the whites in one dry warmed bowl and the yolks in another. Add to the yolks:
   ¼ cup plus 2 Tbs. warm water (¾ dL)
   1 Tbs. sugar
   2½ tsp. salt
Beat at high speed with an electric mixer for 2 to 3 minutes or until the mixture dropping from raised beaters forms a ribbon. Move along quickly once the yolks have been beaten and don't let yourself be interrupted. Have the yolks, green onions (at room temperature), flour, and egg whites on the counter in front of you. Also have a large spatula for folding and a large wire whisk.

   Using clean beaters, beat the whites with an electric mixer until they fill the bowl with white foam and are approaching the soft-peak stage. This will not take very long (a minute or so). The whites should still be runny.

Quickly fold the green onions into the yolk mixture. Sift one-third of the flour over the yolks. Give the whites a 2-second beating with the whisk, then dump one-third of them over the flour. Fold quickly.

Using the wire whisk, beat the whites for 4 or 5 seconds, just to get them smooth again and perhaps to get them just a tad stiffer. Add half the remaining flour to the yolks and half the remaining whites. Fold quickly.

Sift over the last of the flour. Give the whites another 4- or 5-second beat with the whisk to get them smooth again. By now they should be almost stiff peaks, but *not overbeaten*. (If you should accidentally overbeat and the whites get a speckled, curdly look, quickly add a new egg white. Beat it in for just 2 or 3 seconds, then proceed with the recipe.) Dump on the last of the whites, then fold. Pour the batter in an even layer into the angel-food pan.

TO BAKE AND COOL Bake the cake in a preheated 350°F/180°C oven for 25 to 30 minutes or until the top is lightly browned and a cake tester inserted in the center of the cake is clean when removed.

"Hang" the cake to cool by poking the neck of the bottle you have selected into the *top* of the pan's tube. Invert the pan and bottle, and let the cake cool while hanging on the bottle for 1 hour or longer.

The cake is *very delicate*. Do not handle at all until it is completely cool and be careful even then. If doing this a day ahead, refrigerate the cake in the tin.

TO HEAT AND SERVE Several hours ahead of serving, run a knife all around the edge of the chilled cake to free it. Gently push out the removable bottom while using the knife to free the cake from the center tube and from the bottom part of the tin. Leave the cake on the tin's removable bottom.

Wrap the whole thing carefully in foil, tucking the foil in the top hole of the center tube and not letting the foil touch the top of the cake if possible.

About 30 minutes before serving, place the cake still wrapped in the foil in a preheated 350°F/180°C oven. Heat for 25 to 30 minutes or until warmed through. At the last minute, heat eight 8-inch (20-cm) salad plates. Also have ready:

> 1 stick butter (4 oz. or 115 grams), melted and warm
>
> 1 cup chicken broth or other good broth, heated

Cut the cake into eight wedges. Do this neatly with a serrated knife or an angel-food-cake cutter. Pour 2 tablespoons hot broth on each serving plate. Dip both cut sides of each cake wedge into the melted butter, then place in the broth on the plate. Serve at once.

FRIED SQUAB BREASTS AND LEGS

6 servings

This is an elegant, delightful appetizer. The breast meat is lifted off the bone on each side of a squab with the thighs and legs attached to make two nice, compact little packages. The squab is salted, lightly floured, and fried in oil just long enough to turn crispy and brown outside but remain slightly pink inside. It is a lovely, succulent morsel.

Two or three small, fresh white figs heated in stock, then tossed in butter with the chopped livers, make an unusual and attractive accompaniment. If you can't find fresh figs, white grapes are very nice.

If you can afford and find it, squab is more elegant and more exciting, but Cornish game hen makes an excellent alternative.

---

3 squabs or Cornish game hens, 12 oz. (340 grams) each (or heavier)
Corn oil (or other oil), ¼ inch (¾ cm) deep
Milk or water
Salt and pepper
Flour

THE BIRDS Have:

> 3 squabs or Cornish game hens, 12 oz. (340 grams) each (or heavier)

Leave the skin on. Using a sharp knife, carefully bone the breast meat from each side of the bird, bringing with it the thigh and leg still attached. You will get two servings from each. This procedure may sound tricky, but it's not. You will find it easy. The birds can be prepared a day ahead. Keep on a plate in the refrigerator, covered with a damp paper towel. Do not wrap airtight or they can spoil.

TO COOK AND SERVE Fry the squabs just before serving. Select a frying pan that the six pieces will fit into without a lot of extra space (this avoids smoking, burning fat). Pour in:

Corn oil (or other oil), ¼ inch (¾ cm) deep
Heat the oil, not blisteringly hot but as if you were frying chicken. Moisten the squab pieces with:

Milk or water
Sprinkle with:

Salt
Then dip in:

Flour
to coat both sides. Shake off excess flour. Place the pieces in the hot oil, skin side down. Let cook gently (the fat should bubble and sizzle, but not too wildly) for 4 minutes, then turn the pieces over and cook 3 minutes on the second side. Drain briefly on paper towels. Serve with:

Salt and pepper
on the side. Accompany with Fresh White Figs with Squab Livers, the recipe for which follows.

FRESH WHITE FIGS WITH SQUAB LIVERS

6 servings

If you can't find good, sweet-tasting figs for this recipe (look for them in summer, particularly in late summer), then substitute black figs or white grapes. For some reason fresh figs are rarely good in this country. If you've ever had figs in France or Italy, you are ruined forever for enjoying the bland, tasteless ones you generally get here. I haven't given up, though. Once in a while you find good ones. Look for a very ripe, oozy look and you'll have a better chance.

If you decide to use white grapes instead of figs, buy those that look slightly yellow rather than bright green.

---

12 to 18 fresh white figs

3 livers from the 3 birds

Chicken stock, enough to cover the figs to be added

3 Tbs. butter

Salt and pepper

TO PREPARE THE FIGS Buy:

12 to 18 fresh white figs
Cut off the stems. If the figs are too large, you might want to cut them in half. At serving time, have them at room temperature. I am assuming that you will have:

3 livers from the 3 birds
If the market didn't give you the livers, substitute chicken livers or do without the liver.

TO SERVE Chop the livers very fine. In a saucepan bring to a boil:

> Chicken stock, enough to cover the figs to be added

Add the figs and simmer briefly, just enough to heat through. In a sauté pan melt:

> 3 Tbs. butter

Add the livers to the butter in the sauté pan. Right away drain the figs and also add to the pan. Cook, stirring to coat the figs with butter and to finish the livers—they cook almost instantly and should not be overcooked. Sprinkle over:

> Salt and pepper

Serve with the fried birds.

TO PREPARE GRAPES AS AN ALTERNATE Omit heating the grapes in the chicken stock as you do the figs, but just toss briefly in butter with the chopped livers long enough to warm them. Sprinkle with salt and serve. Don't overcook the grapes or they start to look just like those terrible canned ones. For an extra touch, let them sit in brandy beforehand for an hour or two, turning occasionally (¼ cup or ½ dL brandy for 1 pound or 450 grams grapes).

FIRST-COURSE SALADS

Eggplant Cubes with Chopped Tomatoes and Chives

Mixed Greens with Red Bell
Peppers and Toasted Hazelnuts

Shredded Lettuce Salad with Shrimp and Squid

Wilted Lettuce Salad with Shad Roe

Wilted Lettuce Salad with Snails and Mushroom Caps

Here are some more lovely first courses, but in the salad department. They also follow the theme of surprise and delight, the same as the first courses in the previous section, and they are equally nice.

If you have heard that the French always serve their salads following the main course and that first-course salads are strictly something invented by Californians, you are partly right. Be advised, however, that the type of salad that follows the main course in France is always, well almost always, a salad made up exclusively of lettuce. As soon as you add other things, it becomes a composed salad and traditionally must be served earlier in the meal.

To carry all this one step further, the old tradition in France dictated that a first-course salad (*crudités*, for example) be served only at the mid-day meal. Evening meals were smaller and always started with soup. The old traditions are dying quickly, however. The rules were beginning to change even before the *nouvelle cuisine* movement hit, but that certainly speeded up the process and now threatens to all but obliterate the old cooking. The new freedom to create and combine is energizing and exhilarating, but I hope that the good old dishes, many of which are so suddenly and hopelessly out of fashion, do not disappear altogether or become museum pieces.

The five salads in this section precede very well almost any main course you can think of. You might try to avoid following the seafood salads with seafood main courses unless you are deliberately having an all-seafood dinner.

EGGPLANT CUBES
WITH CHOPPED TOMATOES AND CHIVES

6 servings

Here is a lovely appetizer salad. Large cubes of unpeeled eggplant are boiled just until green and barely tender, then cooled. The cubes are arranged on lettuce leaves and dressed with a vinaigrette sauce. At the last minute, chopped tomato and chives mixed with some vinaigrette are spooned over the eggplant, making a very colorful and attractive dish. You will be happy to know that all the ingredients can be prepared a day ahead and combined at the last minute.

1¼ to 1½ lbs. eggplant (565 to 675 grams)
4 quarts water (3¾ L)
2 to 3 tsp. salt
¼ cup good red or white wine vinegar (½ dL)

THE EGGPLANT Buy:
   1¼ to 1½ lbs. eggplant (565 to 675 grams)
Choose eggplants that are dark and shiny, with a nice green stem. I pick the smaller ones because they have fewer and smaller seeds. Peel if you like, but I don't. Cut into 1-inch (2½-cm) cubes. In a

½ tsp. salt
Pepper
¾ cup oil—olive, corn,
    or whatever you like
    (1¾ dL)
1 tsp. Dijon mustard
2 tomatoes
1 small bunch chives
    (or green parts of
    green onions)
6 large or 12 small
    attractive lettuce
    leaves (butter lettuce
    preferred)

large saucepan boil at least:
    4 quarts water (3¾ L)
    2 to 3 tsp. salt
Stir; add the eggplant. Push the cubes down into
the water (they float) and stir around a bit. Cover
the pot. Cook over high heat until the water
returns to a boil, then adjust the heat so the water
continues to boil not too violently. Exactly how
long the cubes should cook seems to depend on the
ripeness of the eggplants, but it won't be long.
After the cubes have been in the water for 3
minutes, I start testing by poking with a fork.
Sometimes they are done in 4½ minutes, but other
times they have needed 6 minutes. It is *critical* for
the appearance of the dish and also for the texture
and flavor that you do not overcook the cubes to
where they lose their shapes and green color or
become wilted and tired. As soon as they are
tender, drain and refresh right away in cold water.
Drain again and spread on a plate to finish cooling.
Refrigerate. Allow to come to room temperature
before serving.

SAUCE VINAIGRETTE Into a mixing bowl or jar put:
    ¼ cup good red or white wine vinegar (½ dL)
    ½ tsp. salt
    Pepper
Whisk well to dissolve the salt. Add:
    ¾ cup oil—olive, corn, or whatever you like
        (1¾ dL)
    1 tsp. Dijon mustard
Whisk or shake the dressing before using.
THE TOMATOES AND CHIVES Have:
    2 tomatoes
Find nice ones that are good and red, with some
flavor. Peel (you can blanch for 10 seconds in
boiling water to speed this along if you like). Cut in
half and squeeze each half, flicking out any juice
and seeds. Chop the pulp into ⅛-inch (½-cm)
pieces. You need 6 tablespoons chopped pulp (a
rounded ⅓ cup or ¾ dL); if you have more, use for
another dish—there's no use overdoing the tomato.
Reserve until serving time.
Also have:
1 small bunch chives (or green parts of green
    onions)

Strip into ⅛-inch (½-cm) pieces or smaller with scissors or cut with a knife. You need 3 to 4 tablespoons. Wrap well in plastic and reserve until serving time. (If you use green onion tops, they will smell awful after a while, but don't worry. They taste fine.)

THE LETTUCE Have:

> 6 attractive large lettuce leaves or 12 smaller
> ones (butter lettuce preferred)

Wash and dry. Keep in a plastic bag in the refrigerator until serving time.

TO ASSEMBLE AND SERVE Add just enough of the vinaigrette to the eggplant cubes to coat well, then stir carefully. Taste and add more salt or pepper or vinegar or Dijon mustard or all of them. Frankly, my taste runs to light and mild, but usually I add more salt and vinegar. Place the lettuce leaves on six 8-inch (20-cm) salad plates, then spoon the eggplant cubes in a mound in the center of each. Arrange the cubes so that most are skin side down. Mix the tomatoes and chives, then stir in ⅓ cup (¾ dL) vinaigrette. Spoon over the eggplant cubes, spreading it out to cover them attractively. Serve at room temperature.

Note: If you don't mind last-minute work, you can boil the eggplant shortly before serving and present this salad warm.

MIXED GREENS WITH RED BELL PEPPERS AND TOASTED HAZELNUTS

6 servings

The mixed greens of this salad set off the brilliant red of the peppers beautifully. The flavor and crunch of the toasted hazelnuts make the salad more festive, very special indeed.

Red bell peppers are available in most parts of the country in August and September, sometimes before and beyond. They simply are green bell peppers that have been allowed to ripen. They have a sweetness and a gentleness of flavor that make them far preferable to the green ones, in my opinion.

There seems to be some confusion between the names hazelnut and filbert. They are essentially the same nut, as I understand it, although filberts are European and hazelnuts are American and there is supposedly a subtle difference in their flavors. You may use either nut for this dish.

4 oz. hazelnuts or
  filberts (115 grams or
  about 1 cup)
¼ cup good vinegar
  (½ dL)
1 tsp. salt
Pepper
¾ cup oil—preferably
  a flavorless one
  (1¾ dL)
3 large red bell
  peppers (about 1 lb.
  or 450 grams)
3 quarts water (2¾ L)
2 to 3 tsp. salt
1 bunch spinach and/
  or watercress
1 head chicory and/or
  lettuce (oak leaf—
  also called
  Australian or salad
  bowl—butter,
  Boston, red leaf, or
  iceberg)

THE TOASTED NUTS Have:
  4 oz. hazelnuts or filberts (115 grams or about 1
    cup)
Spread on a baking sheet and toast in a preheated
350°F/180°C oven for 15 minutes or until the skins
are dark brown and the meat of the nuts is pale
brown. Wrap in a towel and allow to cool. Rub off
and discard the skins. Process the nuts in a food
processor until ground fairly fine. Reserve.

I suppose it is preferable to do this grinding in a
proper nut grinder, which gives nice, powdery bits.
But the oily, moist, minced type of grind that you
get from the processor works just fine in this salad.

THE DRESSING Into a bowl or jar put:
  ¼ cup vinegar (½ dL)—the better the vinegar,
    the better
  1 tsp. salt
  Pepper
Whisk or shake until the salt is dissolved. Add:
  ¾ cup oil (1¾ dL)—any will do, but I like a
    flavorless one for this
  All but 6 Tbs. ground hazelnuts
  (The 6 tablespoons will be sprinkled over the
    salads at the end.)
  ¼ cup water
Water? In a salad dressing? Horrors! Choke, gasp,
sputter! Why bother to dry off the lettuce leaves?
The purpose of the water is to lighten the dressing
after the nuts are added. The dressing is thinned so
it doesn't coat the leaves so heavily. (If you don't
dry the leaves of the greens after washing them,
then you can leave the water out of the dressing.) If
it makes you feel any better, you can add chicken
stock, white wine, orange juice, or red Kool-Aid
instead of that awful water.

Shake or whisk the dressing well before using.

THE PEPPERS Remove the stems and seeds from:
  3 large red bell peppers (about 1 lb. or 450
    grams)
Cut into 1-inch (2½-cm) squares. In a pot boil:
  3 quarts water (2¾ L)
  Add:
  2 to 3 tsp. salt
Add the peppers. Cook at a medium boil for 4
minutes. Drain, then refresh in cold water for a few
seconds to stop the cooking. Drain again and

spread out to finish cooling. Refrigerate until serving time.

THE LETTUCE AND OTHER GREENS Buy one head each of three or four different greens. Choose from iceberg, butter or Boston, red leaf, oak leaf, or any other kind of lettuce. Other greens may be romaine, escarole, chicory, spinach, or watercress. The last time I made this salad I used:

> 1 bunch spinach (tender and young, with short stems)
> 1 head chicory
> 1 head oak leaf lettuce (also called Australian or salad bowl)
> 1 bunch watercress

Wash all and tear (or cut if you are not doing this too far ahead) into attractive bite-size pieces. Try to use more or less equal amounts of each green and stop when you have enough for six people. In preparing watercress, use only the top leafy part of each branch; discard the lower, thicker branch sections. Dry the greens or not (see discussion about water in salad dressing recipe above). Refrigerate until serving time.

If you prefer your salads not too chilled, remove from the refrigerator ½ hour ahead to let come to room temperature.

TO SERVE At serving time, place the mixed greens in a big bowl and the red pepper squares in another bowl. Shake or whisk the hazelnut dressing, then pour enough over the lettuce and also over the peppers to coat each well, but no more. Toss the lettuce a long time, then put onto serving plates. Toss the pepper squares well and spoon over the greens. Over the salads sprinkle the 6 tablespoons of reserved ground hazelnuts. Serve.

SHREDDED LETTUCE SALAD WITH SHRIMP AND SQUID

6 servings

Here is a delightful salad that could start almost any meal. Shrimp, squid, mushrooms, celery, green peppers, green onions, and parsley are tossed in an olive oil vinaigrette and served on shredded lettuce. This salad also would serve nicely as a main course for a luncheon.

1 lb. (about 40 medium-size) uncooked shrimp in the shell (450 grams)
6 cups water (1½ L)
¼ cup vinegar (½ dL)
½ tsp. salt
1½ lbs. squid (675 grams)
½ lb. mushrooms (225 grams)
2 Tbs. dry white wine
¼ tsp. salt
Pepper
1 medium stalk celery
½ medium red or green bell pepper
4 Tbs. sliced green onions
4 Tbs. chopped parsley
¼ cup vinegar (½ dL)
1 tsp. salt
Pepper
1 tsp. Dijon mustard
¾ cup olive oil (1¾ dL)—or any oil
1 head iceberg lettuce, approximately 1 lb. (450 grams)—or any lettuce
1 Tbs. vinegar
1 tsp. Dijon mustard
¼ tsp. salt
Pepper

THE SHRIMP Buy:
   1 lb. uncooked shrimp in the shell (450 grams), about 40 medium-size
Shell and devein. You will end with about 13 ounces (370 grams) of shrimp meat. If you have some fish stock in the freezer, use it. If not, into a saucepan put:
   6 cups water (1½ dL)
   ¼ cup vinegar (½ dL)
   ½ tsp. salt
Bring to a boil. Add the shrimp. Stir well. Keep the pan over medium heat and cook without boiling about 2 minutes. If the water shows the slightest signs of a boil, remove from the heat. Skim out the shrimp with a slotted spoon (save the liquid to cook the squid). Spread on a plate to cool. Cut each in half, butterfly fashion, so that the pieces retain the same shrimp shape.
   Unless you buy them frozen, I recommend buying the shrimp and the squid the day they are going to be eaten. They spoil too quickly to risk keeping them longer than that.
THE SQUID Buy:
   1½ lbs. squid (675 grams)
You will have about 10 oz. or 285 grams after cleaning. If your guests are going to be all giggly about squid, you could cut back to just a pound (450 grams). First clean the squid by poking your finger into the body case and turning and scraping with your finger to detach the intestines and center matter from the case. Grab the tentacles and pull, trying to pull out the intestines. Cut off the tentacles with a knife just where they meet the eyes. Use the tentacles and cases, but throw away the rest.
   Finish cleaning by pulling the two rudder fins

from the body case and at the same time pull off the thin, speckled membrane from the case, leaving it all shiny and white. Remove the clear, plastic-like quill or backbone from the inside of the case. If there is anything left inside the case, scrape with the back of a knife and force it out. Cut the body across into rings about ½ inch (1½ cm) wide.

TO COOK THE SQUID Cook exactly as you did the shrimp. Using the same liquid, return it to a boil, then add the squid (body rings and tentacles). Stir, then cook for 2 minutes over medium heat. Remove from the heat if the water shows signs of starting to boil. Fish out the squid with a slotted spoon (save the cooking liquid). Refrigerate uncovered until thoroughly chilled, then wrap.

THE MUSHROOMS Have:

　　½ lb. mushrooms (225 grams)

Rinse in three waters, putting them quickly in and out so that they soak up as little as possible; dry. Place in a saucepan that accommodates them in one layer. Sprinkle over:

　　2 Tbs. dry white wine
　　¼ tsp. salt
　　Pepper

Cover, then simmer for 2 to 3 minutes or until barely tender. Cool and cut into a ½-inch (1½-cm) dice. Reserve.

THE CELERY AND GREEN PEPPER Have:

　　½ cup celery (½ dL), cut into ⅜-inch (1-cm)
　　　　dice (1 medium stalk)
　　½ cup green or red bell pepper (1 dL), cut into
　　　　½-inch (1½-cm) dice (½ medium pepper)

Bring the shrimp-squid cooking liquid to a boil. Add the celery and pepper and cook exactly 2 minutes. Strain, saving the broth, then plunge the celery and pepper quickly into cold water for 5 seconds. Drain, spread on a plate, and chill. Cover when cold. This can be done a day ahead. The broth can be used as a soup or sauce base, or you can freeze it for poaching fish or shellfish another day.

THE GREEN ONION AND PARSLEY Prepare:

　　4 Tbs. green onion sliced thin crosswise (about
　　　　½ bunch); use 4-inch (10-cm) sections of
　　　　white and pale green
　　4 Tbs. chopped parsley

Both can be prepared a day ahead, wrapped in

plastic, and refrigerated.

SAUCE VINAIGRETTE Into a bowl or jar put:

 ¼ cup vinegar (½ dL)

 1 tsp. salt

 Pepper

 1 tsp. Dijon mustard

Whisk or shake well to dissolve the salt. Add:

 ¾ cup olive oil (1¾ dL)—or any oil

Whisk or shake well before using.

THE LETTUCE You can prepare the lettuce 4 to 5 hours before eating. Have:

 1 head iceberg lettuce, approximately 1 lb.

 (450 grams)—or any lettuce

Remove the outer leaves. I do not wash iceberg lettuce because it never seems to be sandy or buggy. I understand that the outside leaves grow first and the inner leaves grow from the inside, and therefore even if the lettuce were sprayed, the inner leaves would not be affected. Remove the white core, then slice the lettuce into ⅛-inch (½-cm) slivers across the head. Put in a bowl. Refrigerate.

TO ASSEMBLE AND SERVE Several hours before eating, assemble the shrimp-squid salad. Put everything except the lettuce and dressing in a bowl: shrimp, squid, mushrooms, celery, green pepper, green onions, and parsley. Mix well and return to the refrigerator. Bring out 1 hour before serving so the mixture will not be too cold.

When ready to serve, whisk or shake the vinaigrette sauce. Pour onto the shredded lettuce to coat well, but don't pour on too much. Toss the lettuce until it glistens. Make beds of lettuce on six individual salad plates. Add to the remaining vinaigrette:

 1 Tbsp. vinegar

 1 tsp. Dijon mustard

 ¼ tsp. salt

 Pepper

The sauce must be more highly flavored for the seafood and vegetables or you can't taste it at all. Whisk or shake, then add enough to the shrimp mixture to coat well. Toss and taste. Add more vinegar, salt, or mustard if necessary until you like the taste. Spoon portions of the salad over the beds of lettuce. Place the tentacles and the shrimp in prominent places. Serve.

WILTED LETTUCE SALAD WITH SHAD ROE

6 servings

Shad roe comes along only once a year. It appears sometime in May, is around for about a month, and then it's gone, presumably because what once was roe is now a bunch of little fish. There are a lot of substitutes for it in this salad, which I will tell you about later, but first I may have to talk you into looking for shad roe if you have never eaten it. I hope you will make an effort to get some and try it. It is an odd but wonderful delicacy.

I was born and grew up in south Jersey. When I was a kid and shad roe was in season, my father drove us down to a little town called Bivalve where the fishing boats came in. He would buy shad roe and take it home, where Mother cooked this once-a-year treat we all loved.

Shad roe is mild and delicate and has texture like a lot of little eggs, which of course it is. The roe is wet and tender and lovely cooked simply in butter with salt and a little bit of pepper. It is important not to overcook roe because it dries out and the eggs get hard. Then it has all the appeal of raw cornmeal.

Now, about those substitutes. You can use slices of lobster tail, scallops, squid, and fish or butterflied shrimp. Also, if you can't find kohlrabi, you can substitute turnips or avocado slices.

You also may not be familiar with the other non-lettuce ingredient in this salad. Kohlrabi, also around in May and June, is an interesting-looking vegetable of the cabbage family with a bulb that looks and tastes like a mild turnip. The turnip wins where the texture of the vegetable is concerned although, to me, the kohlrabi is more pleasant.

One simple way to try kohlrabi is to peel it, grate it fine, and eat raw on a crudités plate, with or without vinaigrette sauce. Or peel, slice, cook briefly, and serve with butter and parsley as you would carrots or potatoes. For this salad I cook the kohlrabi briefly and serve it warm.

---

1 head romaine lettuce
2 or 3 bulbs kohlrabi, each 2 to 2½ inches (5 to 6½ cm) in diameter
1 pair shad roes, approximately ½ lb. altogether (225 grams)
3 Tbs. butter
½ cup oil (1 dL)—corn, olive, or any vegetable oil
¼ cup good wine vinegar (½ dL)

THE LETTUCE Have:

1 head romaine lettuce

Wash and dry well, then cut or tear into pieces the size of a calling card. The edges of the leaves won't turn dark if you cut them no more than 4 or 5 hours ahead. To judge whether you have enough romaine, lay out a salad plate you will use and portion out the romaine six times. Refrigerate in a bowl, but bring out to the room 2 hours before serving.

THE KOHLRABI Have:

2 to 3 bulbs kohlrabi, each 2 to 2½ inches (5 to 6½ cm) in diameter

Peel, then slice into 1 × 1 × ⅛-inch pieces (2½ ×

½ stick butter (2 oz. or
   60 grams)
Salt and pepper

2½ × ½ cm), enough to make about 2 cups (½ L). Blanch in boiling salted water just until barely tender, 4 to 5 minutes. Drain and refresh in cold water for a few seconds to stop the cooking. Drain again, then spread on a plate and refrigerate uncovered until chilled, then cover. This can be done up to a day ahead. Bring out to the room 2 hours before serving.

THE SHAD ROE Buy:
> 1 pair shad roes, approximately ½ lb.
>   altogether (225 grams)

On the morning of the dinner, sauté the roes very briefly as follows, just to firm the outside so they will slice neatly and can be cooked later without the slices becoming messy. Into a sauté pan put:
> 3 Tbs. butter

Heat until foamy. Don't have the pan too hot or the roes will spatter and spit. Add the roes and cook barely 10 to 15 seconds per side or just until the outside seems to be cooked. Remove and put on a plate. Refrigerate for 1 or 2 hours uncovered until chilled. Cut into ¼-inch (¾-cm) slices diagonally so you get larger slices. The roes will still be raw inside. Refrigerate until serving time.

TO ASSEMBLE AND SERVE THE SALAD Measure and have ready:
> ½ cup oil (1 dL)—corn, olive, or any vegetable oil
> ¼ cup good wine vinegar (½ dL)
> ½ stick butter (2 oz. or 60 grams)

Just before serving the salad, follow this plan:
1. Sprinkle salt and pepper over the romaine and toss well.
2. Pour the oil in a nonstick sauté pan (I like T-Fal pans) and heat for 1 minute or until the oil starts sputtering and making other noises.
3. Add the kohlrabi slices to the warm oil and stir for a few seconds until heated through.
4. Dump the kohlrabi and oil onto the romaine. Toss well.
5. Add the butter to the sauté pan and heat until melted and foaming. Don't have the pan too hot. Add the roe slices and cook a bare 10 to 15 seconds per side, just enough to finish cooking.

6. Remove the roe slices to a plate, but leave the butter in the pan. Add the vinegar to the butter, heat for a few seconds, and dump onto the salad.
7. Toss the salad and distribute onto serving plates.
8. Portion the roe slices over the salads. Serve immediately while warm.

WILTED LETTUCE SALAD WITH SNAILS AND MUSHROOM CAPS

6 servings

People all over the world have come to love snails, thanks to the French and their great escargots in garlic butter. It seems time, however, to figure out another good way to serve them. In Spain I had snails in a tomato-base sauce loaded with hot pepper, which really didn't do it for me. So I dreamed up this wilted lettuce salad as something a little different. Not wanting to take too many chances, I kept the garlic butter and just added lettuce, mushroom caps, a little vinegar, and some small toasts to soak up the butter. I think it's a good dish. When I've made it in cooking classes in different parts of the country, it has always met with great success.

1 or 2 heads curly lettuce, preferably escarole or curly endive, or spinach

36 small or 30 medium raw mushrooms (5 or 6 caps per person)

3 Tbs. butter

36 to 40 snails packed in water (extra large or *extra gros* preferred)

½ lb. butter at room temperature (2 sticks or 225 grams)

2 Tbs. finely minced green onions

3 or 4 large garlic cloves, minced fine

THE LETTUCE, MUSHROOMS, AND SNAILS These can all be prepared a day ahead. Have:

1 or 2 heads curly lettuce, preferably escarole or curly endive, or spinach

Wash and dry well, then tear into bite-size pieces. Portion out the lettuce onto a salad plate six times to make sure you have enough for six servings. Allow for a little more because the lettuce wilts down some when the hot ingredients are poured over it. Reserve. Wash:

36 small or 30 medium raw mushrooms (5 or 6 caps per person)

Then cut the stems even with the caps. (Use the stems, too, if you like, although they won't look as elegant.) If you have to use larger mushrooms, cut them into halves or quarters. Into a saucepan put:

3 Tbs. butter

Heat until melted, then add the mushrooms. Sauté for 5 minutes or until cooked and lightly browned,

4 Tbs. finely chopped
     parsley
½ tsp. salt
Pepper
Nutmeg (careful, not
     too much)
6 slices whole wheat
     bread
3 to 4 Tbs. vinegar

keeping the heat high enough to keep the juices evaporated. Reserve. Have:

> 36 to 40 snails packed in water (extra large or *extra gros* preferred)

Drain, then rinse well in several waters. Set aside.

SNAIL BUTTER Prepare this at least one day ahead and put the snails in it so they can pick up the flavor of the garlic butter. Into a small saucepan put:

> ½ lb. butter at room temperature (2 sticks or 225 grams)
> 2 Tbs. green onions, minced fine
> 3 or 4 large garlic cloves, minced fine
> 4 Tbs. parsley, chopped fine (measure after chopping)
> 1½ tsp. salt
> Pepper
> Nutmeg (careful, not too much)

Heat until the butter is melted, but be careful not to let the butter sizzle hard or it will be indigestible. Stir, then add the snails. Push the snails down into the butter as best you can, refrigerate until chilled, then cover.

THE TOASTS Cut 2½-inch (6½-cm) squares from the centers of:

> 6 slices whole wheat bread

Toast in a toaster. Reserve.

THE FINAL ASSEMBLY Just before serving, warm six salad plates. Have the lettuce in a mixing bowl at room temperature. Place one toast square on each warmed plate. Heat the snails in the butter in a saucepan until the butter is bubbling and the snails are warmed through. Add the mushrooms and stir until the mushrooms are heated. Right away dump the contents of the saucepan onto the lettuce and toss well. Into the saucepan put:

> 3 to 4 Tbs. vinegar

Heat the vinegar, swirling well to clean out the pan. Pour over the salad and toss. Spoon out onto the toast squares on the plates. Make sure everyone gets approximately six snails and six mushroom caps. Work quickly and get the plates out to the table while all is still warm.

MAIN COURSES:
SEAFOOD AND POULTRY

SEAFOOD

*Sea Bass Fillets with Salmon Mousse
Baked in a Crust*

*Fish Fillets with Peppers and Fruits

*Fish Slices with Shredded Snow Peas

POULTRY

Chicken Breast Scallops with Prosciutto

Chicken with Whole Wheat Dumplings

Roast Ducks with Crisp Skins

*Roast Frying Chickens

*Turkey Sausage Patties

*Special quick dishes

This section, the first of two dealing with main courses, contains dishes of great variety in terms of style. It has one very elegant, formal dish, Sea Bass Fillets with Salmon Mousse Baked in a Crust; one hearty, country dish, Chicken with Whole Wheat Dumplings; several simple dishes suitable for weeknight suppers, Fish Fillets with Peppers and Fruits, Fish Slices with Shredded Snow Peas, and Roast Frying Chickens; a breakfast or brunch sausage patty; and a simplified version of Peking Duck. The dishes are all very special, very unusual, and very good.

I would like to suggest two menus based on some dishes I especially like from this section. As a dividend, all but one of the recipes in both menus carry stars, meaning they are relatively quick and easy to prepare.

A SUMMER MENU

Zucchini Alfredo

Fish Fillets with Peppers and Fruits
Bulgur and Barley Pilaf

Lettuce Salad, Sauce Vinaigrette†

Blueberry Tart

A WINTER MENU

Green Onion Appetizer Cake

Roast Frying Chickens
Brown Rice with Toasted Pine Nuts
Shredded Cabbage with Grated Banana Squash

Lettuce Salad, Sauce Vinaigrette†

Truffled Pears

---

†For a recipe for Sauce Vinaigrette, see Shredded Lettuce Salad with Shrimp and Squid. For the lettuce, use any type you like or a combination, washed and dried.

Sea Bass Fillets with Salmon Mousse Baked in a Crust

8 servings

This recipe is a simplified version of one of the most spectacularly beautiful and elegant dishes of all French cuisine. Don't be misled by the title. The dish sounds complicated and gooey and rich, but it isn't. Inside a very thin layer of dough are plain, steamed fish fillets with a layer of ground salmon (or shrimp) mixed with cream and a few seasonings. A simple sauce of thickened cream with dill and lemon juice accompanies the fish. This is a beautiful dish. It has an absolutely delicious, clean, wholesome taste.

Make one batch of rapid puff paste (recipe follows). Or to make this dish really fast and easy, make two double batches (4 cups flour in all) of the instant food processor dough that you will find in the recipe for Pear Pie. Once the dough is made, assembling this dish does not take long. If you have made the dough ahead, bring it out of the refrigerator to warm up before starting the assembly so the dough is soft enough to roll easily.

RAPID PUFF PASTE USING THE FOOD PROCESSOR This puff paste is much easier to work with than classic puff paste. In this version, called *feuilletage viennoise*, the classic proportions of 1 pound flour to 1 pound butter remain the same, but almost half the flour is worked into the butter, which makes the butter much easier to handle and also lessens elasticity problems with the flour "package" because there is so much less of it. This means you can move right ahead with the process without the long waits. The dough can be done from start to finish in 45 minutes or less, including two 15-minute waits! Another benefit of this procedure is that using less flour to make the dough package means that much less water is required to make the dough. This results in a puff paste different in consistency and much more tender than the classic version. A disadvantage (sorry to bring this up) is that, if baked too long, the dough tends to be dry and powdery.

2½ cups sifted flour (300 grams)
3 Tbs. cold butter (50 grams)
1 tsp. salt
½ cup plus 1 Tbs. cold water
1 egg yolk

THE DOUGH Into the container of a food processor fitted with the metal blade put:

    2½ cups sifted flour (300 grams)

    3 Tbs. cold butter (50 grams), cut into pieces

Process until like coarse meal. Into a small bowl put:

    1 tsp. salt

    ½ cup plus 1 Tbs. cold water (Don't cheat! Use full measures.)

    1 egg yolk

Mix and add to the container with the flour and butter. Process until the dough comes together into

1½ cups sifted flour (180 grams)

1 lb. minus 3 Tbs. chilled hard butter (400 grams) cut into ½-inch (1½-cm) cubes

7 oz. skinned and boned raw salmon (200 grams)

½ tsp. salt

Cayenne pepper

Nutmeg (easy!)

1 cup chilled whipping cream (¼ L)

2 lbs. sea bass fillets (900 grams)—or snapper, rock cod, swordfish, halibut, etc.

1 egg

2 cups whipping cream or sour cream or half-and-half (½ L)

1 Tbs. cornstarch

2 Tbs. lemon juice

1 tsp. salt

White pepper or cayenne (black pepper doesn't look good in a white sauce) (optional)

½ tsp. dried dill weed (or 1 to 1½ tsp. fresh dill)

a ball. Don't overwork the dough. If it doesn't come together within 10 to 15 seconds, add 1 tablespoon more cold water, then process again. Remove the dough and form into a ball. Wrap and refrigerate while you work with the butter package.

BUTTER PACKAGE Again using the metal blade, into the processor jar put:

    1½ cups sifted flour (180 grams)

    1 lb. minus 3 Tbs. chilled hard butter (400 grams) cut into ½-inch (1½-cm) cubes

Process until homogenous. Actually, this will clog the machine and make it stop. Remove from the container and form into a disk. Refrigerate until ready to use, but no more than 30 minutes or the butter will become too hard to roll.

TO ASSEMBLE DOUGH AND MAKE THE TURNS Move right along; it is not necessary to wait. Using a knife, cut a cross going halfway down into the ball of dough. Pull open the top four knobs as if they were the petals of a flower. Roll the dough to a 12- or 14-inch (30- or 35-cm) cloverleaf shape into a good, solid, thicker-center platform that is at least 5 inches (13 cm) square. Place the butter package in the center and fold over the dough "petals" to encase the butter completely so that it cannot ooze out when you roll it. Roll the dough into a rectangle somewhere around 8 × 18 inches (10 × 45 cm). Fold in thirds in the traditional letter fold, then turn the dough 90°. Roll out again to the same 8 × 18-inch rectangle, but this time fold both ends into the center until they touch, then fold the package in half. Wrap and refrigerate for 15 minutes.

Then roll out the rectangle and make only one "fold-into-center-fold-again" turn, which is called a double turn. Refrigerate for another 15 minutes, then roll and make a final double turn. Supposedly the dough is better if you wait and do this last turn shortly before you are going to use the dough, but I don't think it's too important. After the dough has rested 20 minutes, it is ready to use. It can also be frozen at this point.

TO DEFROST DOUGH AND USE Transfer from the freezer to the refrigerator 24 hours ahead. Then an hour or so before you are going to use it, bring out to the room to let warm and soften a little. Do not try to work with this dough when it is too hard and cold or you will work it too much and it will become elastic and impossible to roll.

THE SALMON MOUSSE Place in a food processor:

> 7 oz. skinned and boned raw salmon (200 grams)

You will have to buy 10 ounces (285 grams) or so of tail fillets or salmon steaks to get 7 ounces of salmon skinned and boned. Fresh salmon is preferable, but frozen will do. It must be raw, however. Cooked, canned salmon will not work. Raw shrimp or raw lobster meat also is fine for this. Add:

> ½ tsp. salt
> Cayenne pepper
> Nutmeg (easy!)

Process until the salmon is well ground. Dribble in slowly down the feed tube:

> 1 cup chilled whipping cream (¼ L)

Refrigerate until ready to use.

THE SEA BASS Have:

> 2 lbs. sea bass fillets (900 grams)—or snapper, rock cod, swordfish, halibut, etc.

It is easier to use larger fillets (½ to ¾ inch or 1½ to 2 cm thick) so you can make an even platform of fish, but I think you can use any fish there is. Thinner fillets can be placed on the dough in double or triple layers. Thicker fillets can be sliced thinner and cut and pieced together. Just make sure that there are no bones and skin. Keep the fish in the refrigerator until time to assemble the dish.

TO ASSEMBLE Cut the puff paste or instant dough in half and roll each piece separately into two large rectangles approximately ⅛ inch (½ cm) thick. Use firm, hard, steady pressure and try to get where you're going in as few strokes as possible.

Select the largest baking sheet that will fit in your oven. Place a piece of parchment or brown paper on the sheet to keep the bottom of the crust from burning. Place one sheet of dough on the paper. Arrange the fish fillets on the dough in such a way as to make the body and head of a fish. (Design the fish to go from corner to corner to get maximum length.) Your "fish" can be fat like a flounder or streamlined like a fast-moving fish. Once you have a shape with the fish fillets, spread the salmon mousse in an even layer on top. Into a saucer put:

1 egg

Beat with a fork until well mixed. This will be both the "glue" to bind the two pieces of crust together and the glaze for the crust. Using a pastry brush, paint an inch-wide band of egg all around the pastry at the base of the fish fillets. Don't brush on too much egg or the dough won't stick together well. Paint a larger area around the tail section to create a proper tail. Place the second sheet of dough over the fish and press down to seal.

Now comes the creative part. Cut out a fish shape, leaving a ¾-inch (2-cm) border all around the fish stuffing and cutting out a beautiful tail and two or three nice fins. You can use a ravioli wheel or a knife. Once the fish is cut out, press down with a fork all around the outside border and tail area to seal the dough well (the way you sometimes seal the edge of a pie).

Paint the whole fish with the egg glaze. Then, using the dough scraps that are left, cut out a strip about 3/16 inch wide and 5 inches long (about ¾ cm by 13 cm). This will be a "gill." Place it in the proper area across the head. Use a pastry-tube tip with a ½-inch (1½-cm) hole or a knife to cut a hole where an eye should be (this will also serve as a vent for steam). Cut out a ring-shaped piece of dough (with a ½-inch hole) and place this over the eye hole to emphasize the eye. Using a fork, press lines to make fins and tail look bony. Using the pastry-tube tip again, make rows of crescent-shaped cuts into the dough all over the fish's body to look like scales. Add lips cut out of the scraps or make a rounded V-shaped notch for a mouth. You are done!

Refrigerate the "fish," but bring out to the room 1 hour before baking to come to room temperature. The fish can be prepared to this stage on the morning of the dinner or even a day ahead if you have to.

TO BAKE Preheat the oven to 450°F/230°C. Paint the fish with a final coating of egg glaze and bake 20 minutes or until starting to color. Turn the oven down to 375°F/190°C and bake another 20 to 30 minutes or until done. Test with an instant-reading meat thermometer. The temperature should be at least 130°F/54°C in the center of the fish. When done, let sit 5 minutes out of the oven before serving. Serve squares of this with the following sauce.

LEMON CREAM SAUCE WITH DILL This is the easiest, best sauce you ever ate. It's great on any fish dish. What a pity it's not low calorie. Into a saucepan put:

> 2 cups whipping cream or sour cream or half-and-half (½ L)

Into a small saucer put:

> 1 Tbs. cornstarch
> 2 Tbs. lemon juice

Mix, then add to the cream in the saucepan. Bring to a boil over high heat, whisking all the time until the mixture thickens and boils. Let simmer 3 minutes, whisking occasionally. Add:

> 1 tsp. salt
> White pepper or cayenne (black pepper doesn't look good in a white sauce) (optional)
> ½ tsp. dried dill weed (use 2 or 3 times this much fresh dill)

You can make this a day ahead. To keep a skin from forming on top, touch a piece of butter to the surface of the warm sauce, leaving just a tiny film all over. Refrigerate uncovered until chilled through. To serve, reheat to boiling. Be careful not to boil very hard or the sauce can separate. Whisk well to make sure it is smooth. Add more salt or more lemon juice if you think either is needed. Serve. This sauce makes the dish, so serve it all.

SUGGESTED ACCOMPANIMENTS Either plain white rice or boiled potatoes (could be parsleyed), plus a colorful green vegetable such as string beans or broccoli. Keep the vegetables somewhat plain and let the fish be the star of the show.

Note: This dish could be served alone as a small first course at an elaborate, multi-course meal.

FISH FILLETS WITH PEPPERS AND FRUITS

6 servings

This is a wonderful, colorful dish that has the added advantage of being very quick and easy to prepare. The fruits used in it are bananas and pears, and before you pull back in horror, think for just a moment, please, how the French must have scoffed the first time Véronique brought out her now famous filets de sole. Can't you just hear them? What? White grapes with fish? Quelle scandale!

This dish may sound odd, but it doesn't taste odd, and it is really good. Tail fillets of salmon are lovely used in it, but any good fresh fish fillet will do. The fish is quickly pan-fried, then served in its own instant butter sauce garnished with chunks of sautéed bananas, crunchy, not-quite-ripe pears, and red and green bell peppers. By being heated and combined with the peppers, butter, and salt, the fruits somehow are lifted out of the dessert category into that of a valid vegetable accompaniment. Although its lineage may be somewhat questionable, the dish is festive, has good texture and color, and is perfectly delicious.

1½ to 2 lbs. fish fillets (675 to 900 grams) in 6 serving-size pieces
1 lb. green bell peppers (450 grams)
1 lb. red bell peppers (450 grams)
4 or 5 small bananas (about 1¼ lbs. or 565 grams)
1¼ lbs. pears (565 grams)
Lemon juice
½ lb. butter (225 grams) at room temperature
Salt and pepper
Flour
Chopped parsley (optional)
Lemon slices or wedges

THE FISH FILLETS Have:

1½ to 2 lbs. fish fillets in 6 serving-size pieces (675 to 900 grams)

Use any fresh or frozen fillets of quality. Check the fillets and remove any bones still remaining. Tweezers or small pincer-type wire cutters or pliers work best for this, I think. Refrigerate until serving time.

THE BELL PEPPER AND FRUIT GARNISH Have:

1 lb. green bell peppers (450 grams)
1 lb. red bell peppers (450 grams)

If you cannot find red bell peppers, use all green ones. Fortunately, red peppers seem to be more and more available at different times of the year. You definitely should be able to find them in late summer and early fall, but they also are appearing in February and other surprising months.

To prepare the peppers, cut off the stem ends, cut in half lengthwise, and remove the seeds and pithy veins. Bring a large pot of water to a boil. Add the pepper halves and cook exactly 2 minutes and not a bit longer. Right away plunge into cold water to stop the cooking. Drain and cool completely. Cut into ½-inch (1½-cm) dice. Reserve. Have:

4 or 5 small bananas (about 1¼ lbs. or 565 grams)
1¼ lbs. pears (565 grams)

The bananas should be ripe, but not overly; don't peel until serving time. Bartlett, Bosc, or Winter Nellis are the preferred pears, but others will do. Ideally the pears still should be somewhat green and hard, but at the stage where they would be good for out-of-hand eating in 2 or 3 days.

Cut the pears in half and remove the stems and fibrous parts. Cut out the center cores with a melon-ball scoop and immediately rub the cut surfaces with:

Lemon juice

to prevent darkening. Reserve in the refrigerator until serving time.

TO COOK AND SERVE Heat the oven to 200°F/95°C and warm six serving plates in it. Have ready:

½ lb. butter (225 grams) at room temperature

Portions of the butter will be used at various stages in the following instructions until all is eventually used up. On both sides of the fish fillets, sprinkle:

Salt

Then dust on both sides with:

Flour

Shake off excess. Into a large sauté pan (or two pans if all the fillets will not fit side by side) put 5 tablespoons of the butter. Heat carefully over medium heat so the butter does not discolor. Add the fillets and cook 1 or 2 minutes per side or longer, depending on the thickness. The timing rule for fish fillets is no more than a total of 10 minutes per inch of thickness. The fish should cook gently, but with a little sizzle. Do not overcook.

Arrange the fillets on the warmed serving plates and put back into the warming oven while you finish the peppers, fruit, and sauce.

Pour out and discard any butter remaining in the sauté pan(s), but don't wash. Add 4 tablespoons more of the butter to be used for cooking.

Quickly cut the pears into bite-size chunks. Peel and cut the bananas into bite-size trapezoid shapes.

Melt the butter in the sauté pan. Add the pears, bananas, and bell pepper squares. Heat, stirring occasionally and gently, just enough to get all hot throughout. Do not overcook to where the fruit becomes mushy and the peppers lose their crunch. Add:

Salt and pepper

Cover the pan for 30 seconds or so to help speed along the heating.

Remove from the heat and add the rest of the room-temperature butter cut in chunks. (About 7 tablespoons will be left.) Remove the fish plates from the oven, stir the fruit and peppers in the butter sauce, and divide both sauce and the chunky bits over the fillets. Sprinkle with:

Chopped parsley (optional)

Garnish with:

Lemon slices or wedges

Serve.

ACCOMPANIMENT You need only one vegetable to serve with this. A baked or boiled sweet potato is a good choice because of its color and compatibility with the fruits and peppers. Traditional white potatoes or rice also would be fine.

FISH SLICES WITH SHREDDED SNOW PEAS

6 servings

Here is a colorful dish that is about 80 percent Chinese and 20 percent French. Small fish slices are sautéed in butter, then combined with peapods that have been blanched and cut into strips. Green onions and a few flavorings are added to complete the dish. I had this one night, served with a small baked potato and half an ear of corn. It was easy, pretty, and a sumptuous Monday night supper.

2½ to 3 lbs. fish fillets (1¼ kg or more)
½ to 1 tsp. salt
3 to 4 Tbs. dry white wine (Noilly Prat dry vermouth is fine)
2 Tbs. cornstarch
1 lb. snow peas (450 grams)
1 bunch green onions (scallions)
1 stick plus 6 Tbs. butter

THE FISH For a dish like this, the Chinese use a firm-textured fish such as rock cod or sea bass. Halibut, swordfish, salmon, or shark also do well. If you like, you can use the more delicate flounder (sole, etc.) or trout types, but you must be awfully careful because they crumble and fall apart with overcooking or too much handling. Have:

2½ to 3 lbs. fish fillets (1¼ kg or more)

Slice the fish in such a way as to end up with pieces in the neighborhood of 1½-inch (4-cm) squares, about ¼ inch (¾ cm) thick. You will have to slice some fish on the diagonal. Place the fish slices in a bowl. Add:

½ to 1 tsp. salt

**½ cup fish stock or
  clam juice or
  chicken stock (1 dL)**

3 to 4 Tbs. dry white wine (Noilly Prat dry
  vermouth is fine)
2 Tbs. cornstarch

Stir well, then let sit for 1 or 2 hours or longer, up
to 3 or 4 hours.

THE SNOW PEAS Buy:

1 lb. snow peas (450 grams)

Pick the smaller ones if you have the patience.
Snap off the stem ends and string the pods down
both sides. The smaller pods (2 inches long or
under) may not need stringing. Blanch for 1 minute
in 2 or 3 quarts (2 to 2¾ L) of boiling water, then
remove and plunge into cold water to stop the
cooking. Drain, then cut the pods into coarse
shreds about ¼ inch wide by 2 inches long (¾ cm
by 5 cm). Simply cut the small pods in half
lengthwise, and cut the larger ones into three or
four strips each, on the diagonal. Reserve in the
refrigerator until serving time. You can do this a
day ahead.

THE GREEN ONIONS Have:

1 bunch green onions (scallions)

Cut off the root ends, then slice across into ¼-inch
(¾-cm) round slices. Stop when you have ⅓ cup (¾
dL). Cover with plastic and refrigerate until serving
time.

TO COOK AND SERVE Use a large frying pan or sauté
pan, nonstick if possible. Sauté the fish slices in
two batches. Into the pan put:

3 Tbs. butter

Heat, then add half of the fish slices. Dump them
into the pan and separate them with two forks so
that they are in one layer. Let cook 30 to 60
seconds, then turn them with a spatula. Cook
another 30 to 60 seconds or until the fish pieces are
barely done. Do not overcook. Remove to a plate,
then add another:

3 Tbs. butter

Sauté the second batch. When they are done, add
to the rest of the fish slices. Put the snow peas into
the sauté pan, adding:

½ cup fish stock or clam juice or chicken stock
  (1 dL)

Turn the heat to high and quickly get the greens
hot. Add the fish slices to the pan, then cover with
a lid and steam for 1 minute over very high heat or

until everything is really hot. Check and add more stock if the mixture looks too dry. There must be enough liquid to furnish some steam. When everything is hot, remove the pan from the heat, then add:

> ½ to 1 stick (2 to 4 oz. or 60 to 115 grams) butter, sliced, at room temperature
> Reserved ⅓ cup sliced green onions

Carefully stir to mix. Taste and add more salt if you like. Serve.

CHICKEN BREAST SCALLOPS WITH PROSCIUTTO

6 servings

This exciting dish is a variation of the great Italian saltimbocca. Chicken breasts are sliced and pounded flat, seasoned with a few leaves of fresh cilantro, and topped with thin pieces of Italian ham. All is cut into 2-inch (5-cm) squares and held together with a toothpick. At dinnertime, you quickly sauté the squares and serve with a very simple deglaze (clean-out-the-pan) sauce.

In the classic saltimbocca, thin scallops of veal are used instead of chicken and fresh sage leaves instead of cilantro. I began using chicken during a veal shortage some years ago and found that in some dishes I preferred it. Because I am a cilantro lover and cilantro is a lot easier to find than fresh sage, that substitution is a practical one for me.

Cilantro, a parsley-like green, is very popular in the cooking of China and Mexico. So if you have any significant population in your town from either of those countries, you won't have trouble finding cilantro (the Mexican name) or Chinese parsley as it also is known. Fresh basil leaves, dried basil, or dried sage are herbs you can substitute if you can't find cilantro or don't like its unusual flavor.

---

20 slices of good, pink prosciutto
3 chicken breast halves, approximately 8 oz. or 225 grams each
1 bunch cilantro (also called fresh coriander or Chinese parsley)
Flour
1½ sticks butter

THE PROSCIUTTO Have ready to use:

> 20 slices of good, pink prosciutto

Good prosciutto can be a problem to find. Your best bet is a fine Italian market or delicatessen. The meat, which is uncooked ham that has been made ready-to-eat by salt-curing, must be sliced paper-thin or it is not interesting to eat. The meat itself should be a lovely pale red, not a color reminiscent of sturdy walking shoes. The slices should bend like skins that can be wrapped around something or draped. Some merchants who don't realize this sell ⅛-inch-thick pieces (way too thick) that are completely unyielding and about as tasty as slivers

About ½ cup dry
white wine (1 dL)
About ¼ cup (½ dL)
chicken stock
(optional)
Salt and pepper

off the top of your old Motorola. If you can't find prosciutto, substitute thin baked or boiled ham.

THE CHICKEN BREASTS Buy:

> 3 chicken breast halves, approximately 8 oz. or
> 225 grams each

Bone the breasts or have the butcher do it. Detach the little filet-like pieces that you find on the underside of each breast, then remove the tendons. Reserve the filets. Trim off any fat or hanging-on bits from the breast halves. Fluff up each breast half to make it fatter, then slice each into two pieces, cutting the flat way as if to butterfly.

You will end with two very thin scallops from each half breast. Lay these side by side on waxed paper, along with the filet-like pieces, leaving plenty of space between. Cover all with waxed paper and pound with a mallet to get neat, even scallops ⅛ inch (½ cm) thick or thinner. Be especially gentle with your pounding on the little filets because they are very tender. Peel off the paper. Have:

> 1 bunch cilantro (also called fresh coriander or
> Chinese parsley)

Wash, pull the leaves off the stems, and place two clumps or four or five leaves in the middle of each end of each scallop. (Later you will cut each scallop in half, so you want a cilantro clump for each half.)

Notes on herb substitutes: If using fresh basil, use one leaf for each half scallop. If using dried sage leaves (not the powdered stuff), be careful not to use too much! One or two of the little sage leaves per half scallop is enough; more will ruin them.

Cut a piece of prosciutto to the same size and shape of each scallop and lay on top. Press down to seal the meats together. Cut each scallop in half; the results will be two approximately square pieces about 2 × 2 inches (5 × 5 cm). Fasten the prosciutto to each piece by passing a toothpick in once and out, casually. One pick is enough for each piece. The stickiness of the chicken helps keep it attached to the prosciutto, even after the cooking. The picks give a little peace of mind to the cook. The scallops can be prepared a day ahead. Keep refrigerated, covered but not airtight.

TO COOK AND SERVE Cook at the last minute. This dish can't be held at all. The cooking will go faster if you use two large sauté pans but can be done in one pan with two batches. Have ready:

Flour

Flour the scallops very lightly. You cannot do this ahead or they get soggy. Shake off the excess flour. Heat the sauté pan(s) with:

3 or 4 Tbs. butter (in each pan)

When the butter foams, add the scallops, chicken side first. Ideally, there should be no space between the scallops or the butter will burn, but since you can't make two layers, you may have to compromise with the ideal here. Let the scallops sizzle gently over medium heat for 1 or 2 minutes or until the chicken is slightly brown.

Turn the scallops and let cook 30 seconds only on the prosciutto side.

Remove to a heated pan. If you have to make a second batch, keep the scallops in a warming oven (170°F/77°C). Be sure to use more butter for the second batch (3 or 4 tablespoons more). When all the scallops are cooked, pour out the excess fat and add to the sauté pan:

About ½ cup dry white wine (1 dL)

Cook, stirring and scraping to dissolve any brown in the pan. If you need still more liquid, you also can add:

Chicken stock, about ¼ cup or ½ dL (optional)

This is a moistener rather than a sauce, so don't worry if it is thin. Off the heat, swirl or whisk in:

Butter at room temperature (try ½ stick or more)

Taste to see if you will need:

Salt and pepper

Pour the sauce (moistener, that is) over the chicken pieces. Serve.

SUGGESTED ACCOMPANIMENTS White or brown rice would be simple and nice, and for the second accompaniment, Cauliflower with Watercress Sauce (see Vegetables) would be beautiful and delicious and it doesn't involve very much last-minute work. The final stages of putting out this dish are going to be a wee bit frantic, so ask one of your guests to give you a hand in putting things on plates so that everything gets to the table hot.

CHICKEN WITH WHOLE WHEAT DUMPLINGS

6 servings

Chicken and dumplings, the quintessential country American dinner, ought to be served on a Sunday afternoon in a small town by somebody's aunt or grandmother. I am neither, but I offer you a splendid version of this great dish.

I have worked harder to perfect this "simple country dish" than I normally do on the most complicated pastries. Those blasted dumplings almost did me in. I cooked so many clunkers that I got to be afraid to lift the lid off the pot to face the results of each new experiment. And I had to taste them all. But finally, a breakthrough. I used a sponge-cake technique of mine to fold in six beaten egg whites, and the dumplings are now as light as the proverbial cloud, even though they contain half whole wheat flour.

2 roasting chickens (5 lbs. or 2¼ kg each), including the chicken pieces (hearts, necks, giblets) and chicken fat

2 onions, sliced thin

2 carrots, sliced thin

2 stalks celery, sliced thin

6 to 8 cups boiling water (1½ to 2 L) or enough to just barely cover the vegetables

Homemade chicken stock (optional)

½ cup "rendered-type" chicken fat skimmed off the stew (1 dL)

½ cup flour (60 grams)

6 cups reduced stock (1½ L)

1½ tsp. salt

4 or 5 medium carrots (or enough for 6 people)

1 or 2 barely ripe avocados

¾ cup whole wheat flour (75 grams)

COOKING THE CHICKEN You can do this part of the recipe a day ahead. Buy:

2 roasting chickens, 5 lbs. each (2¼ kg), cut into serving pieces

I tried using stewing hens, cooking them longer, of course, but by the time they were tender enough to use, the meat was dry and not of a nice texture. Put the chicken fat pieces into the freezer to be chopped and added to the dumplings later.

Select a pot to cook the chicken in. The ideal is a heavy pot with an opening wide enough (about 9 inches or 23 cm) so that the dumplings can sit on top of the chicken to steam and have plenty of room to expand. However, use the best thing you have. If necessary, you can just dump the dumplings (I love that) on top in one big cake-like layer and serve cut in wedges. Into the pot put:

Chicken pieces, hearts, necks, giblets—in short, everything except the livers

2 onions, sliced thin

2 carrots, sliced thin

2 stalks celery, sliced thin

6 to 8 cups boiling water (1½ to 2 L) or enough to just barely cover the vegetables

If you want to use the chicken livers, slice and sauté in a little chicken fat for 1 minute or until barely done; chop and add to the gravy just before serving. If you want an even more spectacularly flavorful dish, use homemade chicken stock instead of water for the liquid. (See any basic French cookbook for a recipe for stock.)

Whether to add salt at this point or later, just

1½ tsp. baking powder
1 tsp. salt
1½ Tbs. minced
   chicken fat pieces
   (optional)
4 Tbs. chopped
   parsley (optional)
6 eggs at room
   temperature
⅓ to ⅔ cup milk (¾ dL
   to 1½ dL)
¾ cup sifted flour (90
   grams), unbleached
   all-purpose
   preferred

before the dish is done, is controversial. Some people claim that salt draws the juices out and makes the meat drier. It is a very subtle point, I believe, and almost not worth mentioning, but I do add the salt at the end just to go along with it all.

Return the pot to the boil, then cook uncovered at a very slow simmer until the chicken is tender. During the first half hour, you might attempt to remove some of the frothy scum that will rise to the top. How long to cook is difficult to say. Since chickens these days are fed to reach roasting weights much sooner, the younger ones may take only 45 to 50 minutes to be tender. Old-fashioned farm-raised chickens can take 1½ hours. Check with a fork and stop the cooking when nicely tender. Remove the chicken pieces and let cool. Refrigerate uncovered until chilled, then cover.

Strain the chicken juices (taste the vegetables and decide whether you want to return them to the gravy later or not), then cool and refrigerate uncovered until chilled and the fat has set. If you are going right on to serve the dish, skim off the fat and continue. In any event, save the fat if you are going to use it for the gravy.

TO MAKE THE GRAVY You can do this by the "fat" method or the "nonfat" method. The first will taste better and the other, the more traditional actually, will have fewer calories.

To make it the lean way, put ½ cup flour (60 grams) in a bowl and add 6 cups (1½ L) of the reduced broth in a slow stream, whisking well so the flour doesn't lump. Then cook the same as for the following "fat" method. Place in a saucepan:

   ½ cup "rendered-type" chicken fat skimmed
      off the stew (1 dL)
Heat gently to melt, then add:
   ½ cup flour (60 grams)
Whisk together, then cook over medium heat for 30 seconds. Add:
   6 cups reduced stock (1½ L)
Bring to a boil, whisking constantly to keep smooth. Add:
   1½ tsp. salt
Cook 2 or 3 minutes, whisking occasionally to break up the skin that forms on top. Cool, then place plastic wrap in contact with the surface. Refrigerate.

TO PRECOOK THE CARROTS Scrape:

>   4 or 5 medium carrots (or enough for 6 people)

If large, cut the carrots in half both ways. Cook in boiling, salted water 7 or 8 minutes or until barely tender. Drain and run under cold water to stop the cooking. Reserve.

TO MAKE THE DUMPLINGS AND FINISH THE DISH
Approximately 30 minutes before serving, put the sauce in a cooking pot. Add the strained-out vegetables and chopped liver if you have decided to use either or both. Layer in the chicken pieces, cooked carrots, and prepare:

>   1 or 2 barely ripe avocados

Peel and seed the avocados; coat with lemon juice if desired to prevent darkening. Reserve while making the dumpling batter.

For the dumplings, you can have these dry ingredients measured and mixed in advance. Into a bowl put:

>   ¾ cup whole wheat flour (75 grams)
>   1½ tsp. baking powder
>   1 tsp. salt

Toss a few times to distribute the baking powder, then mix in:

>   1½ Tbs. minced chicken fat pieces (those saved and frozen; it's easy to chop the fat while frozen, too) (optional)
>   4 Tbs. chopped parsley (optional)

Now choose between the following options. *For a more solid, whole-egg dumpling,* into a bowl put:

>   6 egg yolks at room temperature
>   ⅓ cup milk (¾ dL)

Beat 1 minute or until frothy. Here is the other option.

For a really light dumpling: Instead of the preceding yolks and milk, just add ⅔ cup (1½ dL) plain milk with no yolks. Add to the whole-wheat flour mixture and stir in just until moist. Reserve. Measure:

>   ¾ cup sifted flour (90 grams), unbleached all-purpose preferred

Reserve. In another bowl put:

>   6 egg whites at room temperature

Beat to soft peaks. Sprinkle one-third of the reserved flour over the batter, then add one-third of the beaten whites. Fold, turning the bowl and cutting down with a rubber spatula through the mixture and across the bottom of the bowl. Give the whites another 5-second beat to get them creamy again; then add another one-third of the flour and another third of the egg whites. Fold again, beat the whites again, and add the remaining one-third of the flour and the rest of the whites. Fold in thoroughly, but not a stroke more than necessary.

Bring the pot of chicken and carrots to a simmer. Meanwhile, cut the reserved avocado in 1-inch (2½-cm) cubes. *Important:* Set the heat so the chicken is just simmering slowly. (Test the heat by putting a lid on the pan; almost no steam should force itself up and out under the lid.) Add the avocado and mix in.

Immediately put big blobs of the batter onto the surface of the stew. (I scoop it out with a ⅓-cup measure and scrape it out of that with a rubber spatula. Sorry, the batter is soft and will not make round dumplings, but flattened ones.) The dumplings will sit up out of the liquid and will steam on the top. When all the batter is in, cover the pot and do not lift the cover for 20 minutes. (Again, make sure that the chicken barely simmers and almost no steam forces itself from under the lid.) After 20 minutes, test the dumplings by poking with a toothpick, which should come out clean. Place the dumplings, chicken, and vegetables on a serving platter or individual plates. Spoon lots of gravy over. Serve.

ROAST DUCKS WITH CRISP SKINS

6 servings

These are dark and delicious roast ducks with wonderful crispy skins. The ducks are split, flattened, and coated with a glaze, which is allowed to dry for two days in the refrigerator. The ducks are then seasoned and roasted.

Probably you have noticed that this method has a strong Chinese influence. Yes, this duck is a "country cousin" of the citified Peking (Beijing) Duck, but it is prepared in an extremely simplified way: no bicycle pump for blowing air between the skin and flesh so the skin will be super crisp, no sewing up, no three days suspended in a breezy north window, and no hanging while roasting in special ovens. Several days are necessary for the preparation, but the labor involved is simple and so is the roasting.

---

2 ducks, 5 lbs. (2¼ kg) each or heavier, including gizzards, hearts, necks, livers
3 Tbs. cornstarch
2 Tbs. cold water
1½ cups water (3½ dL)
1 Tbs. honey
2 Tbs. vinegar
Duck gizzards, hearts, backbones, wing joints, necks
Cold water or chicken stock to cover plus 2 inches
¾ stick butter (3 oz. or 85 grams) or ⅓ cup rendered fat (¾ dL)
⅓ cup flour (40 grams)
6 cups duck stock (1½L), previously prepared
1 tsp. 5-spice powder
2 tsp. salt
2 tsp. sugar
Duck livers
Hoisin sauce (optional)
Salt and pepper

THE DUCKS Have:

2 ducks, 5 lbs. (2¼ kg) each or heavier

Ducks of 5 pounds serve three persons, with each person receiving two-thirds of a breast half plus a piece of thigh or leg. Also there will be lots of extra pieces for the big eaters to gnaw on. If you can't find ducks this heavy, roast three instead of two, but you had better have two ovens because three ducks may be difficult or impossible to fit into a standard-size oven.

If the ducks are frozen, remove from their plastic bags and let them thaw uncovered in the refrigerator. This will take a day or two. Don't worry if the skins dry out. This actually will help make a crispy skin during the roasting.

TO FLATTEN AND COAT THE DUCKS Two or three days before roasting, remove the end (pointy) wing joints of each duck. Using a heavy, sharp knife, cut out and remove the backbones and any meatless parts of the upper backs. Open the ducks and flatten them out, skin sides down. Remove the wishbones from each. Without cutting through the meat, carefully detach each wing bone at the socket where it is attached to the breast. Also cut through the breastplate without cutting through the meat or skin to divide the bony part of each duck in two. The reason for all this bone cutting is to make sure that the ducks will stay flat while roasting.

Line two jelly-roll pans with foil, shiny side up. Spread each duck on the foil, skin side up. (The pans don't really have to be jelly-roll pans just because that's what I use. Any large-enough baking pan with a rim to contain the rendered fat will do. I like a jelly-roll pan because the rim is low and does not keep the heat from reaching the duck.)

THE DUCK COATING Into a small bowl put:

3 Tbs. cornstarch
2 Tbs. cold water

Mix until smooth. Pour into saucepan and heat:

1½ cups water (3½ dL)

Before the water boils, add the cornstarch mixture in a stream, whisking all the time. Continue bringing to a boil and whisking until the mixture suddenly thickens. Once it boils and is smooth, lower the heat and allow to burp and bubble for 2 or 3 minutes, whisking occasionally. Remove from the heat, then add:

> 1 Tbs. honey
> 2 Tbs. vinegar

Mix well. Brush this thick mixture over the entire skin areas of the ducks. Lay it on well and use it all. Refrigerate the ducks uncovered for two or three days or until the coating dries.

DUCK STOCK This will be used to make a sauce. A sauce is not necessary with these ducks, but if you have the time and want to make one, a sauce is nice. Preheat the oven to 450°F/230°C. Lay in a roasting pan:

> Duck gizzards, hearts, backbones, wing joints, necks (in short, everything you have left except the livers, which should be put back in the freezer)

Roast for 30 minutes or until nicely browned. Transfer the pieces to a saucepan, then add:

> Cold water or chicken stock to cover plus 2 inches

Bring to a boil. Pour some of this liquid into the roasting pan, scrape up any good brown stuff, and return all to the saucepan. Cover and simmer for 2 to 3 hours; strain. If necessary, return stock to saucepan and heat to reduce to 6 cups (1½ L). Reserve in the refrigerator or make and reserve the sauce.

DUCK SAUCE This can be made one or two days ahead. Technically it is a velouté sauce, but it's pretty close to what my mother would call gravy. First make a *roux*. Into a saucepan put:

> ¾ stick butter (3 oz. or 85 grams) or ⅓ cup rendered duck or chicken fat (¾ dL)
> ⅓ cup flour (40 grams)

Heat until the butter melts. Whisk the mixture together, then let it foam up and cook for 30 seconds. Remove from the heat and add:

> 6 cups duck stock (1½ L), previously prepared

Bring to a boil, whisking well; then let simmer for 5 to 10 minutes, whisking occasionally, until thickened. Film the sauce after removing from the heat by touching a stick of butter to its surface so a tiny film of butter melts. This keeps the sauce from forming a floury skin. Reserve in the refrigerator.

SEASONING THE DUCKS For this you need 5-spice powder, available in Chinese groceries or in some nationally distributed spice lines. Five-spice has a strong anise smell and flavor. You could substitute the French mixed spices called *quatre épices* or "four spices"; not the same, but nice.

On the day you serve the ducks, bring them out 1 to 2 hours before roasting to come to room temperature. Turn them over so the skin sides are down, but handle carefully. You don't want to disturb the dried coating. In a small bowl mix well:

    1 tsp. 5-spice powder
    2 tsp. salt
    2 tsp. sugar

Carefully rub the mixture into the parts of the duck that are up. Turn the ducks over again so the coated skin sides are up.

TO ROAST THE DUCKS Preheat the oven to 450°F/230°C. About 1 hour before the ducks are to be eaten, roast for 25 minutes. After this time, they should be colored a deep brown with some spots that appear almost burned. Remove from the oven.

Using a bulb baster, remove most of the rendered fat from the pans. Cover the ducks with *loose* sheets of foil, then return to the oven for another 20 to 35 minutes. (Total roasting time is 45 minutes to 1 hour.) Transfer the ducks to a plate and return to the turned-off oven with the door slightly ajar. Meanwhile, finish the sauce.

TO FINISH THE SAUCE Reheat the duck sauce. Pour all the duck fat out of the roasting pans and discard. Pour some of the duck sauce into one roasting pan. Carefully scrape up the good brown bits from the foil. A pastry brush is nice and gentle for this. Transfer the sauce to the other roasting pan and deglaze in the same fashion. Return all the sauce to the saucepan. Remove from the freezer:

    Duck livers

Mince fine by hacking away on a board with a large, sharp knife. Toss into the sauce and simmer for 1 minute. Some people would strain out the livers and discard them after they have flavored the sauce, but I leave them in. For a sneaky little Peking Duck touch, you might like to add:

> Hoisin sauce (available in Chinese groceries), to taste (optional)

Taste and add if necessary:

> Salt and pepper

Keep warm.

TO CUT AND SERVE THE DUCKS Using a heavy knife and/or poultry shears, cut each duck down the center of the breast, separating it into halves. Cut off each wing joint, then remove each leg and thigh in one piece. Cut each breast in half, cutting across the short way so the meat is equally divided. (You may need shears to cut through the bones.)

You will now have eight nice breast servings. Cut legs and thighs apart; you will have four legs and four thighs.

You should have warmed serving plates for each guest. Pour onto each a puddle of the sauce. Onto the sauce, place one piece of breast and one thigh or leg, skin sides up. Add the vegetables you plan to serve and take to the table.

Pass around extra breast pieces, legs, wings, and extra sauce for those desiring seconds. If you have succeeded in achieving a crisp skin for the ducks, make sure that you don't ruin it by dumping hot, wet sauce all over it.

SUGGESTED ACCOMPANIMENTS Two very interesting accompaniments to the duck would be the somewhat chow-mein-like Spaghetti with Three-Color Vegetable Shreds (see Main Courses: Soups and Pasta) and Baked Cubes of Butternut Squash (see Vegetables), which you could squeeze into the oven underneath the ducks. However, if you have two ovens, it would be easier to bake the ducks and the squash separately.

ROAST FRYING CHICKENS

6 servings

This is going to be one of the easiest dishes you ever prepared and one of the best-tasting, if you can get chickens that have not been frozen. It is two plain, lightly oiled, and salted roast chickens. No trussing. No basting. No mincing or chopping. Just throw the birds into a hot oven (on a pan, of course) and wait 60 minutes. Remove, let sit 15 minutes, and serve. That's all.

ON ROASTING CHICKENS AT HIGH TEMPERATURES Many people are astonished to learn that small fowl can be roasted at very high temperatures. It would seem more logical to roast small fowl and smaller pieces of meat at low temperatures and large fowl and larger pieces of meat at high heat. Actually, due to the laws of physics, the reverse is the case. The most important things to consider in roasting are (1) to cook the meat until it is done and (2) to cook it so that it tastes good. The browning of fat plus the caramelizing of sugars in the meat cause the meat to taste good to us. A 3-pound chicken must be roasted at high heat, at 450°F/230°C or thereabouts, for the proper browning to take place without overcooking the meat. If you cook chicken longer at a lower temperature and take it out while still juicy and nice, caramelization will not have had time to take place and the chicken will not taste as good. Larger pieces of meat can stay in the oven at lower temperatures long enough for the heat to penetrate the center and also for the proper browning to occur.

---

2 3-lb. (1350-gram) chickens that have not been frozen
A little oil
Salt

TO ROAST THE CHICKEN Buy:

  2 3-lb. (1350-gram) chickens that have not been frozen

Bring the chickens out to room temperature 2 or 3 hours before roasting if you think of it. Remove any chicken fat from just inside the cavities. Rub the outsides with:

  A little oil

Then sprinkle lightly inside and outside with:

  Salt

Select a roasting pan with low sides that the chickens just nicely fit into without a lot of empty space where juices and fat can spatter, burn, and smoke. If you were going to present the chickens at the table whole, you would truss them so they'd look pretty, but since you are not going to, you won't bother. Merely plunk the chickens in the pan, breasts up. Preheat the oven to 450°F/230°C. Roast for 1 hour (add an extra 10 minutes if you prefer them a little more well cooked). To test for doneness, lift up the chickens. The last drops of juice that run from the cavities should be almost clear. Remove and let rest 15 minutes on a plate before carving into pieces. Serve.

SUGGESTED ACCOMPANIMENTS Try the Steamed Millet with Onions and Oregano for an interesting and different dish to serve with this. Shredded Cabbage with Grated Banana Squash (see Vegetables) would be a colorful and good-tasting second accompaniment. If you want to keep it really quick and simple, throw in some potatoes to bake along with the chicken (I even bake medium-sized redskin "boiling" potatoes at 450°F/230°C for about an hour and they turn out fine) and have some string beans or peas on the side.

By the way, I do not object to serving two starches on the same plate. A baked potato plus corn on the cob, for example, tastes fine to me, as does the combination of fresh peas and a baked or boiled potato. This is one conventional "no-no" that I believe should not be followed slavishly.

TURKEY SAUSAGE PATTIES

6 servings

Since I discovered this, I can't stop eating it. One of the best things about it is that it's so easy to do. I don't know why we seem to eat sausage made only with pork. Turkey is marvelous in sausage, and I'm sure many other meats are, too. In this recipe, I use the breast cutlets that you buy right from the poultry case. This is the simplest way, but you could use meat boned from the leg and thigh (the dark meat might taste even better). If you don't have a food processor, use a meat grinder or do it the Chinese way, by putting everything on a board and hacking away with two cleavers or two of the heaviest knives you own. It works more quickly than you'd think and it's fun!

1 lb. turkey breast pieces (450 grams), cut into 1-inch (2½-cm) squares
½ lb. chicken fat pieces (225 grams), cut into ½-inch (1½-cm) cubes (not rendered fat, but pieces cut from chickens)
2 tsp. salt
½ tsp. white or black pepper

THE SAUSAGE You can cook and eat this sausage as soon as you make it, but if you make it a day ahead, the spiciness is magically accentuated. Into the container of a food processor put:

1 lb. turkey breast pieces (450 grams), cut into 1-inch (2½-cm) squares)
½ lb. chicken fat pieces (225 grams), cut into ½-inch (1½-cm) cubes (not rendered fat, but pieces cut from chickens)
2 tsp. salt
½ tsp. white pepper (or black)
½ tsp. thyme
1/16 tsp. nutmeg (2 "knife points")
1/16 tsp. powdered ginger

½ tsp. thyme
⅟₁₆ tsp. nutmeg
  (2 "knife points")
⅟₁₆ tsp. powdered
  ginger
⅟₁₆ tsp. cinnamon
⅟₃₂ tsp. cloves (take it
  easy; cloves take
  over!)

⅟₁₆ tsp. cinnamon
⅟₃₂ tsp. cloves (take it easy; cloves take over!)

Process on and off until the meat is ground, but do not grind very long. Sausage is nicer, I think, if somewhat coarse so that it has a chewy texture. As soon as the fat seems to be smashed up a bit, stop. Place in a bowl; cover and refrigerate for one or two days.

TO COOK AND SERVE Shape the sausage into twelve patties 2 inches (5 cm) in diameter and ½ inch (1½ cm) thick. Place the sausages in a cold frying pan and cook over moderate heat approximately 3 minutes per side or until nicely browned. The patties should be done in the center (cut into one and check), but don't cook them so long that you evaporate all the juices and fat and make them dry.

SUGGESTED ACCOMPANIMENTS These sausages would be great to serve at a brunch. If you care to try something a little different, serve them alongside the Fat, Broiled Pancake with Pecans (see Breads). Sauté some cherry tomatoes (or plum tomatoes if you can find them) in butter very briefly just to warm and add them to the plate.

MAIN COURSES:
BEEF, LAMB, AND PORK

Roast Filet of Beef, Minced Mushroom Sauce

* *Sautéed Beef Cubes*

Tournedos, Basil Béarnaise

* *Beef Skillet Cake*

* *Double-Thick Sirloin Steak with Mustard*

Broiled Double Loin Lamb Chops with Kidneys

Lamb Noisettes with Green Peppercorns

* *Roast Saddle of Lamb with Rosemary and Garlic*

Pork Cutlets, Arlesienne Style

Pork Mousselines, Green Beurre Blanc

*Special quick dishes

In this section you will generally find dishes that are fairly simple. In cooking and entertaining, I favor a formal, multi-course style of serving. At a dinner I like to present a small first course, sometimes followed by a small fish course, then a main course, salad, sometimes cheese, and a fancy dessert or desserts. For this style of entertaining, it becomes impractical to serve complicated main courses such as rich, hearty stews or rolled, stuffed breasts of this or that. The tone of those dishes is wrong for long, complicated meals. They are too wet, too rich, and too filling. Please don't get me wrong. I love hearty dishes, particularly at lunch. I love eating them in other people's houses and in the country and in restaurants that specialize in them, but at home they just don't fit into the way I entertain.

What you will find in this section, with the exception of the Beef Skillet Cake, is a group of broiled, roasted, or sautéed tender cuts of meat with simple sauces or with no sauces at all. They are meant to be accompanied by interesting vegetables and to be preceded and followed by varied first courses and desserts.

The following three menus will give you examples of what I am referring to. The final one is a kind of all-stops-out, knock-'em-dead menu such as I serve occasionally when I really feel like runnin' wild.

A SUMMER MENU

Shredded Lettuce Salad with Shrimp and Squid

Tournedos, Basil Béarnaise
Summer Vegetable Chunks with Black Olives
Cornmeal Polenta Swiss Style with Gruyère

Fresh Summer Fruits with Watermelon Ice

A WINTER MENU

Oysters on Saffron Bean Threads

Roast Filet of Beef, Minced Mushroom Sauce
Fresh Chestnut Puree
Cauliflower with Watercress (or Spinach) Sauce

Lettuce Salad, Sauce Vinaigrette

Spiced Apple and Pear Cobbler

A FANCY SPRING MEAL OF MANY SMALL COURSES

Asparagus, Beurre Blanc, with Green Pineapple

Wilted Lettuce Salad with Snails and Mushroom Caps

Lamb Noisettes with Green Peppercorns

Three Colorful Vegetable Purees:
Butternut Squash   Broccoli†   Beet-Potato

Cheese

Strawberries Three

Blueberry Tart‡

Chocolate Whipped-Cream Truffle Cake

†Substitute broccoli for string beans in the recipe elsewhere in this book.
‡Using canned wild blueberries as mentioned in the recipe.

I realize that this last menu is going to horrify many of you who have never served or eaten this kind of meal before. It looks like a week's work, and it might well be. I don't mean to shock you, but there are some of us around who enjoy performing this kind of *tour de force*. If you are wild enough to attempt meals of this sort, and if you keep the courses properly small, and if you do everything right, or almost right, you will be very happy with the results and will find, perhaps to your surprise that (1) many of your guests will deem this the most exciting meal they have ever eaten in their lives; (2) your guests will leave the table feeling filled, but not stuffed; and (3) no one present will ever invite you for dinner again.

ROAST FILET OF BEEF, MINCED MUSHROOM SAUCE

6 servings

The filet of beef, or tenderloin, is the tenderest piece of meat on the animal. A whole piece of filet sometimes is difficult to find because many butchers slice the middle of the steer's back (the filet runs the length of it) into T-bone and sirloin steaks, both of which therefore contain a slice of the filet. Or they sell the tenderloin sliced into filets mignons and the rest of the back boneless as New York or sirloin steaks. However, if you order ahead, most butchers will find you a filet for roasting.

A filet or piece of filet
for roasting
½ stick plus 3 Tbs.
butter
½ lb. mushrooms (225
grams), minced fine
¼ cup Madeira (½ dL)
1 tsp. salt (you could
use a little less)
Pepper

THE BEEF FILET Buy:

A filet or piece of filet for roasting

You will need a trimmed piece of meat weighing a total of 1½ to 2 pounds (675 to 900 grams). The filet or tenderloin is an expensive piece of meat. You will find it, however, in various sizes and can save money by obtaining a smaller one. Another possibility of saving money is to ask your butcher if he will sell you an 8- or 9-inch (20- or 23-cm) piece from the head, or thicker end, of the filet. If he will, that could cut your expense almost in half. If you are forced to buy the whole tenderloin, you can economize by cutting off an 8- or 9-inch piece from the head end yourself. Serve that to your guests, saving the rest for another meal. The head end will provide enough meat to serve six people European-type portions (not huge), which is the way I prefer to serve when entertaining.

Some tenderloins are sold completely trimmed. If the one you bought was not, then trim it of all fat and membrane. Tie the sausage-shaped roast into a neat cylinder by wrapping and tying string around in seven or eight places, not too tight. The tying gives the roast a better shape after it is cooked. Arrange the meat in a roasting pan small enough to hold the meat nicely without a lot of empty space in the pan. Refrigerate. This can be done a day ahead.

TO ROAST Remove the meat from the refrigerator 1 or 2 hours before roasting to let it come to room temperature throughout. Preheat the oven to 450°F/230°C. The timing is tricky and will depend upon the thickness of the piece of meat. A smaller roast will be done in 20 to 25 minutes; the larger ones take 25 to 30. Ask your butcher if the tenderloin you have purchased came from a large animal or a smaller one. Take that into consideration when roasting. Guess on a roasting time and when that is up, test with an instant-reading meat thermometer. The temperature should fall between 120° and 130°F (49° and 54°C). If you take it higher than that, you risk having the meat end up brown all the way through (which ruins it, as far as I am concerned).

Let the meat sit 15 minutes before carving, then remove the strings and cut into slices less than ¼ inch (¾ cm) thick. Serve one or two slices to each guest, partly topped with the following sauce. (Don't hide all the pretty red color of the meat with the sauce.)

MINCED MUSHROOM SAUCE This is an interesting sauce that I discovered somewhat by mistake. I was fooling around one day, working on a composed butter sauce with a *duxelles* base. I tried my concoction on lamb chops for supper that night and it was—"undistinguished" is the best word I can think of. The leftover sauce sat for a week in the refrigerator. Then one day I began wondering what would happen if I heated the sauce and served it hot. This simple additional step magically turned my undistinguished *duxelles* butter into a sort of sauce that I think is really good.

THE SAUCE First you make a *duxelles*, but without the onion classically used. Into a saucepan put:

   3 Tbs. butter

Heat just to melt, then add:

   ½ lb. mushrooms (225 grams), minced fine

Brush or wash the mushrooms by dunking quickly in three changes of cold water. Slice, then mince fine with a knife (arduous) or, using the food processor fitted with the steel blade, throw in a handful of whole mushrooms and, working in small batches, pulse the machine on and off until the mushrooms are chopped fine.

Cook the mushrooms in the butter over medium/high heat to keep the juices evaporating. When the excess liquid is gone, add:

   ¼ cup Madeira (½ dL), a drier type such as
      Rainwater or Sercial
   1 tsp. salt (you could use a little less)
   Pepper

Cook, stirring occasionally, until the wine boils down and the excess liquid is reduced but not gone. This is going to be a sauce and it should not be too dry. Spread the *duxelles* out on a dinner plate and let cool. When it has come to room temperature, add:

   ½ stick softened butter (2 oz. or 60 grams)

Mix together to a paste. Reserve in the refrigerator up to a week or use it right away.

TO HEAT AND SERVE THE SAUCE Cut the chilled sauce into pieces and place in a saucepan. Over medium heat stir with a wire whisk until the sauce just barely comes to the boil. Remove from the heat. It will separate and look oily around the edges, but if you give it a good whisking, it will come back together again. You can add a tablespoon or two of water if it looks too impossibly thick. Serve.

SUGGESTED ACCOMPANIMENTS For a pretty and unusual combination of foods, try serving this with Cornmeal Polenta Swiss Style with Gruyère (see Rice, Grains, and Legumes, Misc.) and Cucumber "Noodles" (see Vegetables).

SAUTÉED BEEF CUBES

6 servings

Most marinades are nothing more than vinaigrette sauce with variations. In this recipe, beef cubes are marinated in the classic vinaigrette ingredients: olive oil, vinegar, Dijon mustard, salt, and pepper. This simple marinade gives a nice flavor to the filet cubes, which otherwise would not be very exciting.

This is a simple dish. I buy filets mignons from the supermarket down the street, cut them into large chunks, and let them marinate for 1 or 2 hours while I take my afternoon nap. Then I pan-fry them very briefly and just serve. They are delicious and easy and everybody likes them. The beef cubes can be cooked outdoors on a barbecue or hibachi if the grill is narrow enough to keep them from falling onto the coals.

2 lbs. beef tenderloin steaks (900 grams), preferably cut 1¼ inches (3 cm) thick
1 Tbs. vinegar
½ tsp. salt
1½ Tbs. olive oil
1 tsp. Dijon mustard
Pepper
3 Tbs. olive oil, cooking oil, or fat rendered from beef trimmings

THE BEEF Buy:
    2 lbs. beef tenderloin steaks (900 grams),
        preferably cut 1¼ inches (3 cm) thick
This will be about six *filets mignons.* You can use other tender beefsteak cuts from the loin or rib area, but I find the little round ones from the tenderloin most convenient. The meat is very lean and very tender, and you don't have to worry about veins of fat or about chewy or tough sections. The only bad thing about filet or tenderloin is the price. (For a cheaper version of this dish, use flank steak, but slice it on an angle.)

The reason for having the meat cut so thick is that thicker pieces are easier to cook correctly. You want the cubes to be lovely and brown on the outside and still rare inside.

Trim off any exterior fat. Cut the steaks into 1¼-inch (3-cm) cubes. You should get about five cubes from each steak, which means you will end up serving five cubes per guest.

THE MARINADE Into a bowl put:

1 Tbs. vinegar
½ tsp. salt

Whisk until the salt is dissolved, or almost. Add:

1½ Tbs. olive oil
1 tsp. Dijon mustard
Pepper

Mix, add the beef cubes, and stir to coat with the marinade. Let sit out in the room for 1 to 2 hours or up to 3 or 4. Stir once in a while if you think of it.

TO SAUTÉ THE CUBES At serving time, drain the meat cubes on paper towels to keep the fat from spitting when they're added. Put on an apron. Warm the serving plates. Use a frying pan or sauté pan that will hold all the cubes in one layer and put over high/medium heat. Add:

3 Tbs. olive oil, cooking oil, or fat rendered
     from beef trimmings

Heat until the pan is very hot and the fat just starts to smoke. Turn the heat to high. Add the beef cubes as quickly as possible.

Let cook for 1 minute or until brown on one side; don't touch them meanwhile. Turn over and cook about 1 minute or until browned. That ought to do it, but you do have to use some judgment. Do they look good to eat? If not, give them a great stir and let them cook a few seconds on an unbrowned side. Be worried. You don't want to overcook them. Using a finger or fork, jiggle a cube. If it wiggles like raw liver, the meat inside will be awfully rare. If it still wiggles a little but has firmed some, the inside is perfect. (When meat feels firm, it has overcooked.) If you have ever wondered how great steakhouse chefs or Japanese *yakitori* cooks get the meat just right, this is how. With a little practice in touch-testing and a lot of experience, you'll soon be able to cook meat to order like a professional.

If you like, sprinkle over more:

Salt

Serve right away.

Note: If you want to be wilder with your

marinade, there are many possible variations. Instead of salt, use some soy sauce. Instead of vinegar, use other acids or tangy things like wine, lemon juice, or exotic juices of pomegranate or green pineapple. For more complex flavors, add cayenne pepper, minced fresh ginger, minced garlic, or herbs like oregano, basil, thyme, or crumbled bay leaf.

Other things that are frequently added to marinades, like brown or white sugar, tomato catsup, Worcestershire sauce, Tabasco, or powdered ginger, may be good but are not considered very chic.

SUGGESTED ACCOMPANIMENTS If it's summertime, try serving the beef cubes with a ratatouille variation of mine called Summer Vegetable Chunks with Black Olives (see Vegetables). Ears of corn or fresh peas or boiled potatoes would go well as the third item on the plate. In winter, try Shredded Cabbage with Grated Banana Squash (see Vegetables) along with a baked potato.

TOURNEDOS, BASIL BÉARNAISE

6 servings

One of the most appealing things to the human palate—most certainly to the European and Western palate—is a thick beef filet, fried in a pan, served with Béarnaise sauce. However sophisticated you become, somehow each time you eat a steak with Béarnaise, you smile in the realization that few foods are so good to eat.

In this most-popular and well-loved sauce, I substitute basil for the traditional tarragon. The change is subtle. I like the basil version as much, if not more, than the classic tarragon.

Basil works magic. The Italian pasta and rice dishes that feature basil are among the best dishes man has devised. If you are not already among the many who worship this unusual herb, just put a bouquet of it to your nose and take a big whiff. You will experience one of life's greatest olfactory pleasures. You will need no further words from me to convince you that basil in any form is worth a try.

1 bunch fresh basil, sometimes called sweet basil

SAUCE BÉARNAISE WITH BASIL If you have a wide-mouthed Thermos, you can make this sauce 4 or 5 hours ahead. Otherwise, make it at the last minute

¼ cup white vinegar
  (½ dL)
4 Tbs. chopped
  shallots or green
  onion
Salt and pepper
2 sticks butter (½ lb.
  or 225 grams)
3 Tbs. cold water
3 egg yolks
6 slices good white
  bread (regular, not
  thin, slices)
6 tournedos, 5 to 6 oz.
  each (140 to 180
  grams), about 1¼
  inches (3 cm) thick
3 Tbs. rendered beef
  fat or cooking oil
1 Tbs. chopped basil
Chopped parsley
  (optional)

because reheating without separating is tricky. When you are ready to start the sauce, preheat the Thermos by filling with hot water and letting it sit while you make the sauce. Have:

  1 bunch fresh basil, sometimes called sweet
    basil

If you buy the basil ahead, keep the bouquet wrapped in paper or plastic and place the stems in a glass of water as if it were a bouquet of violets. Do not wash until just before you use it or the leaves can turn black. The bouquet will keep for days in the refrigerator like this. When ready to make the sauce, remove the leaves and discard the stems. Wash the leaves and dry. Chop fairly fine with a stainless steel knife. You need ¼ cup (4 Tbs.) chopped leaves for this sauce.

  Use a small, heavy saucepan. (Do not use uncoated aluminum or the sauce will turn gray. Calphalon works fine.) Into the pan put:

  ¼ cup white vinegar (½ dL)
  2 Tbs. chopped fresh basil
  4 Tbs. chopped shallots or green onion (chop
    very fine)
  ½ tsp. salt
  Pepper, lots

Bring to a boil and cook down until the moisture almost disappears. While this is reducing, into another saucepan put:

  2 sticks butter (½ lb. or 225 grams)

Heat until melted. Set aside to cool a little. When most of the moisture has disappeared from the basil mixture, remove its pan from the heat and add:

  3 Tbs. cold water
  3 egg yolks

Using a wire whisk, stir briskly and constantly over low heat (not too low or it takes forever) until the sauce thickens to the consistency of mayonnaise. Remove the pan from the heat and allow to cool a little. When both the yolk misture and the melted butter are still very warm but not boiling hot (test with a finger), add the butter to the yolk mixture in a very thin stream (actually, I add it in blobs), then stop and whisk. Turn the sauce round and round with the whisk. Be especially careful at first. It is very easy to ruin the sauce at this point. You must stop adding butter every few seconds and beat until the sauce is smooth again. Continue until all the butter has been added and the sauce is smooth. Add:

1 more Tbs. chopped basil

Dump the hot water out of the Thermos, then pour the Béarnaise in. Cover with both lids and reserve until serving time. (Wrap the remaining tablespoon of chopped basil in plastic and reserve until just before serving time.)

THE TOASTS This French touch is optional. The toasts do make the amount of meat on the plate look like more. They also absorb some of the meat juices and are rather pleasant to eat as a result. Have:

6 slices good white bread (regular, not thin, slices)

Using a cookie cutter or a glass or whatever will work, cut out six bread disks from the centers that are about the size of the steaks after they are tied. Toast in a toaster or broil quickly, first on one side and then on the other, under a hot broiler close to the heat. The idea is to toast both sides while leaving the center soft. Reserve until serving time.

THE TOURNEDOS Steaks from the small end of the beef tenderloin filet are called *filets mignons*. Those from the other, thicker end are known as *chateaubriand*. The medium-size steaks from the center are called *tournedos*. Have:

6 tournedos, 5 to 6 oz. each (140 to 180 grams), about 1¼ inches (3 cm) thick

Try to get them all more or less the same thickness and same diameter. This ensures that all will cook the same and that some guests won't be eyeing other guests' larger portions enviously. Trim steaks *completely* of fat and any membrane (fascia). (You can dice the fat and cook it in a frying pan with about ¼ cup (½ dL) water until it renders some fat to use for frying the meat. Or you can use cooking oil.)

Tie the steaks into nice round shapes with one or two circles of string. These neat servings look very stylish on the toasts. Reserve in the refrigerator, but bring out to room temperature 1 or 2 hours before cooking. Cook and serve at the last minute.

TO COOK AND SERVE THE STEAKS Use a frying pan that the steaks fit into fairly closely. Although you should not jam them in, it's far worse to have lots of empty space between them. The fat is likely to burn and spit all over the place. Add to the pan:

3 Tbs. rendered beef fat or cooking oil

Get the pan very hot, until just starting to smoke. Add the steaks. Get them in fast. If they are 1¼ inches thick, they will take 3 or 4 minutes per side, depending on how rare you like them. Set a timer and keep watch. It is a sin to overcook beautiful and expensive steaks. Sometimes 1 or 2 minutes makes the difference between perfect and ruined. The heat all this time should be adjusted up and down to keep the steaks sizzling pleasantly and noisily, but not smoking and crackling so madly that your kitchen is a mess and the steaks become indigestible.

After the first 3 or 4 minutes, turn the steaks over quickly and set the timer again for 3 or 4 minutes. Salt the steaks. When they should be done, jiggle the meat with your finger or with a fork. If too soft and wiggly like raw liver, give them another minute. If they are starting to firm up and don't wiggle too much, get them out instantly. Arrange on the toasts and cut the strings. Stir into the Béarnaise in the Thermos:

Reserved 1 Tbs. chopped basil

Spoon the Basil Béarnaise onto the steaks. You can sprinkle over:

Chopped parsley (optional)

Add the vegetables that accompany this dish to the plates. Serve.

SUGGESTED ACCOMPANIMENTS If you are using fresh basil because it is summer, I suggest you try a wonderfully colorful dish, Sautéed Zucchini, Snow Peas and Tomatoes. On the side, serve a simple baked or boiled potato or steamed rice.

BEEF SKILLET CAKE

6 servings

This skillet cake is wonderfully hearty and good, but not very elegant. Therefore it's suitable as the main course for an informal lunch or supper and perfect for a small brunch.

The ground beef, potato, and cheese flavors combined here are the same, although in a slightly different form, as those which have helped to sell umpteen billion Big Macs with fries. People seem to like these flavors, however they are combined. You will like this very easy dish. Almost everybody does.

1 lb. medium boiling
   potatoes (450 grams)
   (red ones are good)
1 lb. ground beef (450
   grams)
1 tsp. salt
4 to 5 Tbs. butter
4 oz. grated Gruyère
   or Swiss cheese (115
   grams)

THE POTATOES Have:
   1 lb. medium potatoes (450 grams) (red ones
      are good)
Put the potatoes in a pot of water, bring to a boil, and cook for 20 minutes. They will be almost but not quite done. Cool and chill. When cold, cut into coarse shreds with a hand shredder or a food processor fitted with the shredding disk. Shred unpeeled. Refrigerate covered. This can be done a day ahead.

TO PREPARE THE DISH AND SERVE In spite of the title of the recipe, the ideal pan to use is a nonstick frying pan measuring 10 inches (25 cm) in diameter at the top rim. This keeps the cake from sticking, and the pan's light weight also makes turning the cake easier. You can use a traditional iron skillet if you keep scraping to keep the cake from sticking.

The skillet cake should be cooked at the last minute, but you can mix the beef and potatoes ahead. In that case, don't add salt until the last minute because it changes the color of the beef and makes it look like corned beef.

Start the preparation 10 minutes before serving time. Put into a mixing bowl:
   1 lb. ground beef (450 grams)
As a kid, I was sent by my mother to the butcher shop with instructions to ask for the top of the round, ground twice. If you have any choice, that is still good advice. Add the cooked, shredded potatoes and:
   1 tsp. salt
   2 to 3 Tbs. butter, cut into pieces (optional)
Cut and toss with two knives until well mixed. Into the frying pan put:
   2 Tbs. butter

Heat to melt, then dump in the beef-potato mixture. Pat down into an even cake. Cook over fairly high heat for 3 minutes, then turn the cake this way: Over the top of the pan, place a dinner plate, platter, or tray that is larger than the pan. Carefully but quickly reverse the whole business. The cake will fall onto the plate. Return the pan to the stove. Then slide the uncooked side of the cake back into the pan. Right away sprinkle over:

> 4 oz. grated Gruyère or Swiss cheese (115 grams)

The heat of the cake will melt the cheese to some extent. Cook the second side of the cake for another 3 minutes or until browned as you like. Serve cut in wedges.

TO MAKE LARGER QUANTITIES I have tried doubling the recipe and cooking one really fat beef cake, but somehow it doesn't taste as good as the thinner one. Besides, the trauma of turning such a thick cake is tremendous and just not worth it. I suggest you use two pans and cook two cakes simultaneously.

For serving even more people, you may make as large a batch as you like and form the mixture into individual patty shapes, just like (I hate to say this) cheeseburgers.

SUGGESTED ACCOMPANIMENTS For a breakfast or brunch, serve with scrambled eggs and Sautéed Plum Tomatoes (see Vegetables) or cherry tomatoes. For a mid-week supper, serve with Steamed Carrot Shreds (see Vegetables) plus a green vegetable such as peas or string beans or broccoli.

DOUBLE-THICK SIRLOIN STEAK WITH MUSTARD

6 servings

Here is a dish for people who like to build a meal around a good piece of beef. A double-thick sirloin steak is roasted with a coating of Dijon mustard, fresh ginger, and garlic, then served in slices cut at a slight slant. Speaking of easy, dishes don't come any faster and simpler than this one, and if you're a beef eater, you are sure to like it.

A double-thick sirloin steak about 2 inches (5 cm) thick, weighing approximately 3 lbs. (1350 grams), with the tenderloin piece removed

4 Tbs. Dijon mustard
1 tsp. soy sauce
2 cloves garlic, minced very fine
4 slices fresh ginger
2 Tbs. oil

THE BEEF Have:

A double-thick sirloin steak about 2 inches (5 cm) thick, weighing approximately 3 lbs. (1350 grams), with the tenderloin piece removed

Trim the meat of any excess exterior fat. Reserve.

THE MUSTARD COATING Into a small bowl put:

4 Tbs. Dijon mustard
1 tsp. soy sauce
2 cloves garlic, minced very fine (2 tsp.)
4 slices fresh ginger, thick diagonal slices, skin scraped off, minced, but not too fine (3 to 4 Tbs.)
2 Tbs. oil

Stir to a smooth paste. Two hours before roasting time, brush the steak all over with the coating, then place in a roasting pan, spreading the last of the coating in a thick layer on the top. Let sit in the room for 2 hours.

TO ROAST AND SERVE Preheat the oven to 475°F/245°C. Place the meat in the center of the oven and roast for approximately 20 minutes or until the internal temperature of the meat reaches 125° to 130°F (52° to 54°C). Remove from the oven and let sit 6 or 7 minutes, then serve. Slice on the diagonal into thin or thick slices as you prefer. I prefer about ¼ inch (¾ cm) thick.

SUGGESTED ACCOMPANIMENTS For a good but plain American dinner, serve with a baked potato (the potatoes can bake at 475°F/245°C along with the steak, but bake them 50 minutes to an hour), along with fresh asparagus, string beans, or broccoli. For something a little different, instead of the green vegetable, try the pretty orange and yellow Sliced Carrots and Yellow Summer Squash.

BROILED DOUBLE LOIN LAMB CHOPS WITH KIDNEYS

6 servings

There is a well-known and highly thought-of restaurant in San Francisco called Jack's. One of their specialties is called simply Mutton Chops. It really isn't mutton. It's older or mature lamb, but whatever it is, it's good. When I first tasted this dish years ago, I

thought it was one of the most satisfying chunks of good, red meat I had ever eaten. I still think so. This is my version of that dish.

6 double loin lamb
  chops,
  approximately 2 to
  2¼ inches (5 to 6 cm)
  thick
3 lamb kidneys
3 Tbs. butter
6 slices bacon
Minced garlic
Oil
Salt and pepper

LAMB THAT HAS BEEN AGED There is a big difference in the flavor and tenderness of lamb when it has been aged by the butcher. Really fine shops have a special refrigerator where they age the more tender cuts of lamb and beef. The refrigerators are set between 33° and 34°F (1° and 2°C). In the case of lamb, particularly young lamb, they hang the meat for one to two weeks. As it ages, the tissues break down and the meat becomes more tender and more flavorful. On the outside, particularly if there is not a very thick fat covering, the meat will rot and turn black. The butcher is obliged to cut this off, thereby losing some of the meat he has to sell. So the price per pound must be higher. Some of the more sensitive souls among you are probably on the floor by now. Sorry, but this is what aging is all about, and I highly recommend that you try to buy aged lamb or the dish will not be as good as it should be.

THE LAMB CHOPS Buy:

> 6 double loin lamb chops, approximately 2 to 2¼ inches (5 to 6 cm) thick

Order these well ahead. If you have a nice butcher who likes you and you happen to catch him when he's not too busy, he may take six short loins and give you one good double chop from the sirloin end of each loin. This way you get a fat filet piece on each chop. Bone the chops and trim away all fat and membrane. You will end up with two pieces of meat for each chop, which you will later tie together with string. Reserve these in the refrigerator. The fatty flap, which you will discard, has a piece of meat on it that you can trim out and save for a lamb stew later in the week.

THE KIDNEYS Buy:

> 3 lamb kidneys

Call early in the week and ask the butcher to save these for you. There are only two per animal and they are often gone by the end of the week. Cut them in half as if to butterfly them, then cut out the white cores with the funny fat "fingers" as best you can. Sauté the kidneys briefly, approximately 30 seconds per side, in:

> 3 tbs. hot butter

Use a low/medium flame so you do not overheat
the butter. The kidneys should brown and be
cooked outside but still be pink inside. Remove to a
strainer over a bowl and let the kidneys drain. Red
juices will come out, which you should discard.
This removes the strong taste. Refrigerate and allow
to chill thoroughly before assembling the chops.

TO ASSEMBLE THE CHOPS Have ready:

6 slices bacon (thin or regular)

Place a chilled kidney half between each two pieces
of chilled lamb chop while sprinkling over the meat
inside (so it will be wrapped inside the meat after
all is tied together) some:

Minced garlic

If the chops you bought did not have much of a
filet piece, you will just have to wrap the one big
piece of meat around the kidney half as best you
can. Then wrap a slice of bacon around each lamb
"sandwich" and tie string around the bacon. Do
not tie too tight because the meat will expand a
little as it cooks. Keep in refrigerator.

TO BROIL THE CHOPS I would advise strongly that
you buy a few extra chops and do a trial run on the
dish for supper the night before. The size of chops
differs enormously, and stove broilers all have their
peculiarities. You are taking a chance if you expect
to get these right the first time. My broiler is gas. I
broil with the tops of the chops about 3 inches (8
cm) from the flame and the oven door closed.

Preheat the broiler at least 15 minutes ahead.
Brush the broiler pan with oil, then brush or rub
the chops (they should be completely at room
temperature) with:

Oil

Put the chops in the pan. Broil 4 minutes on the
first side, then turn. Sprinkle the second side with:

Salt and pepper

Broil 3 minutes more. Turn the broiler off; open the
door and let the chops rest 4 or 5 minutes before
serving. Turn the chops over when placing on
plates, then salt and pepper the top side.

DO-AHEAD NOTES You can assemble the chops
completely a day ahead. You can even do them
further ahead and freeze, but you will lose quality.
Just be sure they are fully at room temperature

when you broil them. A cold kidney between warm lamb is not a treat

SUGGESTED ACCOMPANIMENTS The French love the combination of lamb and beans. I do, too. Try Fresh Black-eyed Peas with Pesto or make that dish using small white beans instead of the black-eyed peas. For a second vegetable, choose any colorful green or orange one or a combination of the two.

LAMB NOISETTES WITH GREEN PEPPERCORNS

6 servings

Lamb noisettes are small loin lamb chops boned and tied into pretty little round medallions, or noisettes. In this recipe they are pan-fried and served on toast rounds with a deglaze sauce featuring green peppercorns.

To deglaze means to add liquid and scrape up the good stuff that sticks to the bottom of the pan you cook the meat in. The liquid in this case is reduced cream.

You can buy green peppercorns (they are simply underripe peppercorns) in little cans in "gourmet" food shops. If you can't find them, leave them out and at the very end, just before serving, add a large amount of freshly ground pepper (white is preferred for appearance) to the sauce.

6 large lamb chops from the "small loin," 1¼ to 1½ inches (3 to 4 cm) thick
1 loaf good white bread
1½ cups whipping cream (3½ dL)
1 Tbs. lemon juice
3 Tbs. dry Madeira
½ tsp. salt
1 tsp. Bovril or 1 beef bouillon cube (optional)
3 Tbs. green peppercorns, drained, rinsed, and crushed or chopped not too fine

THE LAMB Buy:
6 large lamb chops from what is called the "small loin," 1¼ to 1½ inches (3 to 4 cm) thick

All "small loin" lamb chops are relatively small; but you should avoid getting the very smallest, which have only a bite or two of meat on them, because you are going to serve only one per guest. (You may want to buy some extra ones for bigger eaters in the crowd.) Frequently you can buy the chops right out of the butcher case, but it might be better to ask your butcher well ahead to cut the number you want so that you are sure to obtain them. If your butcher likes you and if he sells that much lamb, he may give you the nicest two chops (those that have the largest pieces of filet) from three or four different loins.

At home, cut out the bones and tie the meat from each with one or two circles of string to form neat, round steaks about 2 inches (5 cm) in

3 Tbs. fat (rendered lamb fat, oil, half butter and half oil, or whatever)

¼ cup good brandy or Cognac (½ dL)

diameter. This can be done a day ahead. Reserve in the refrigerator, loosely covered, but not airtight or the meat can spoil.

THE TOASTS Have:

1 loaf good white bread

Cut six little bread rounds to go under each of the *noisettes*. I use a cookie cutter approximately 2½ inches (6½ cm) in diameter. Preheat the broiler, then place the bread rounds on a rack and broil very close to the heat source for 1 minute or so per side (careful, they burn quickly) or until both sides are nicely browned. You could use a toaster instead. Remove and reserve.

THE SAUCE Most of this can be prepared ahead.

Place in a large saucepan (to prevent boiling over):

1½ cups whipping cream (3½ dL), preferably the heavy, old-fashioned type

Cook over high heat, whisking well now and then, until the cream thickens and reduces to about half. Add:

1 Tbs. lemon juice

3 Tbs. Madeira (Rainwater or Sercial, the drier types)

½ tsp salt

1 tsp. Bovril or 1 beef bouillon cube (optional)

3 Tbs. green peppercorns, drained, rinsed, and crushed or chopped not too fine

Mix. Reserve until serving time. You can make this much a day ahead.

TO COOK THE LAMB Have the lamb and the reduced cream sauce at room temperature. At serving time, place in a frying pan:

3 Tbs. fat (rendered lamb fat, oil, half butter and half oil, or whatever)

Get the pan very hot. The fat should start to smoke. Quickly put in the lamb and cook over high heat a bare 1½ minutes per side. For my taste, the steaks should be cooked medium rare. Remember that, because they are small in diameter, they will cook faster than large steaks. Salt after turning. When done, place on the toasts on a platter; with scissors cut and remove the strings. Keep warm in a 170°F/77°C oven while you finish the sauce. Pour all the remaining fat from the frying pan and discard it. Add to the pan:

¼ cup good brandy or Cognac (½ dL)

Heat, scraping up any brown bits from the bottom of the pan. You can flame this if you like, but don't set yourself on fire. Add the reserved cream sauce. Stir, taste, spoon over the steaks, and serve as quickly as possible.

SUGGESTED ACCOMPANIMENTS For something really different, try serving the noisettes with Steamed Millet with Onions and Oregano. To go along with this, it is critical to serve something with lots of color—Sautéed Zucchini, Snow Peas, and Tomatoes, for example, or Shredded Yellow Squash with Red Bell Pepper. Also, any of the suggested accompaniments for the previous lamb dish would work very well with the *noisettes*.

ROAST SADDLE OF LAMB WITH ROSEMARY AND GARLIC

6 servings

This serves six, just barely. The saddle is a luxurious, very expensive cut of meat. It will cost you about the same per guest as serving each a 1¼-pound (565-gram) lobster flown in live from the state of Maine. If you are not willing to mortgage your house for this, I suggest you serve a butterflied, boned leg of lamb with rosemary and garlic instead (see the end of this recipe for cooking instructions). It will cost about a third as much as the saddle.

A saddle is not a very well known cut of meat. It consists of two rows of little loin lamb chops not yet cut apart, from the back of the animal where a saddle would be put if anybody rode around on lambs. Many butchers may not even know it by name, if at all; but they will probably understand if you order a double short loin, still attached, with the skin flaps or flanks left on and the fell removed. It is a very compact roast, almost square, that weighs around 5 pounds, trimmed weight.

1 saddle of lamb, approximately 5 lbs. (2¼ kg)
1 tsp. thyme
½ tsp. rosemary, chopped or crumbled between your fingers
2 or 4 cloves of garlic, sliced thin
Pepper

THE LAMB Buy:

1 saddle of lamb, approximately 5 lbs. (2¼ kg)
Trim away all but a ⅛-inch (½-cm)-thick layer of fat from the main, top part of the roast. Turn it over and open the flaps. Trim all the fat that you see from this area, trimming down to the actual filet strips that you will see there. Also trim some of the fat from the flaps themselves. Fold the flaps over this area and cut them off so that they just meet and do not overlap.

TO PREPARE FOR ROASTING Make sure to bring the

meat out of the refrigerator 3 hours or so before roasting to allow to come to room temperature. One or 2 hours before roasting, open the flaps and sprinkle over the filet area:

> ½ tsp. thyme
> ¼ tsp. rosemary, chopped or crumbled
>   between your fingers
> 1 or 2 garlic cloves, sliced thin
> Pepper

Fold the flaps over this, then tie in three or four places with string to keep the flaps closed. Place the meat, flaps down, in a roasting pan that just fits it nicely. You can place it on a rack if you like. Sprinkle over:

> Thyme, rosemary, and pepper

in the same amounts that you did on the under side. Make slits in the fat covering and poke in slivers of:

> Garlic

TO ROAST Preheat the oven to 450°F/230°C. Place the roast in the oven for 10 minutes. Lower the heat to 350°F/180°C and cook another 45 minutes or until done. This can vary quite a bit, depending upon the size of the lamb. To test for doneness, insert a trussing needle or cake tester into the spinal column, right up through the backbone of the animal. Let it remain there for 10 seconds, then remove and touch the end of it to your lips. It should just feel nicely warm for the roast to be medium rare or lovely and pink inside. Let the roast sit out 10 to 15 minutes before carving. This gives time for the heat to distribute to the center of the roast. *Note:* Because of the shape of a saddle, I find using a meat thermometer impractical. The test for doneness just given works for me.

TO CARVE The saddle is usually carved vertically into long, thin slices. The first cut should be a long, thick one to remove the fatty flap from one side. Set the flap meat aside and serve as seconds or thirds later. With the saddle in the same position it was in when roasted and with your knife cutting straight up and down, cut long, thin slices of meat less than ¼ inch (¾ cm) thick, first from one side, then from the other, each slice coming nearer to the center. The slices will stay attached at the bottom. Then you will slice across the bottom to free the slices. For the first serving, give everyone two of these long, thin slices.

When anyone is ready for seconds, turn the roast over and bone out the two long, fish-shaped filets. Cut them across into 1-inch (2½-cm) chunk-like pieces and give everybody one or two. Anybody who wants to come back for thirds gets pieces of the flaps, which are a little chewy but good.

SUGGESTED ACCOMPANIMENTS This is an elegant cut of meat and it needs quite an occasion for serving it. One of my favorite times for presenting this roast is at an intimate Christmas Eve dinner for four or five or six. As an accompaniment at such a dinner, I love to serve Fresh Chestnut Puree, plus a colorful mixture of at least three sautéed, cooked vegetables in the style of Sautéed Zucchini, Snow Peas, and Tomatoes. Cut and cook the vegetables ahead, then carefully reheat at the last minute in butter. Pick your own combination. Broccoli flowerets, sliced carrots, and sliced zucchini, for example, would be nice.

Other possibilities for accompanying the saddle of lamb are the traditional French potato dishes Gratin Savoyarde or Gratin Dauphinoise (see any good, traditional French cookbook for recipes) and a green vegetable.

BUTTERFLIED BONED LEG OF LAMB You could use the same herb and garlic treatment for a boned leg of lamb. Have your butcher bone a leg of lamb for you. Trim completely of all exterior fat and membrane (or leave some fat on if you prefer). Cut between the muscles just so that the leg will spread out and lie lumpy but more or less flat. Two hours before roasting, oil the meat well all over, sprinkle with herbs and salt, and insert garlic slivers here and there. Broil the meat in a preheated broiler, keeping it still somewhat pink in the center, with the one really large muscle still rather rare. In my gas broiler, I broil 5 inches (13 cm) from the flame, about 18 minutes per side, with the broiler door closed.

PORK CUTLETS, ARLESIENNE STYLE

6 servings

Arles is a city in the south of France where tomatoes, peppers, onions, and garlic are very popular cooking ingredients. These pork cutlets are done in the style of that city.

This dish is one that I have been cooking for years with great success. It is festive and can be completely done a day ahead. I learned it at the Cordon Bleu in Paris. There they used veal instead of pork, but I find the pork a nice variation and it is certainly easier to find. The dish works equally well using chicken breasts, butterflied and pounded. The combination of meat with the layer of tomatoes, peppers, onions, and garlic plus cheese seems to appeal to everyone.

6 rib pork chops
½ cup flour (60 grams)
1 tsp. salt
Pepper
2 eggs
½ cup olive oil (1 dL)
7 or 8 slices of good
   white or whole
   wheat bread
4 Tbs. fat
4 Tbs. olive oil
1 onion, minced
1 green pepper,
   chopped coarse
1 or 2 garlic cloves,
   minced
6 medium tomatoes
   (about 2 lbs. or 900
   grams)
1 tsp. dried basil (or 2
   to 3 tsp. fresh)
1 tsp. salt
Pepper
Thin slices of Gruyère
   or Swiss cheese
   (about 6 oz. or 180
   grams)

THE PORK You start this recipe first by making Wiener Schnitzel, only with pork instead of veal. Wiener Schnitzel, which translates literally as "Viennese little slice," actually is a breaded, sautéed veal scallop. People say that the Viennese took this dish from the Italians. The Mexicans seem to bear this out, since they call breaded, sautéed pork scallops *Milanese de puerco*, giving credit to the Milanese. To confuse the matter even further, the French call this style of breading and sautéing *panée à l'anglaise*. So there you are. I was hoping that this might clear matters up, but I can see that it hasn't. So just buy:
   6 rib pork chops
The ideal pork chops are large in meat area and about ¾ inch (2 cm) thick, with a nice round of meat in one solid piece. If you find a great white veining of fat within the meat, so much the better.

Cut the meat away from the bones, then trim off the fat, leaving a ¼-inch (¾-cm) border. Butterfly by starting to cut through the area that has the border of fat. Open up the pieces, then pound between sheets of parchment or brown paper to make even scallops about ⅛ inch (½ cm) thick.

TO BREAD AND COOK THE PORK Have three dinner plates. On the first put:
   ½ cup flour (60 grams)
   ½ tsp. salt
   Pepper
On the second, add and mix with a fork:
   2 eggs

½ cup olive oil (1 dL)
½ tsp. salt
Pepper
On the third put:
　　Fresh bread crumbs, not the toasted kind
(Remove the crusts from seven or eight slices of
good white or whole wheat bread and process to
crumbs in a food processor or blender.) Press each
pork scallop into the flour mixture, first on one
side, then on the other. Shake off the excess, then
dip each side into the egg mixture. Lift with a fork,
then shake the scallop a bit, letting the excess egg
run off. Put the scallop in the crumbs, turn over
and press down, sprinkling over more crumbs if
necessary until well coated.

　　Place on a plate and continue until all are
coated. You can cook the meat right away or let it
dry for an hour or longer in the refrigerator. Some
people say that the coating stays on better if dried,
but I don't think there's much difference.

4 Tbs. fat　　TO PRECOOK THE PORK In a large sauté pan or
frying pan put:
　　4 Tbs. fat
(You can use lard; half butter, half oil; peanut,
corn, olive, or other vegetable oil; all butter or
clarified butter. If you use all butter, cook the
scallops over low heat because butter burns
quickly.) Sauté the scallops in the hot pan for 1½ to
2 minutes per side or until lightly browned. Drain
on paper towels and cool. Wipe out and clean the
pan between batches and add new fat each time.
THE VEGETABLE TOPPING In a large sauté pan heat:
　　4 Tbs. olive oil
Add:
　　1 onion, minced
　　1 green pepper, chopped coarse
Soften the onion and pepper in the oil over low
heat for 5 minutes. Don't let it color. Add:
　　1 or 2 garlic cloves, minced
Cook 1 minute, then add:
　　6 medium tomatoes (about 2 lbs. or 900 grams),
　　　　peeled, seeded, and chopped coarse
　　1 tsp. dried basil (or 2 to 3 tsp. fresh)
　　1 tsp. salt
　　Pepper

Cook uncovered over very high heat for 5 minutes or more, stirring occasionally until some liquid from the tomatoes evaporates and the mixture holds together somewhat like a paste. Spread the mixture on a plate to cool and to evaporate more moisture.

TO ASSEMBLE THE DISH Spread each pork scallop with one-sixth of the vegetable mixture, in an even layer as if you were peanut-buttering a piece of bread. Refrigerate uncovered until the meat and topping are chilled, then cover with plastic. This much can be done a day ahead.

TO HEAT AND SERVE Bake in a preheated 350°F/180°C oven for 10 minutes. Remove and top with:

> Thin slices of Gruyère or Swiss cheese (about 6 oz. or 180 grams)

Bake 5 minutes more, just long enough to heat the cheese. (The cheese does not brown, but just gets soft and hot. When I tried more time to brown the cheese, it all just melted and ran off the meat.) Serve.

SUGGESTED ACCOMPANIMENTS I have served this dish many times with Brown Rice with Pine Nuts (see Rice, Grains, and Legumes, Misc.) and Cauliflower with Watercress Sauce (see Vegetables). I highly recommend that combination. The green sauce on the cauliflower and the vegetable topping on the pork cutlets make this a beautiful and colorful plate. The taste and texture combinations are also wonderful.

PORK MOUSSELINES, GREEN BEURRE BLANC

6 servings

These pork mousselines *are really exciting and simple.* Mousselines *have been around for years and for a long time have been the big specialty of the great three-star restaurants of France. Barrier in Tours makes his with sweetbreads (Darioles de ris de veau); the Haeberlin brothers at the Auberge de l'Ill do theirs with frogs' legs (Mousselines de cuisses de grenouille); Alain Chapelle at Mionnay does his with chicken livers (Gateau de foies blonds de volaille). Restaurants all over France and the United States offer fish* quenelles, *which in most cases are not* quenelles *at all (that is, made with flour and frequently egg yolks) but* mousselines.

The big restaurants featured mousselines *in the old days because they were something unique to offer and because making them required hours of pounding and sieving, which nobody at home would take the time to do. The arrival of the food processor changed all this. It is now a simple matter to make your own at home.*

Perhaps you are wondering what a mousseline *is. It is ground fish or poultry or meat mixed usually with egg whites, heavy cream, and seasonings, then baked most often in individual molds. The resulting "cake" or "pudding" is soft, light, heavenly, and a wonderful vehicle for showing off a great sauce. Some* mousselines *have surprise clumps of solids hidden in their interiors, but most do not.*

Mousselines can probably be made of any protein, providing it is raw. They can be done with fish: pike, sole, sea bass, catfish, trout, shark, squid, you name it. They can be done with shellfish: scallops, shrimp, lobster, crab (but try getting raw crabmeat out of the shells). They can be made with chicken, veal, pork, beef, lamb, goat, moose, beaver, and aardvark. The strange thing is that everything you try seems not only to work but to be delicious.

I decided to use pork for my mousselines *as a little reverse chic. I approached the project very much afraid of ending up with just an elegant hot dog—or Spam. I was happily surprised with the results. I think they are divine.*

First, here is how to do the sauce.

---

1 bunch spinach
4 or 5 quarts boiling water (3¾ or 4¾ L)
1 or 2 Tbs. salt
¾ lb. unsalted butter (3 sticks or 340 grams) cut into tablespoon-size pieces
2 Tbs. shallots or green onions, minced fine
3 Tbs. white vinegar
¼ cup dry white wine or vermouth (½ dL)
½ tsp. salt
Softened butter
1½ lbs. lean pork meat (675 grams)
3 egg whites
2¼ cups cream (5¾-dL)
1½ tsp. salt
⅛ tsp. cayenne pepper

GREEN BEURRE BLANC This sauce is simply *beurre blanc* with some cooked spinach blended into it. The sauce turns a lovely green and has a spinach taste that is so subtle you almost have to imagine it. (If your kids won't eat spinach, let 'em try this.) The spinach is there mainly for the color. The *mousselines* taste so wonderful in themselves that I feel they should not be overpowered by too strong a green taste.

If you use this sauce for another dish and want a greener taste, you can add other things such as fresh tarragon, chervil, parsley, chives, or watercress. Blanch the fresh greens for 30 seconds, then add with the spinach.

THE THERMOS If you have a Thermos (a wide-mouthed one is preferable), you can do the green *beurre blanc* about 5 hours before it is to be eaten. Otherwise, it must be done at the last minute. While you are making the sauce, preheat the Thermos by filling it with water as hot as it comes from the tap. With this quantity, you are safe with that kind of heat, but with smaller batches of *beurre blanc,* be careful and use less or the extreme heat can melt the sauce.

THE SPINACH Buy:
    1 bunch spinach
You could use frozen leaf spinach for this, about one-third package. Let it defrost, then get rid of as many of the stems as you can. If using fresh spinach, wash well, then remove all the stems. In a large saucepan have:

4 or 5 quarts boiling water (3¾ or 4¾ L)
Add:
    1 or 2 Tbs. salt
Add the spinach and cook for 1 minute. Drain in a colander, then run cold water over the spinach to stop the cooking, thus preserving the color. Chop briefly, then squeeze out excess water. Reserve. The spinach should be warm or at room temperature when added to the sauce.

THE BEURRE BLANC AND THE GREENING OF IT The sauce will be described for the Thermos technique (see above), which can be done 4 or 5 hours ahead. If you are making the sauce at the last minute, simply omit the Thermos instructions, proceeding to the next steps.

Pour hot water as hot as it comes from the tap into the Thermos, then cover and set aside. Have a large, heavy saucepan that is not of uncoated aluminum. I use a 4½-quart (4-L) Calphalon pan for this, but a smaller one will do. Have ready on the side in the refrigerator:
    ¾ lb unsalted butter (3 sticks or 340 grams), cut
        into tablespoon-size pieces
Into the saucepan put:
    2 Tbs. shallots or green onions, minced fine
    3 Tbs. white vinegar
    ¼ cup dry white wine (½ dL) (I use Noilly Prat
        dry vermouth)
    ½ tsp. salt
Cook over high heat until the liquid has reduced to about 2 tablespoons. *Be careful not to reduce this any further or the sauce will not work.* Reduce the heat to medium and right away add two-thirds of the butter pieces to the pan. Whisk around quickly in the pan. The pieces will gradually soften, liquefy, and turn a very yellow-white color, but they will not actually melt and turn oily yellow unless you overheat. Keep whisking constantly and, as the pieces dissolve, check the temperature of the sauce by putting your finger in it. It should be the temperature of warm bathtub water or a little hotter. If it is too cold, increase the heat; if too hot, remove the pan from the heat for a while. If by mistake it gets so hot that you see some melting of the butter around the edges, quickly pour the sauce into a bowl and whisk it. When it has lost its extreme heat, pour back into the pan and continue.

Whatever you do, don't panic. People are scared to death of *beurre blanc,* and frankly, it ain't that big a deal.

When there are only two or three small, solid pieces of butter left in the sauce, remove the pan from the heat and whisk until all the butter is dissolved. Dump the water from the Thermos and pour in the *beurre blanc,* pouring it, if you wish, through a strainer to remove the shallots. Cover the Thermos and keep warm until serving time. Reserve the rest of the butter in the refrigerator, but keep the spinach out so that it stays at room temperature.

TO FINISH THE SAUCE AND SERVE Just before serving, pour the sauce from the Thermos into the container of a food processor fitted with the steel blade. Add the reserved chopped, cooked spinach at room temperature or slightly warmed. Process until smooth, about 2 minutes. Return the sauce to a heavy saucepan and place over medium/low heat. Whisk again, and as soon as the sauce reaches warm bathtub temperature, add all the remaining chilled butter pieces. Whisk quickly until the butter dissolves. Keep checking the temperature of the sauce and adjusting as you did when adding the first portion of butter. When all the pieces have dissolved and the sauce is smooth, serve.

THE MOUSSELINES You need six 6-ounce (1¾-dL) glass or metal ovenproof custard cups (or equivalent). Butter them well with:

Softened butter

Into the container of a food processor fitted with the steel blade (you will have to do this in two or three batches because there is too much bulk) put:

1½ lbs. lean pork meat (675 grams), cut into ½-inch (1½-cm) cubes

(I use the "eye" or the lean part from 3 pounds (1350 grams) of center-cut rib chops and make sausage from the leftover scraps, but loin chops or leg steaks or tenderloins would do fine.) Process on and off at first, then let the machine run for 1 or 2 minutes or until meat is chopped fine. Add:

3 egg whites
2¼ cups cream (5¾ dL)
1½ tsp. salt
⅛ tsp. cayenne pepper

Process until pureed smooth. Spoon into the

buttered cups. Zigzag a toothpick through the paste
to break up air pockets, but avoid touching the
buttered sides of the cups. Bang the cups down on
a crumpled dish towel (don't break them) to get rid
of more air and to level the paste. Preparation can
be done to this point the day before. Refrigerate
until the meat is chilled, then cover with plastic
wrap.

TO SERVE Bring the molds out to room temperature
1 or 2 hours before baking. Preheat the oven to
375°F/190°C. Fill a pan with boiling water to set the
cups into when baking. The water should come 1
inch (2½ cm) up the sides of the cups. Place a sheet
of foil over the cups, shiny side down, to prevent a
skin from forming. Put all this in the oven and bake
for 45 minutes. (This is longer than necessary to set
the *mousselines,* but since we are dealing with pork,
we must be careful.) Check the internal
temperature of several of the *mousselines* with an
instant-reading meat thermometer. The temperature
should read 138°F/59°C. If it does not, bake another
5 minutes.

Drain the juices from the molds, then unmold
onto warmed serving dishes. The dishes must not
be cold or the butter sauce will congeal when it hits
the plates. Strange as it may seem, you must let the
mousselines cool off just a tad or the butter sauce
may melt. This is fine anyway, since it gives you
ample time to add the accompanying vegetables to
the plate. When everything is ready to go out to the
dining room, pour the *beurre blanc* from the
Thermos over the *mousselines.* Serve.

SUGGESTED ACCOMPANIMENTS A wonderful
accompaniment to this dish would be the three
vegetable purees described in the Vegetable section:
butternut squash, string beans, and potato-beet.
Try to picture the brilliant colors on the plate with
the two greens, the orange, and the purple. It is a
truly beautiful and great-tasting combination of
foods.

MAIN COURSES:
SOUPS AND PASTA

SOUPS

Mixed Seafood Soup with Wild Rice and Vegetables

Soup with Beef Slices and Whole Wheat Noodles

PASTA

Spaghetti with Three-Color Vegetable Shreds

MIXED SEAFOOD SOUP
WITH WILD RICE AND VEGETABLES

6 servings

This is an exciting soup . . . finally. Getting the blasted thing to turn out just right almost drove me crazy. In the early stages, my usual careful approach to seasoning—aiming for lovely, mild flavors—got me absolutely nowhere. I kept throwing in tons of fish and vegetables but ending up with nothing but dishwater.

Finally, abandoning all caution, I went stark wild with herbs, seasonings, and strong-flavored fish. The result is a soup that is really *soup. The key to success with this wonderful concoction is the amount of herbs and seasonings and, perhaps more important, the types of fish.*

You must choose fish with lots of character. By that I don't mean fish that's old and smells bad. What I do mean is forget the trout, sole, and delicate white fish. Concentrate on those like bass, cod, and especially mackerel. Don't be timid. Don't think, "Yuck! I can't stand mackerel, it's so strong. I'll leave it out." For this dish you must have it.

In terms of preparation time, this is not a simple soup. But if you consider that it is a main course and such a delicious one, I think you'll agree that the time is well worth it.

Ideally this soup should be eaten the day it's made. It definitely is better the first day. However, it is still good if reheated the next day. If you do the soup ahead, be very careful to chill as quickly as possible and don't cover until thoroughly cold.

---

8 oz. wild rice (225 grams)
A 1½-lb. mackerel (675 grams)
A 2-lb. rock cod or other cod or rockfish (900 grams)
A 1-lb. sea bass (450 grams)
1 lb. squid (450 grams)
4 oz. medium-size shrimp (115 grams)
4 oz. scallops (115 grams
2 Tbs. cornstarch
1½ tsp. salt
2 Tbs. dry white wine or good dry vermouth (I use Noilly Prat)
1 bunch leeks
2 onions, peeled and sliced thin

THE WILD RICE Have:

8 oz. wild rice (225 grams)

Wild rice is not cheap. If you don't feel like splurging for it, substitute 1½ cups brown rice (measured before cooking) and cook according to instructions in one of the brown rice dishes elsewhere in this book.

To prepare the wild rice, wash very well in three or four waters, ending with running water through it in a strainer. Pour in a bowl. Heat 6 cups (1½ L) of water to boiling and pour over. Let steep for 30 minutes. Drain. Repeat this process two more times. Reserve.

If you are finicky about not overswelling your wild rice and if you are doing the soup a day ahead, you can eliminate the third steeping and let steeping in the soup take its place. I tend to like the grains fully swollen and open, so I do three steepings. I have noticed a difference in batches of wild rice. The fresher, sturdier rice holds up better and improves with four, even five, steepings. But older batches tend to fall apart with this much soaking.

2 carrots, sliced thin
2 celery stalks, sliced thin
3 or 4 large sprigs parsley
1 large bay leaf
1 tsp. thyme
½ tsp. rosemary
2 tsp. salt
Heads, tails, skin, and bones from the fish; or 1 cup (¼ L) or more bottled clam juice
8 cups water (2 L)
2 cups dry white wine or good dry vermouth (I use Noilly Prat)
1 unpeeled baking potato (about 8 oz. or 225 grams)
3 Tbs. butter
½ cup celery
½ cup diced carrot
½ cup diced turnip
1 tomato (about 8 oz. or 225 grams)
1 head butter lettuce (also called Boston or garden lettuce)
1 stick butter (4 oz. or 115 grams) (optional)
6 Tbs. butter
Salt
Pepper

THE FISH AND THE SHELLFISH Here is a good combination of fish and shellfish. If you can't get the same ones, feel free to substitute. Just make sure to use fish of "high character" and to have at least 1½ to 2 pounds (675 to 900 grams) of mackerel or a mackerel-type fish. If you don't know what to substitute, ask your fish seller to suggest other strong-flavored fish. If you can't find squid, use crab or increase shrimp and/or scallops or fish to make up for it. Have:

A 1½-lb. mackerel (675 grams)
A 2-lb. rock cod or other cod or rockfish (900 grams)
A 1-lb. sea bass (450 grams)
1 lb. squid (450 grams)
4 oz. shrimp of medium size (115 grams)
4 oz. scallops (115 grams)

Buy the fish whole if you can. Have the fish merchant gut and fillet them, then skin the fillets. Ask him to give you all the heads, tails, bones, and skin, which you will use for your stock. If you cannot get whole fish, buy a total of 1½ pounds (675 grams) fillets and use clam juice in the stock instead of the heads and bones. This is an amazingly good substitute. An 8-ounce (¼-L) bottle probably will be enough, although possibly part of another bottle will be needed. But don't use too much. You shouldn't taste the clam juice in the finished soup.

TO SLICE THE SEAFOODS AND MARINATE This is a Chinese approach. The fish will be sliced and marinated until cooking time, which is right before serving time. Use tweezers to pull out any bones in the fillets. Cut into 1-inch (2½-cm) strips, then slice into ½-inch (1½-cm)-thick pieces, cutting on a slant as you do when cutting flank steak. When cutting the mackerel, don't discard the dark brown flesh. It is good. Put the fish slices in a bowl, preferably glass or china.

Clean the squid (see how to do this on page 25). Cut the squid bodies into rings ¼ inch (¾ cm) thick. Cut the tentacle clumps into halves or thirds.

Shell and devein the shrimp. Cut each in half lengthwise, cutting through the deveined areas as you would for butterflying. Trim off and discard any little hard nibs from the edges of the scallops, then slice ¼ inch (¾ cm) thick. Add the squid, shrimp, and scallops to the fish slices. You'll now have a total of 2½ to 3 pounds (1125 to 1350 grams) of seafood. Add to it:

2 Tbs. cornstarch

1½ tsp. salt

2 Tbs. dry white wine or good dry vermouth (I use Noilly Prat)

Mix well and refrigerate until serving time.

THE FISH BROTH Sand can be a problem if you don't wash the vegetables (especially the leeks) very well before adding to the broth. Wash the leeks carefully, getting down inside the stalks, then slice them across. You need:

1 bunch leeks

Put the green parts in a large saucepan or small stockpot. Cut the white parts in ¼-inch (¾-cm) dice, measure 1 cup (¼ L), and reserve; any extra white part also can go in the pot. To the pot also add:

2 onions, peeled and sliced thin

2 carrots, sliced thin

2 celery stalks, sliced thin

1 bouquet parsley (3 or 4 large sprigs)

1 large bay leaf

1 tsp. thyme

½ tsp. rosemary

2 tsp. salt

Heads, tails, skin, and bones from the fish; or 1 cup (¼ L) or more bottled clam juice

8 cups water (2 L)

2 cups dry white wine or good dry vermouth (½ L) (I use Noilly Prat)

1 unpeeled baking potato (about 8 oz. or 225 grams)

Bury the potato in the broth-to-be. Bring all to a boil, then let cook at a low boil for 30 minutes. Strain and discard all solids *except* the potato. If the potato is not done, cook in the strained stock until it is. Then peel and put into the food processor with 1 cup (¼ L) of the stock. Puree until smooth. Return to the stock.

THE VEGETABLE GARNISH Into a heavy saucepan put:

3 Tbs. butter

Heat over medium/low heat, then add the reserved 1 cup of diced leeks plus:

½ cup celery, cut into ¼-inch (¾-cm) dice
(1 stalk)

Cook over medium/low heat for 5 minutes, stirring occasionally, until translucent and slightly soft. Add to the fish stock along with:

½ cup carrot, cut into ¼-inch (¾-cm) dice
(1 carrot)

½ cup turnip, peeled and cut into ¼-inch
(¾-cm) dice (about 1 2-inch or 5-cm turnip)

1 tomato (about 8 oz. or 225 grams), peeled, seeded, and cut into ½-inch (1½-cm) dice

Also add the wild rice that you previously prepared. Bring to a boil. Simmer 5 minutes. Cool and reserve until serving time. Have:

1 head butter lettuce (also called Boston or garden lettuce)

Wash and dry the leaves. Cut into long shreds a little under ¼ inch (¾ cm) wide. Reserve.

THE FINAL COOKING Do just before serving. Have a large frying pan or sauté pan ready. I have a 12-inch (30-cm) T-Fal pan (the flat bottom area measures 9 inches or 23 cm) that is perfect for this. Have the bowl of marinated seafood and the shredded lettuce on the side, as well as:

1 stick butter (4 oz. or 115 grams) at room temperature (optional)

This butter will be floated on the tops of the individual soups. Do not use it for cooking the fish. The butter you need for that purpose is specified below.

Bring the soup to a boil over high heat. At the same time, put in the frying pan:

3 Tbs. butter

Get the pan hot, but don't burn the butter. Then add half the seafood. Spread it out on the pan and let cook 30 to 60 seconds without stirring. Turn with large gestures of a spatula. Let cook another 30 to 60 seconds without stirring. Don't worry if some of the seafood is not completely cooked. It will finish in the soup. Dump the seafood into the soup, which should be boiling by now. Let the fish cook for 2 or 3 minutes while you do the rest of the seafood. Add to the frying pan:

Another 3 Tbs. butter

Cook the same way and dump into the soup. Add the shredded lettuce; don't stir but push down into the broth. Let cook 1 minute. Taste and add if necessary:

   Salt and pepper

Use a large ladle for serving, dipping down to make sure that everybody gets some of the wild rice, which tends to sink. Portion out so the shreds of lettuce stay on top where their nice green color can show. Put a tablespoon-size piece of the reserved butter in the center of each bowl. This soup is nice served with homemade Whole Wheat Bread with Scotch Oats (see recipe in Bread section).

SOUP WITH BEEF SLICES AND WHOLE WHEAT NOODLES

6 servings

When I was studying in Taipei in the spring of 1976, friends and I stopped at noodle stands, frequently late at night, to order a soup that translates literally as beef soup mein. It consisted of lots of spaghetti-like noodles in a light broth with some fried beef slices and a few vegetable strands on top. This is what the Chinese eat for quick meals and for between-meal snacks, at those times most Americans have a hamburger, pizza, or taco. I've also had this soup in this country in Chinese noodle houses and in regular Chinese restaurants. It is wholesome, delicious, and cheap.

   This recipe, a variation of that soup, makes a great main course. I have added some whole wheat flour to my noodle dough (you won't be hungry an hour later), and I cut the noodles into a skinny tagliarini shape with a pasta machine. This shape is popular for noodle soups in some of the Cantonese noodle houses here in San Francisco. I have added toasted sunflower seeds to this dish because I like toasted sunflower seeds.

   You can make this soup easier, of course, by using canned broth and store-bought pasta.

   You may be interested in knowing that there are chicken, duck, and seafood variations of this soup, which are equally good.

---

1 cup unbleached all-purpose flour (120 grams)
¾ cup whole wheat flour
½ tsp. salt
3 eggs
1 tsp. oil

THE PASTA Into the container of a food processor fitted with the metal blade put:

   1 cup unbleached all-purpose flour (120 grams)
   ¾ cup whole wheat flour
   ½ tsp. salt

Mix a little with the machine off by twisting the blade, grabbing it by the center plastic nob. Add:

   3 eggs
   1 tsp. oil

1 lb. flank steak (450 grams)

3 Tbs. flour or cornstarch

¾ tsp. salt

3 Tbs. dry vermouth or dry white wine

1 head Chinese cabbage

1 bunch green onions (scallions)

1 bunch cilantro

1½ to 2 oz. raw, shelled sunflower seeds (45 to 60 grams)

3 cans (14½ oz. or 4½ dL each) chicken broth or 6 cups (1½ L) homemade broth

1 tsp. soy sauce (taste and add more if you like)

6 Tbs. oil

Process until the dough comes together. It may be too dry or it may be too wet, depending on the flours you use, the size of the eggs, and just plain luck. If it won't come together, dump it out and knead it a bit. It should be slightly sticky, like a good bread dough. If it isn't, break up the dough and return to the processor. Break another egg into a saucer, beat with a fork, and add 1 tablespoon of it to the pasta; process again. Add more egg if necessary until the dough is right. If the dough is too wet, knead 1 or 2 tablespoons more flour into it, until it feels just slightly sticky.

When the dough seems right, divide it in half, flatten out the two pieces, and pass them one at a time through the rollers of a pasta machine with the space between the rollers adjusted to the maximum openness. Fold and pass the pieces through four or five times. This kneads the dough.

Now bring the rollers closer together one notch at a time and pass each strip through once at each setting until you reach one position short of the thinnest space between the rollers. Flour very, very lightly as necessary, rubbing the flour over the bands of dough as you go along. You must be careful that the pasta is not so sticky as to give you trouble.

Cut the pasta sheets into 12-inch (30 cm) lengths, then pass these through the very narrow cutting rollers. This thin shape is called tagliarini. Toss the pasta strips on the countertop, flouring again a very little bit. Allow the pasta to dry for a half hour. Make sure it is floured enough or it can stick in a nasty lump and never separate again. Once the pasta is dry but not brittle, put in a plastic bag and freeze. Bring out to defrost a couple of hours before using.

THE BEEF Have:

1 lb. flank steak (450 grams)

Trim away all the fat and membrane, then cut the meat into long strips approximately 1 inch (2½-cm) wide. Cutting on a severe slant, slice the strips into pieces about ⅛ to 3/16 inch (between ½ and ¾ cm) thick. Place the slices in a bowl. Cover, but not airtight, and refrigerate. The meat can be sliced a day ahead. One or 2 hours before serving, add to the meat:

3 Tbs. flour or cornstarch

¾ tsp. salt

Mix well with your hands to coat lightly with the flour and salt. Add:

3 Tbs. dry vermouth or dry white wine

Mix with your hands. Marinate the beef for 1 or 2 hours unrefrigerated.

THE CABBAGE Have:

1 head Chinese cabbage (the kind called celery cabbage, which looks like an elongated head of lettuce)

Wash, then cut the white stalks from each leaf. (Use the stalks for another dish or salad.) Cut the leafy parts into shreds about ¼ × 2 × 3 inches (¾ × 5 × 8 cm). Stop when you have filled 6 cups, firmly pushed down. Use a stainless-steel knife for the cutting and do not cut more than 4 to 5 hours ahead. Refrigerate.

THE GREEN ONIONS Have:

1 bunch green onions (scallions)

Trim off the roots and wash. Cut the white, pale green, and dark green parts crosswise into ⅛-inch (½-cm) slices, to measure ¾ cup (1¾ dL). Cover and refrigerate. These smell awful after they sit for a while, even in the refrigerator, but don't worry— they will taste fine in the soup.

THE CILANTRO Cilantro is also called fresh coriander or Chinese parsley. Plant coriander seeds, even those in your spice cabinet, and the parsley-like plant that comes up is the same as what you buy. The people of Mexico and China use this herb quite a bit in cooking and as an edible garnish.

If you can't find any, leave it out and relieve yourself of a minor worry—whether your guests are going to like cilantro or not. There's no substitute for it, not even ground coriander seeds. Because cilantro has a very pungent, strange smell and flavor, it is an acquired taste for most people. You will frequently find pieces of it shunted aside on the plates of a few people when a meal is over. When you like this herb, however, you love it. For me this dish loses a great deal without it. Buy:

1 bunch cilantro

Wash, then remove and discard the stems. Use only the leafy sprigs. Cilantro doesn't keep quite as well as parsley, so don't count on keeping a plastic bag of it in the refrigerator as long, whether in bunch or sprig form.

THE SUNFLOWER SEEDS Have:

> 1½ to 2 oz. raw, shelled sunflower seeds (45 to 60 grams)

You can find raw, shelled seeds in health food stores. Toast by spreading on a baking sheet and baking for 5 to 7 minutes in a preheated 350°F/180°C oven, until lightly browned. To save time and trouble, you can use the roasted, salted seeds sold in cellophane bags or cans in the supermarket. They're not as good, though, and you definitely lose points if you use them.

THE BROTH Have:

> 3 cans (14½ oz. or 4½ dL each) chicken broth or 6 cups (1½ L) homemade broth

If using canned, add water to make a total of 6 cups. Add:

> 1 tsp. soy sauce (taste and add more if you like)

TO PRECOOK THE BEEF Ideally you should cook the meat at the last minute, but it saves bother to do it ahead. I suggest that about 1 hour before guests are to arrive you put into a 10-inch (25-cm) heavy sauté pan or wok:

> 3 Tbs. oil

Get the oil very hot, then add the amount of meat slices that will fit in one layer. They can be pretty well crowded in. I dump in the meat, then spread it out quickly so at least part of each piece is touching the bottom of the pan. Give the meat 20 to 30 seconds without stirring, then scrape and turn over. Work quickly and keep the heat high so that the juices evaporate and don't collect in the pan. Give the meat 20 to 30 seconds without stirring on the second side, then quickly remove from the pan. Spread out on plates to cool quickly and let sit uncovered in the room until serving time.

Rinse out the pan and scrape all the stuff from the bottom. Reheat, then add another:

> 3 Tbs. oil

Cook a second batch the same way. Continue until all the meat is cooked. *Note:* Cook all the meat pieces just until medium rare, not medium. Flank steak toughens if cooked fully.

THE FINAL ASSEMBLY This is a little tricky, so I give you this procedure in schedule form.

DO AHEAD

1. Have a spaghetti pot with 6 to 8 quarts (or liters) of boiling water ready to cook the noodles.
2. Have the chicken broth simmering in a saucepan ready to cook the cabbage.
3. Have a colander in the sink ready to receive the cooked noodles.
4. Have ready six soup bowls with a capacity of at least 2 cups (½ L) each.
5. Have the meat, green onions, sunflower seeds, and cilantro ready on the side.

AT SERVING TIME

Keep cool while juggling all these last-minute acts.

1. If frying the meat at the last minute instead of precooking it, do it first; cook as in instructions for precooking and set aside. If the meat has already been precooked, begin with step 2.
2. Place the noodles in the boiling water and cook for 2 to 3 minutes or just until hot and no longer floury-tasting. If using dry commercial pasta, cook according to the package directions, but be sure not to cook too soft.
3. About 1 minute before you think the pasta will be done, add the cabbage to the hot broth. Let cook 1 minute, then remove pan from heat.
4. Put the sauté pan or wok over heat; add 2 tablespoons oil.
5. Drain the pasta in a colander, then portion out evenly in the six soup bowls.
6. Ladle 1 cup (¼ L) of broth with cabbage into each bowl on top of the pasta.
7. Reheat the beef by dumping all at once into the hot oil in the sauté pan. Stir over high heat for 30 seconds, not too madly. Put a lid on the pan, let the meat steam 20 to 30 seconds, remove the lid, and stir again. Continue, covering to keep the heat in, until the beef is hot. Distribute over the noodles in the bowls.
8. Sprinkle the green onion slices over the soup and then the sunflower seeds (approximately 1 tablespoon per bowl). Finally, scatter four or five cilantro pieces over each soup. Serve immediately.

Eat this soup by first fishing out most of the noodles and meat with chopsticks or fork. Then sip the rest with a soup spoon or Chinese ceramic spoon.

SPAGHETTI WITH THREE-COLOR VEGETABLE SHREDS

6 servings

This wonderful dish could be served as a small first course or as a main course at a vegetable lovers' dinner. It is a sort of vegetarian Italian chow mein. Spaghetti is tossed in a butter sauce with minced onions and garlic plus fine-shredded carrots, broccoli stems, and turnips. The colors are beautiful and the dish is really delicious.

2 to 3 carrots
2 to 3 small turnips
2 or 3 large fresh
   broccoli stems
1½ sticks butter (6 oz.
   or 180 grams)
2 onions, minced fine
3 large cloves garlic,
   minced fine
1 cup water (¼ L)
1 tsp. salt
Pepper
12 oz. spaghetti (340
   grams)
Grated Parmesan
   cheese (optional)

THE VEGETABLES Peel or scrape:
   2 to 3 carrots
Cut into 1½-inch (4-cm) sections, then place in the feed tube of a food processor fitted with the shredding disk. Process by letting the carrot pieces sink down very slowly, hardly pushing on the plunger unless you have to, so the carrots will be shredded as fine as possible. You should end up with 1½ cups carrot. Next peel:
   2 to 3 small turnips
Cut into chunks roughly the size of the carrot pieces and shred the same way so that you have 1½ cups shredded turnips. Finally, peel:
   2 or 3 large fresh broccoli stems
Peel by catching hold of the fibrous skin at the thick end of the stalk between your thumb and a small knife. Pull the skin off in thin sheets. Cut the stems into chunks roughly the size you cut the carrots and turnips. Shred the same way, to get 1½ cups.

Ideally the sauce should be made just before serving the dish, in which case you should refrigerate these three vegetables until just before serving time. However, you can make the sauce in advance, which I think I'd do.

THE SAUCE Into a large saucepan put:
   1½ sticks butter (6 oz. or 180 grams)

Heat just to melt, then add:

    2 onions, minced fine

    3 large cloves garlic, minced fine

Cook over medium heat for 5 minutes or until the onions are softened and translucent. Add the shredded carrot, broccoli, and turnip. Stir to coat well in butter. Increase the heat and let the vegetables cook for 1 or 2 minutes, stirring occasionally. Add:

    1 cup water (¼ L)

Stir, cover the pan, and let the vegetables steam for 1 minute. Add:

    1 tsp. salt

    Pepper

If not serving right away, spread on a platter to cool as quickly as possible and refrigerate uncovered until chilled through, then cover. The sauce can be done a day ahead.

TO COOK THE PASTA AND ASSEMBLE THE DISH Have:

    12 oz. spaghetti (340 grams)

Cook in lots of boiling salted water (try 8 quarts or liters of water with 3 tablespoons salt) according to package directions, but probably for less time. Taste now and then and stop when the pasta is barely done, still chewy or *al dente.* Have the sauce reheating on the side and add more water if it seems too dry. Have a colander ready in the sink.

    When the pasta is done, save 1 cup (¼ L) of the cooking water and drain the pasta in the colander. Then return to the pot you cooked it in. Dump in the heated sauce. Toss well. If it looks dry, add some or all of the reserved cooking water. Taste and correct seasonings if necessary. Serve. If you like, you can pass around at the table:

    Grated Parmesan cheese (optional)

SUGGESTED ACCOMPANIMENTS Serve this with bread, a side salad, and a dessert and you will have a nice little meal. If you like, you can serve it as a small first course as the Italians do with almost all their pasta. It also can be served as a side "vegetable" along with dishes such as Roast Ducks with Crisp Skins, or any sautéed chicken, veal, or pork scallop dish.

HOT DISHES FOR BUFFETS

Valentina's Lasagne Verde alla Bolognese

Coulibiac of Chicken (Deep Dish)

Honeyed Lamb with Dried Figs and Almonds

White Beans with Spicy Ground Pork

*Italian Sausages with Mushrooms and Sour Cream
(Sausages Stroganov)*

Buffet entertaining is very popular these days. It is a wonderful way to host large groups of people and can be festive and fun. Unfortunately, we have all been to many buffets that were neither. I would like to suggest two things you can do that will make your buffets special and even memorable occasions. The first is to serve good food, and the second is to be a good host or hostess. It sounds easy, but read on.

As far as the good food is concerned, you need to make an honest effort. I find that people often seem to spend more time and concern getting their houses cleaned and decorated than they do on the food. There's no time left, so at the last minute they put out cold cuts, pretzels, and potato chips and that's about it. Phooey. Even if you're not a show-off cook, you should be able to do better than that.

For starters, the secret of good buffet food, in my opinion, is to serve at least one major hot and hearty dish. Fill the space on the table with easy things or with things that you have bought, if you must, but serve at least one good, hot dish that you've made yourself. This gives a focus and some body to the buffet. I also believe buffets should have a dessert, or desserts, preferably one being a cake-type, but more about that in the dessert section.

The five hot dishes in this chapter are ideal center dishes for buffets. They can be made ahead and reheated at the last minute. They are hot, well seasoned, relatively dry (the sauces won't run all over the plate—or on your carpets), contain no bones or things to spit out, and they taste good. They may require a little effort, but they are worth it, and all can be made ahead and frozen. I like all five dishes, although if forced to name some favorites, I would choose the lasagne, the sausage dish, and the coulibiac, in that order.

These next remarks may not seem appropriate for a cookbook, but they pertain to buffets and are just as important as the food. They concern being a good host or hostess. If you invite an interesting and varied group of guests to your party, as I hope you will, you should keep in mind that many of them will not know one another. Their enjoyment depends upon you doing your job, *creatively*. The job is introductions, and doing it creatively does not mean dragging Mary and Jane together and saying, "Jane, this is Mary; Mary, this is Jane," then running off to the kitchen to load platters or make drinks. To do it right, you must first think hard of a reason to introduce two people: people of the same profession, two women who have small children, two couples who love to travel, two good cooks, people who live close to each other, and so on. Get these people together, mentioning why you want them to meet and telling each a little about the other. Stay with them until their conversation is well launched, then excuse yourself and look around for more introductions to make.

A good party takes work. If you see clumps of people talking together who have known one another forever, get them apart the same way. Don't let them know what you are doing, but take one person at a time from the group and introduce that person to someone new. Keep going until all the old group is placed in new conversations. They will make new friends and have a better time. Try to con your co-host or -hostess into doing the same thing you are doing and the two of you will set the tone for a really great party. That plus good food and you've got it made. Of course, you should try to get the house straightened up a little.

VALENTINA'S LASAGNE VERDE ALLA BOLOGNESE

18 to 24 servings

Valentina Mascarino is a vigorous, fascinating, earthy Italian lady who may be little and no longer young, but she is no little old lady. Valentina, a couturiere (not to be confused with the Russian couturiere of the same first name), worked in San Francisco until her retirement in 1980. Over the years before that, she created beautiful suits and dresses for many wealthy women of San Francisco.

In addition to having this talent with clothing, Valentina is a fine cook. She was a faithful student in the early days of my cooking school and has become a dear and loyal friend. When she telephones, her rapid-fire communications are always short and frantic, now and then studded with a few salty expletives, which never fail to startle me.

Valentina gave me this wonderful lasagne recipe years ago. Ever since, it has been one of my most treasured possessions. There is an interesting story about how Valentina obtained this recipe. In the late 1940s, she was active in the Italian-American community in San Francisco. Since the war was over, the Italian consulate had reopened. The consul and his wife brought a cook with them from Bologna. They entertained a great deal, and their excellent cook soon became famous in the city for her wonderful, refined version of Lasagne Verde alla Bolognese.

Through her work with Italian organizations, Valentina became friendly with this marvelous cook. Valentina, by this time, was also very well known for her beautiful clothes. One day Valentina's friend said to her, "I wish I had a wool dress made by you, but I could never afford it." Valentina, whose prices even at that time were $300 per dress plus the cost of the fabric, replied, "Fine. I will make you a dress if you will teach me how to make your wonderful Lasagne Verde alla Bolognese."

Valentina, being a practical woman and very wise, specified two more things. She did not want the recipe written down for her. First she would watch her friend prepare the dish. Then Valentina, in her own kitchen, would make the dish with her friend looking on, making sure she did it right. The deal was struck and consummated.

Twenty-five years later, Valentina was kind enough to share this recipe with me, out of friendship. She came over one day, and we prepared the dish together in my kitchen. When you taste it, I think you will see why the recipe was worth three hundred late-1940 dollars to Valentina.

ABOUT THE DISH *To make what well may be one of the best-tasting dishes you'll ever eat, you combine* lasagne verde *(thin sheets of green pasta) with two sauces (a tomato-meat sauce and a quick white sauce) and two cheeses (sliced mozzarella and grated Parmesan).*

If you want to save some time, you can cheat and buy packaged lasagne. But a recipe follows for making the pasta. A nice thing about this dish is that it can be completely prepared one or two days ahead, even frozen, then heated and served.

---

5 Tbs. butter
1 onion, minced
1 carrot, grated or chopped fine
1 stalk celery, sliced fine
1 oz. dried Italian mushrooms (30 grams) (optional)
2 cloves garlic, minced
1 Tbs. chopped parsley
½ tsp. dried thyme
½ tsp. crumbled dried rosemary
1 lb. ordinary ground beef (450 grams)
½ lb. ground pork (225 grams)
1 large can (1 lb. 12 oz.) plus 1 small can (1 lb.) peeled tomatoes (1¼ kg)
3 oz. (½ 6-oz. can) tomato paste (85 grams)
7½ fl. oz. (½ 15-fl.-oz. can) beef broth (4½ dL)
2 bouillon cubes
1 tsp. salt
Pepper

THE SALSA BOLOGNESE (TOMATO-MEAT SAUCE) Use a heavy saucepan, either enameled or stainless steel. Acid sauces should not be cooked in aluminum. Into the pan put:
    5 Tbs. butter
Heat until it melts, then add:
    1 onion, minced
Sauté the onion in the butter over low heat for 5 minutes, then add:
    1 carrot, grated or chopped fine
    1 stalk celery, sliced fine
Cook slowly for 10 minutes, then add:
    1 oz. dried Italian mushrooms (30 grams), soaked 20 minutes in hot water, then squeezed and chopped (optional)
(I stopped using the mushrooms some years back. I am somewhat embarrassed to admit that I prefer the taste of the sauce without them.) Also add:
    2 cloves garlic, minced
    1 Tbs. chopped parsley
    ½ tsp. dried thyme
    ½ tsp. crumbled dried rosemary
Cook 5 minutes, then add:
    1 lb. ordinary ground beef (450 grams)
    ½ lb. ground pork, containing some fat (225 grams)
Don't use too good a quality of ground beef or it will be too lean and therefore too dry. You can brown the beef and pork at this time in some fat for additional flavor if you like. Then add:
    1 large can (1 lb. 12 oz.) plus 1 small can (1 lb.) peeled tomatoes (do not seed), drained (1¼ kg)

½ stick butter (4 Tbs. or 60 grams)
4 Tbs. flour
2 cups milk (½ L)
1 tsp. salt
Pepper
Nutmeg
1 bunch fresh spinach or ½ 10-oz. (285-gram) package frozen spinach
2 cups flour (240 grams)
2 eggs
½ tsp. salt
1 tsp. oil
1 ball mozzarella (about 12 oz. or 340 grams)
1 cup grated Parmesan (3 to 4 oz. or about 100 grams)

3 oz. (½ 6-oz. can) tomato paste (85 grams)
7½ fl. oz. (½ 15-fl.-oz. can) beef broth (4½ dL)
2 bouillon cubes
1 tsp. salt
Pepper

If you prefer, you can use homemade beef broth and eliminate the canned broth and the bouillon cubes.

Simmer the sauce uncovered for 1½ to 2 hours. Keep an eye on it so it doesn't get too dry, stick, or burn. At the end, the sauce should not be too watery. Taste and add more salt and pepper because this sauce should be highly seasoned. Reserve.

THE SALSA BESCIAMELLA (SAUCE BÉCHAMEL OR QUICK WHITE SAUCE) Into a saucepan put:
    ½ stick butter (4 Tbs. or 60 grams)
Heat to melt, then add:
    4 Tbs. flour
Stir together, let foam for 30 seconds, and remove from the heat. Add:
    2 cups milk (½ L)
Return to the heat and let come to a boil, whisking constantly. When boiling, turn down the heat and add:
    1 tsp. salt
    Pepper
    Nutmeg
This amount of salt is large, but the sauce must be highly seasoned. White pepper looks better, but black will do.

Simmer the sauce uncovered for 5 to 10 minutes, whisking now and then. Remove from the heat. If you are not going to use the sauce right away, rub a stick of butter over the surface so a flour skin will not form. Reserve.

THE LASAGNE VERDE (THE PASTA) You can assemble this dough and roll it out using only your hands and a rolling pin. People have been doing it for centuries. However, if your mother or some kind aunt or uncle didn't teach you the old-fashioned but tricky way of doing it, you will find that using a food processor and a pasta machine is a lot easier. Use:
    1 bunch fresh spinach or ½ 10-oz. (285-gram) package frozen spinach

Cook the fresh spinach, drain, cool, chop, and squeeze to get rid of the excess liquid. If you use frozen spinach, just defrost it, chop, and squeeze dry. Put the spinach in the container of a food processor and also add:

> 2 cups flour (240 grams)
> 2 eggs
> ½ tsp. salt
> 1 tsp. oil

Process until the dough comes together. Remove the dough, tear into 1-inch (2½-cm) pieces, return to the container, and process again to get the spinach mixed in more smoothly. Let the dough rest in plastic for 30 minutes. (I don't always do this if I am in a hurry.)

First knead the dough in the pasta machine in the following way. Divide into four pieces. Flatten to tongue shapes. Pass each piece four or five times through the rollers set at the wide-open position (no. 8 on my machine), folding and then flouring the dough lightly each time before putting it through. Usually you fold the dough pieces to make pieces half as long, but if a dough band is getting too wide, fold it the other way, so it is half as wide. After the four or five runs through the rollers, the bands of dough should be about 1 inch (2½ cm) less than the maximum width that the machine will take.

Next roll out the dough by repeatedly passing each strip through without folding, bringing the rollers one notch closer together each time you send the strip through. (On my machine, for example, you set the dial to 7 and pass each piece through once without folding, flouring lightly but often as necessary. Then set the dial to 6 and send each strip through. Continue with 5, 4, and end with 3, where the opening measures about ½2 inch or ⅛ cm.)

The fully rolled pieces will have become quite long. If too long to work with, cut in half. Spread the pasta strips on a floured counter or towels or hang on hangers draped with floured dish towels. Let dry for ½ hour.

TO PRECOOK THE PASTA Fill an 8- to 12-quart (liter) pot with water to two-thirds full. Bring to a boil, then add:

Salt (about 1 Tbs. for each 2 qts. water)
This is a lot of salt. But my little old non-Italian
mother, who learned to cook pasta from my Italian
father, used to say (and still does) that lots of salt in
the water is one of the secrets of good pasta. Stir to
dissolve the salt.

Cut the pasta into 12-inch (30-cm) lengths (no
need to cut it narrow, as store-bought lasagne is).
Add the pieces, one at a time, to the boiling water.
Keep adding quickly, but cook only six or seven
strips at time. Give them a scant 30 seconds in the
water, *no longer!* Fish out with a strainer and dump
right away into cold water. Let sit in the water
while you cook the next six or seven pieces. When
all are done, assemble the casserole.

THE CHEESES Have:

1 ball mozzarella (about 12 oz. or 340 grams),
    sliced thin or shredded
1 cup grated Parmesan (3 to 4 oz. or about 100
    grams)

Note: If you want to pass extra cheese at serving
time, grate extra Parmesan for that.

TO ASSEMBLE THE CASSEROLE Use a 9 × 13-inch (23
× 33-cm) glass baking dish and a small casserole
dish for the leftovers. If you are going to freeze the
casseroles, use baking dishes that can go directly
from freezer to oven without breaking. You should
not defrost the lasagne before baking or it gets
watery, Valentina says. Oil the casseroles.

Have the tomato-meat sauce *(Salsa Bolognese)* at
room temperature or slightly warmed so it is
somewhat spreadable. Warm the white sauce to
where it is no longer a lump of thick paste.

Spread about ½ cup meat sauce in the bottom of
the 9 × 13 casserole dish, then put in a layer of the
cooked pasta (drain and pat dry well as you take it
out of the cold water). Cut and piece as necessary
to get a good, solid layer. Over the pasta distribute
½ to ¾ cup more of the meat sauce, then streak
over 3 to 4 tablespoons of white sauce.

Divide the cheese into seven portions of each.
To the casserole add one portion mozzarella and
one portion Parmesan, distributing evenly over the
sauced pasta layer.

Continue by adding another pasta layer, meat
sauce and white sauce in the same amounts, and

the two cheeses. It probably will take four to five layers of pasta to fill the dish. End with the two sauces and the two cheeses atop them.

Layer the rest of the pasta, sauces, and cheeses in the small casserole by the same procedure.

Refrigerate both uncovered for several hours or until chilled through, then cover with plastic. These can be assembled 1 or 2 days ahead or frozen if you like.

TO HEAT AND SERVE Remove the casseroles from the refrigerator 1 or 2 hours before baking to lose some of their chill. But remember that frozen ones should be baked frozen or they get watery. Preheat the oven to 375°F/190°C. Stick six or seven wooden toothpicks into the lasagne, leaving the ends of the picks sticking up about 1 inch (2½ cm). Cover with a sheet of foil. (The toothpicks hold the foil up and away from the sticky cheeses. The foil is used so the top pasta layer does not get dry and hard, which some people like, but I don't.)

Bake for 30 to 40 minutes or until hot and bubbly. (Frozen casseroles require an extra 15 to 20 minutes, I would guess.) Make sure the center is hot before serving. I sometimes stick my finger (quickly) in the very center to check this, although it might be more sensible to poke a knife in, let it stay 10 seconds, and then feel the knife. Serve.

ABOUT LASAGNE YOU BUY Buy a 1-pound (450-gram) package of green or regular lasagne and cook according to the directions on the box, but don't overcook. Drain in cold water, then assemble as for homemade. This pasta probably will be thicker, and fewer layers will fill the dish. So you may want to use more of the sauces and cheeses per layer.

COULIBIAC OF CHICKEN (DEEP DISH)

24 servings

The word coulibiac *is Russian in origin. The original dish, which this preparation is based on, features salmon, sturgeon marrow, and usually kasha (buckwheat groats). This chicken* coulibiac *is an American variation of a French version of the Russian dish. Its lineage may not be pure, but it is truly delicious and very beautiful with its shiny brown lattice crust. It works very well for buffet serving. Best of all, it can be prepared weeks ahead and frozen. To serve, all you do is bake and take to the table.*

Bill Kuretich of Torrance, California, came to cook with me for a week one summer. It was Bill who had the idea of doing a coulibiac *with chicken instead of salmon. What we tried turned out great. This deep-dish version is easier to serve for buffet entertaining than the traditional loaf shape.*

This dish will serve twenty-four people. Because it is rich and filling, a 2-inch (5-cm) square is a more than ample serving, particularly if you have many other dishes on the buffet.

Batch of brioche
dough
1 whole frying chicken
(about 3 lbs. or 1350
grams)
2¼ cups water (5½ dL)
1 tsp. salt
1 Tbs. butter
1 cup rice
6 eggs
1 lb. fresh mushrooms
(450 grams)
3 Tbs. butter
1 onion, minced
¼ cup dry Madeira
(Sercial or
Rainwater) or
sherry, or dry
vermouth (½ dL)
1 tsp. salt
Pepper
5 Tbs. chopped
parsley
Chilled butter (4 Tbs.)
Salt and pepper
1 egg, beaten

THE BRIOCHE DOUGH Make a batch of food processor brioche dough (for the method see Food Processor Brioche Dough at the end of recipe for Brioche Plum Tart). While the dough is rising and chilling, prepare the rest of the ingredients. I generally get these things all done one day ahead and assemble the *coulibiac* the next day.

THE CHICKEN Preheat the oven to 450°F/230°C. Have:

> 1 whole frying chicken (about 3 lbs. or 1350 grams)

Remove the two leg-thigh pieces at the joint where the thighs are attached to the body. Select a low-sided baking pan into which the carcass with the two leg-thigh pieces arranged at its side just fits. (Cutting the chicken this way means that it will get done faster and that the breast meat will stay more moist.)

Roast the chicken 40 minutes, remove, and cool. Don't worry if it is still a trifle underdone. It will finish cooking inside the *coulibiac* later.

Pull all the meat from the carcass, including the skin if you like (I like). Refrigerate uncovered until chilled through, then cover with plastic.

THE RICE Into a saucepan put:

> 2¼ cups water (5½ dL)
> 1 tsp. salt
> 1 Tbs. butter

(*Note:* Yes, use 2¼ cups water. The normal amount for 1 cup of rice is 2 cups water, but this rice needs to be a little soggier than usual or the *coulibiac* crumbles when served.) Bring to a boil, then add:

> 1 cup rice

Return to the boil. Stir once to level the rice. Cover and cook over low heat for 20 minutes or until the water is gone. (Remove the lid and tilt the pan to check.) Cover again and let the rice sit off the heat for 20 minutes. Turn the rice out on a plate. Refrigerate uncovered until chilled through.

THE EGGS Hard-boil any way you like:

> 6 eggs

(Note: The way I boil eggs seems to avoid that ugly, gray ring around the yolk. Put eggs from the refrigerator in a saucepan and run water as hot as it comes from the tap over them, to about 2 inches [5 cm] above. Let sit 5 minutes for the eggs to warm up throughout. Bring the water to a boil, then remove from heat, cover, and let the eggs sit 15 minutes. Dump out the hot water, immediately run cold water over the eggs, and right away crack all the shells. Peel. Refrigerate in a bowl of cold water.)

THE MUSHROOMS Have:

> 1 lb. fresh mushrooms (450 grams)

To wash so the mushrooms don't soak up unwanted water, dump in cold water, swoosh around quickly, and lift out right away. Change water. Do this three times, then call the mushrooms clean. If you want to cut off and discard any dark slices from the stem ends, do so.

Slice the mushrooms in a food processor with the slicing disk. Load the feed tube with mushrooms, then turn on the machine and push down with the plunger. The machine gives you a pile of slices cut from all angles, plus hacked-up bits and pieces, but for this dish the appearance is not important. If you want lovely slices, do the work by hand.

In a 12-inch (30-cm) sauté pan or frying pan heat:

> 3 Tbs. butter

Add:

> 1 onion, minced

Let the onion soften over low heat for 5 minutes, then add the sliced mushrooms and cook them over high enough heat to keep the juices evaporated. After 3 or 4 minutes, when the mushrooms look soft and cooked, add:

> ¼ cup dry Madeira (Sercial or Rainwater) or
>   sherry or dry vermouth (½ dL)
> 1 tsp. salt
> Pepper

Cook over high heat for 1 or 2 minutes more or until most of the excess liquid has evaporated. Turn out on a plate. Refrigerate uncovered until chilled through.

THE PARSLEY Have:

5 Tbs. chopped parsley

To prepare the parsley, wash and shake dry. Remove the larger stems, then chop in a food processor with the metal blade. The chopping doesn't have to be fine and perfect. Reserve covered in refrigerator.

TO ASSEMBLE THE COULIBIAC Butter a glass or other baking dish about 9 × 13 × 2 inches (23 × 33 × 5 cm). Have the brioche dough, cooked chicken, cooked rice, hard-boiled eggs, cooked mushrooms, and chopped parsley all prepared and chilled. Also have ready some:

Chilled butter (about 4 Tbs.)

Cut off a piece of the dough, about one-third. Return the rest to the refrigerator to keep cold. Roll the piece out, flouring lightly but well, until it just fits the bottom of the baking dish. Transfer the dough to the dish. Distribute over the dough the following ingredients in the order listed. As you do the layering, you may sprinkle lightly with:

Salt and pepper

over each layer. Layer:

1. Half the rice.
2. Half the chopped parsley
3. 2 Tbs. chilled butter, sliced thin
4. Half the hard-boiled eggs, sliced thin or chopped coarse
5. All the chicken, pulled apart into bite-size pieces (even skin if you like)
6. All the mushrooms
7. The remaining hard-boiled eggs, also sliced or chopped
8. The remaining rice
9. The remaining parsley
10. 2 Tbs. more chilled butter, sliced thin

Roll the rest of the brioche dough into a rectangle twice the size of the baking dish. Cut half the dough and place it over the dish as a top crust. Brush off the excess flour. Tuck the dough edges down into the dish.

Have a small bowl with:

1 egg, beaten

This will be used for gluing and glazing the lattice top. (If you want a deeper, richer-looking glaze, try 1 egg yolk plus 2 tablespoons heavy cream.) Brush the entire top of the dough with the glaze, not using too much, but just enough to make the top sticky.

To make the lattice top, cut the remaining piece of dough into ½-inch (1½-cm)-wide strips. Place half of them on the top, starting at a corner of the dish and allowing ¾- to 1-inch (2- to 2½-cm) space between the bands of dough. When the top is covered with parallel strips, brush all of them with egg glaze. Then add another parallel series of strips at right angles, starting from the adjoining corner. Brush with glaze again.

Put the dish in the freezer for 15 minutes to chill the dough so it will not rise. If serving that day or the next, transfer to the refrigerator and cover when chilled through. If you want to keep the *coulibiac* longer, freeze it for 1 hour, wrap well in plastic and foil, and complete the freezing. To defrost, move to the refrigerator for 24 hours.

TO BAKE AND SERVE Preheat the oven to 325°F/165°C. Brush the top of the *coulibiac* a final time with:

Beaten egg glaze

Bake in the center of the oven for 1 hour or until the crust is pretty and brown. I prefer this served hot, but it is very good served at room temperature. Serve with or without a sauce (suggestions follow).

THE SAUCE I like to serve a sauce with this. The one I like best is the easy Lemon-Dill Sauce that accompanies the recipe for Sea Bass Fillets with Salmon Mousse Baked in a Crust (see Main Courses). For a variation, you might use tarragon instead of dill, but frankly I prefer the dill for this.

HONEYED LAMB WITH DRIED FIGS AND ALMONDS

18 to 24 servings

This Moroccan dish is very unusual to Americans, but a very easy one for us to love. The combination of meat with honey and dried fruits is odd but delicious.

This dish is especially suitable for a winter buffet. Do make sure that its sauce is not too thin. People at buffets tend to have odd assortments of foods on their plates and will not welcome a strange sauce running into all the other things.

8 to 10 lbs. boneless lamb shoulder or shank (3½ to 4½ kg)
2 tsp. ground ginger
2 tsp. turmeric (or ¼ tsp. saffron)
½ tsp. ground cinnamon
½ tsp. cayenne pepper
½ tsp. black pepper
4 to 6 large cloves garlic, minced
4 Tbs. oil
4 Tbs. butter
2 lbs. onions, minced (900 grams)
2 cans (1 lb. 12 oz. or 800 grams each) tomatoes
Salt
2 cups raisins (10 oz. or 285 grams)
3 Tbs. oil
10 oz. blanched whole almonds (285 grams)
4 cups chicken broth or water (1 L)
1 tsp. ground ginger
½ tsp. cinnamon
Salt and pepper
Cayenne pepper (optional)
About 50 dried figs (1½ lbs. or 675 grams)
½ cup honey or less (1 dL)

THE LAMB I cook this in a heavy 12-inch (30-cm) high-sided sauté pan (Calphalon). You need a fairly wide pan so that you can reduce the juices and thicken the sauce quickly after the meat is tender. If this reducing takes too long, as it will in a smaller pan, the meat overcooks and starts to fall apart. Have:

8 to 10 lbs. boneless lamb shoulder or shank (3½ to 4½ kg)

Trim off excess fat, within reason, but still leaving a little attached. Cut the meat into 1½-inch (4-cm) squares. Reserve. Next you coat the meat in spices and seasonings, then cook it. First prepare the spice mixture by putting into a small bowl:

2 tsp. ground ginger
2 tsp. turmeric (or ¼ tsp. saffron if you can afford it)
½ tsp. ground cinnamon
½ tsp. cayenne pepper
½ tsp. black pepper
4 to 6 large cloves garlic, minced

Mix well. Divide the spice mixture in half because there is so much meat that you are going to cook half of it at a time. Into the heavy sauté pan put:

2 Tbs. oil
2 Tbs. butter

Heat over moderate heat, then add half the spice mixture and stir to mix. Add half the lamb cubes. Stir the meat until coated, then cook over moderate heat for 3 or 4 minutes, stirring now and then. Adjust the heat so that it is high enough to keep the meat juices evaporated. Turn the meat out onto a plate. Add another:

2 Tbs. oil
2 Tbs. butter

Add the balance of the spice mixture and stir. Add the remaining meat. Cook this batch 3 or 4 minutes, stirring occasionally, then return the first batch of cooked meat to the pan. Add:

2 lbs. onions, minced (900 grams)
2 cans (1 lb. 12 oz. or 800 grams each) tomatoes, drained and chopped

    4 cups water (1 L), or half water and half
      chicken broth
    Salt

The liquid should come about halfway up on the meat. If it doesn't, add a little more water, but not too much. Bring to a boil. Cover and simmer for 1½ hours, stirring occasionally. Add:

    2 cups raisins (10 oz. or 285 grams)

(*Note:* If you want to plump the raisins up first, soak them in warm water for 1 hour.) Boil briskly uncovered so the juices reduce a little and the meat is very tender when tested with a fork. This may take about 30 minutes. Cool, then refrigerate.

THE ALMONDS In a sauté pan heat:

    3 Tbs. oil

Add:

    10 oz. blanched whole almonds (285 grams)

Cook, stirring occasionally, until the nuts are light brown on both sides. Drain and reserve.

TO POACH THE FIGS Into a saucepan put:

    4 cups chicken broth or water (1 L)
    1 tsp. ground ginger
    ½ tsp. cinnamon
    Salt and pepper
    Cayenne pepper (optional)

Bring to a boil, then add:

    About 50 dried figs (1½ lbs. or 675 grams)

Simmer covered for 15 to 20 minutes or until moist and tender. Refrigerate.

    The lamb, the almonds, and the figs all can be prepared one or two days ahead.

TO HEAT AND SERVE Reheat the lamb in its sauce. If the sauce is too thin, let it reduce over high heat, scraping the bottom of the pan most of the time so nothing sticks or burns. Add:

    ½ cup honey or less (1 dL)

(*Note:* You may want to add part of the honey and taste before adding all.) Add the figs and stir to coat with the sauce. When everything is heated through, transfer to a warmed serving platter. Warm the almonds for a minute or two in a dry sauté pan, salting them if you like. Sprinkle the almonds over the lamb with figs and serve.

WHITE BEANS WITH SPICY GROUND PORK

15 to 20 servings

If you like beans and garlic and hot peppers, you will love this dish. It consists of white beans covered with a thick meat sauce of ground pork, garlic, hot little green peppers, and small cubes of the bean curd used in Chinese and Japanese cooking.

Yes, oriental bean curd. The dish isn't Mexican or Tex-Mex, as adapted dishes north of the border are now being called. It is based on the classic Ma Po To Fu *from the Szechuan province of China, an area with a Texas-like climate where the food is similarly highly spiced and hot chiles are abundantly used.*

This happens to be a casserole that can be done ahead, even frozen. Therefore, it would be a perfect hot dish to serve for an informal Fourth of July barbecue or a Labor Day buffet.

I have kept pretty close to the classic Chinese version except for changing the normal rice accompaniment to small white beans and making a few other minor changes so you can use products more readily available in this country.

---

1 lb. small white beans (450 grams)
4 quarts very hot tap water (4 L)
4 tsp. salt
12 to 14 oz. fresh soybean cake (340 to 400 grams)
1½ to 2 lbs. pork meat, including some fat (675 to 900 grams)
¼ cup oil (½ dL)
3 large cloves garlic, minced
1 or 2 small fresh hot chile peppers such as jalapeños or serranos
1 tsp. ground coriander
3 Tbs. soy sauce
3½ cups homemade or canned chicken broth (⅘ L)
3 Tbs. cornstarch
¼ cup cold water (½ dL)
1 bunch green onions (optional)

THE BEANS Buy:

1 lb. small white beans (450 grams)

Soak and cook these according to the directions on the package or as follows, which is the quick method. Look over the beans and discard any little, funny things you don't like the looks of. Place the beans in a pot with:

2 quarts very hot tap water (2 L)
2 tsp. salt

Bring to a boil. Cook for 2 minutes, then cover the pot and let it sit off the heat for 1 hour. Pour the beans into a colander, discarding the liquid. Getting rid of this liquid is supposed to reduce considerably the well-known reaction of beans upon the human digestive system. Put the beans back in the pot and add another:

2 quarts very hot tap water (2 L)
2 tsp. salt

Return to the boil, then simmer for 30 to 45 minutes or until the beans are tender. Taste one to decide. Drain again and discard the water. Spread the beans out on a baking sheet to cool. Reserve.

THE BEAN CURD If you have trouble finding this, leave it out. The bland white custard-like soybean curd doesn't add essential flavor. It does give an interesting texture, more protein at low cost, and the spice of life—variety.

The bean curd, or bean cake as it is sometimes

called, probably is right in your supermarket, either in a produce case or refrigerated somewhere. You'll find it in a small plastic tub with plastic across the top you just rip off, probably labeled *tofu*, the Japanese name. Inside is a rectangle of soft, yet firm soybean custard surrounded by water. Just remove the cake and rinse if you like. It is perfectly good to eat plain without cooking.

Because bean curd is made from soybeans, is almost pure protein, and is fat-free, it is popular with those interested in health food and vegetarian cooking. So look for it at health food stores if your supermarket is behind the times and doesn't stock it. Don't buy any that isn't pure white and smooth. If yellowish and shrinking, it is spoiling and will taste sour. Markets that don't sell a lot of it sometimes will leave it out for sale too long.

For this dish you need:

12 to 14 oz. fresh soybean cake (340 to 400 grams)

Rinse in water and cut into ½-inch (1½-cm) cubes. Reserve.

THE MEAT SAUCE Have:

1½ to 2 lbs. pork meat, including some fat (675 to 900 grams)

You can buy a 1½-pound piece of boneless pork butt (the shoulder) or 2 pounds of any pork chops that have a fair amount of fat to give good flavor. Bone the chops yourself.

Cut the meat into ½-inch (1½-cm) cubes and the fat into ¼-inch (¾-cm) cubes. Place in the container of a food processor, then process with about thirty 1-second on-and-off motions. Don't chop too fine. It's nicer with some texture left.

Into a large, heavy sauté pan or frying pan put:

¼ cup oil (½ dL)

Heat over high heat, then add the chopped pork. Spread the meat over the surface of the pan as best you can. Cook for 30 seconds, then scrape it up, turn over, and stir to break up clumps. Do not stir constantly, but let cook for another 20 to 30 seconds over high heat, then stir again. Continue until you see no more raw bits and the pieces are fairly well broken up. The meat should look crumbly. Add:

3 large cloves garlic, minced

1 or 2 small fresh hot chile peppers such as

jalapeños or serranos, stemmed, seeded, and
chopped fine
1 tsp. ground coriander

For the peppers, I use those little green devils that
are about 2 inches (5 cm) long and hot as hell
(serranos). You can use less or more or none. The
dish is still good without hot peppers, but most
people prefer it with at least a little kick to it. Stir
all around for a second or two, then add:

3 Tbs. soy sauce
3½ cups homemade or canned chicken broth
(⅘ L)

While bringing this mixture to a boil, mix:

3 Tbs. cornstarch
¼ cup cold water (½ dL)

Stir to dissolve the cornstarch. When the meat
mixture has come to a boil, remove from the heat.
Give the cornstarch mixture a final stir, then pour
in a thin stream into the meat, whisking well or
swirling with a chopstick so the cornstarch is mixed
in well before it lumps.

Mix everything well, return to the heat, and
simmer for 1 or 2 minutes. Remove from the heat.
Carefully stir in the bean curd cubes. Let the
mixture cool for ½ hour or longer.

TO ASSEMBLE THE CASSEROLE Oil a glass or other
3-quart (2¾-L) ovenware dish that is 9 × 13 × 2
inches (23 × 33 × 5 cm). Into a mixing bowl put
the prepared white beans and add two-thirds of the
meat sauce. Stir to mix, then put into the oiled dish.
Spoon the rest of the meat sauce over the beans.

Refrigerate uncovered until chilled through. This
can be done one or two days ahead and kept well
covered in the refrigerator, although the garlic
smell will be something fierce. Or it can be frozen
and kept for several weeks.

TO BAKE AND SERVE If frozen, defrost overnight in
refrigerator. Bring out to the room several hours
before baking so the casserole does not go into the
oven too cold.

Preheat the oven to 350°F/180°C. Cover the dish
with foil and bake 30 to 40 minutes or until hot and
bubbly. Sprinkle over:

1 bunch green onions (both white and green
parts), sliced across into ⅛-inch (½-cm)
pieces (optional)

Serve hot, although like most bean dishes this is good warm or even at a summer-day room temperature.

ITALIAN SAUSAGES WITH MUSHROOMS AND SOUR CREAM (SAUSAGES STROGANOV)

15 to 20 servings

I love good pork sausages and don't believe they should be considered too inelegant for entertaining. So here is a delicious treatment of them that you will be proud to serve at even the most formal buffet.

The dish is subtitled Sausages Stroganov because that is essentially what it is. Cooked sausages sliced bite-size are prepared with mushrooms and onions in a sour cream sauce. At the last minute, some fresh spinach leaves are stirred in and just allowed to wilt.

This is wonderful hearty fare that would warm everyone's spirits at a winter brunch or buffet. It would be great après ski or après football, for that matter.

A good accompaniment is rice. If you feel like being fancy, present this in two chafing dishes, with the rice in one and the sausages in sour cream sauce in the other.

A lady I know who readily admits to being raised as a hillbilly, even though she since has done some pretty exotic cookery books, says this dish reminds her of the sausages in cream gravy that are served over hot biscuits throughout the Appalachians, for breakfast, lunch, or dinner. That gravy also is made with the flavorful fat of the sausage. So she suggests giant buttermilk biscuits, split, instead of the rice. They might look very appetizing on the buffet as well.

ABOUT THE SAUSAGES *The sausages are the key to the quality of this dish. Try to find really special ones and, before building the dish around a likely candidate, by all means cook a sample and taste it without benefit of saucing. The sausage should be highly spiced and seasoned or the results won't be exciting.*

I tend to prefer mild Italian sausages—those labeled mild as opposed to hot. The meat is usually coarse, chunky, lean (perhaps too lean), highly seasoned, and slightly peppery without being hot as hell. They also have that special Italian aniseed flavor, which I love.

Many other sausages can be used, though. But stick to raw, fresh pork types and don't use any that are precooked, like hot dogs, garlic sausage, or bratwurst. This is your dish, of course, so use what you like. A friend who now lives in Houston has been singing the praises of the big (of course), fat Texas sausages full of seasoning, which everybody there throws into beans or onto barbecues. They can be purchased with varying degrees of chile pepper. The meat in them is coarse and chunky, too.

Sausages of the breakfast variety, in link or patty form, also work fine. Just fry and cut into bite-size pieces, not too small.

Also, you could make your own sausage. See my homemade turkey sausage recipe elsewhere in this book. If you use homemade sausage, put in more seasoning than you would normally when serving plain.

3 lbs. sausages (1350 grams)

½ cup water (1 dL)

3 onions, about 1 lb. (450 grams), peeled and sliced thin

7 Tbs. butter or fat rendered from sausages

2 lbs. fresh mushrooms (900 grams)

Salt and pepper

3 Tbs. rendered sausage fat or butter if no more fat remains

3 Tbs. flour

3 cups milk (¾ dL)

3 lbs. sour cream (5 to 6 cups or 1350 grams)

2 tsp. salt

Pepper

1½ to 2 bunches fresh spinach or a 10-oz. (285-gram) package frozen leaf spinach

6 cups water (1½ L)

3 Tbs. butter

1 Tbs. salt

3 cups rice (preferably long-grain)

6 Tbs. water

1 Tbs. powdered mustard

1 Tbs. cold water

TO COOK THE SAUSAGES Buy:

3 lbs. sausages (1350 grams)

If using sausage patties or small link sausages, fry about 2 minutes per side or until lightly browned. Don't overcook. They will cook more later when heated in the sauce.

For the typical Italian sausages, which are about 1¼ to 1½ inches (3 to 4 cm) in diameter and in varying lengths, place in a frying pan large enough to hold all. They can be crowded because they will shrink. Add:

½ cup water (1 dL)

Bring the water to boil over high heat, cover, and cook over medium heat for 4 to 5 minutes or until some of the fat has rendered. Uncover to let the excess liquid boil off, about 1 minute. Then over medium heat fry for 3 minutes per side, turning once, or until lightly browned. Let them sizzle nicely. Do not cook more than 6 minutes total or you will dry them out.

Remove from the pan, which you do not wash. You will deglaze the good brown stuff later with the mushrooms. After the sausages are cool, cut them into ⅜-inch (1-cm) slices. Don't be upset if they still are a little pink in the center. They will cook completely later. Reserve.

THE ONIONS AND MUSHROOMS Have:

3 onions, about 1 lb. (450 grams), peeled and sliced thin

Into a heavy saucepan put:

4 Tbs. butter or fat rendered from sausages

Melt over very low heat, add the sliced onions, and stir into the butter. Cook over very low heat for 15 minutes, stirring occasionally. Let the onions soften, but not color. Meanwhile have:

2 lbs. fresh mushrooms (900 grams)

Wash by plunging quickly into a large bowl of cold water. Swoosh around quickly, then fish right out. Do this three or four times, changing the water each time. If you still see dirt after all this, brush them off individually. Slice thin, in the food processor if you like. They don't come out very pretty, but since the sour cream sauce hides them, it doesn't really matter.

Drain and reserve the fat from the frying pan in which you cooked the sausages. Measure about 3 tablespoons and put back into the pan. Save the rest of the fat. Heat, add half the sliced mushrooms, and cook over medium/high heat, scraping the brown stuff from the bottom of the pan into the mushrooms. About 3 or 4 minutes, with occasional stirring, should be enough. Keep the heat high enough so that most of the juices evaporate. Sprinkle with:

> Salt and pepper

Turn the mushrooms onto a dish. Add another 3 tablespoons of sausage fat to the pan and cook the remaining mushrooms. Add the cooked onions to the mushrooms and reserve.

THE SAUCE Into a large saucepan put:

> 3 Tbs. rendered sausage fat or butter if no
>   more fat remains
> 3 Tbs. flour

Heat this *roux,* stirring with a wire whisk, for about 1 minute or until it bubbles and froths for at least 30 seconds. Add:

> 3 cups milk (¾ L)

Bring to a boil, whisking constantly to keep the flour in suspension. Add:

> 3 lbs. sour cream (5 to 6 cups or 1350 grams)
> 2 tsp. salt
> Pepper

Again bring to a boil, whisking occasionally. Remove from the heat and cool until barely warm. Stir in the onions, mushrooms, and sausages.

The dish can be done to this point a day ahead and refrigerated uncovered until chilled through. You can even prepare it two to three weeks ahead and freeze.

THE SPINACH You don't have to add this, but you should. It is really a nice touch, both for flavor and appearance. Have:

> 1½ to 2 bunches fresh spinach or 10-oz. (285-
>   gram) package frozen leaf spinach

Wash the fresh spinach and remove stems as much as a day or two ahead. Whirl in a salad basket or add paper towels to the bag for refrigerating. If using frozen spinach, defrost and remove stems a few hours before using.

THE RICE This recipe makes about 12 cups (2¾ L) or enough for twenty servings of ¾ cup (1¾ dL) each. Cook it the day before the party when you have more time. Reheating in the oven just before serving is easy. Into a 4-quart saucepan put:

6 cups water (1½ L)

3 Tbs. butter

1 Tbs. salt

Bring to a boil. Add:

3 cups rice (long-grain preferable, but short-grain is all right)

Return to the boil, then give a stir to break up clumps and to level. Cover with tight lid and cook over low heat (not too low for this large quantity) for 25 minutes.

Remove the lid and tilt the pan to make sure that all the water has been absorbed. If any remains, recover and cook another 5 minutes or until the water is gone. Remove from the heat. Cover again and let sit 30 minutes for the rice to continue to swell and dry. Fluff with a fork, then allow to cool. Refrigerate uncovered until chilled through, then cover to keep from drying out. Reheat by the following instructions.

TO REHEAT THE RICE Put cooked rice in a 3-quart (2¾-L) ovenware dish. Sprinkle with:

6 Tbs. water

Cover with foil and bake in a preheated 350°F/180°C oven for 45 minutes to 1 hour, or until thoroughly hot. Fluff with a fork and serve or transfer to a chafing dish to keep warm.

TO REHEAT THE SAUSAGE-MUSHROOM MIXTURE AND ADD THE SPINACH If you froze this, partially defrost for 24 hours in the refrigerator. At serving time, put in a large saucepan and bring to a boil over medium/high heat, stirring now and then. This quantity may take 15 minutes or longer to get bubbly and hot again. Keep an eye on it and stir once in a while. The flour in the sauce should keep it from curdling, but boiling hard for very long will cause trouble.

Note: This is not a highly seasoned food. If your sausages are not as exciting as they should be, add to a small saucer:

1 Tbs. powdered mustard

1 Tbs. cold water

Mix until smooth, then let sit for 10 minutes. Mix half into the dish and taste. Then add all if you think it is needed.

As soon as the mixture is bubbling and properly seasoned, *be sure to add the spinach* already prepared, if you are using any. Just as soon as it has wilted, while still a brilliant green, the dish should be served. Taste again at the last minute to see whether more salt and pepper are needed. Also, if the sauce has thickened too much, add water very gradually until just right.

Transfer to a warmed serving dish or put in a chafing dish to keep warm on the buffet table.

VEGETABLES

Cauliflower with Watercress Sauce

Parsleyed Cucumbers with Pearl Onions

My Grandfather's New England Succotash

Summer Vegetable Chunks with Black Olives

Three Colorful Vegetable Purees (Butternut Squash,
String Bean, Beet with Potato)

Sautéed Zucchini, Snow Peas, and Tomatoes

*Baked Cubes of Butternut Squash

*Broccoli Flowerets

*Shredded Cabbage with Grated Banana Squash

*Steamed Carrot Shreds

*Cucumber "Noodles"

*Sliced Carrots and Yellow Summer Squash

*Diced Fennel with Parsley

*Wilted Lettuce Leaves

*String Beans with Minced Garlic

*Shredded Yellow Squash with Red Bell Pepper

*Sautéed Plum Tomatoes

*Special quick dishes

Vegetables have become one of the joys of my life. The more I read about diet and humans, what we were and what we have become, the more I am led to a belief that we were principally meant to eat fruits, vegetables, and grains, accompanied by small amounts of seafoods and even smaller amounts of poultry and meat. We have neglected vegetables and grains for a long time, and I am convinced that we must get back to them, if for no other reason than because we need the fiber they contain to keep our bodies functioning properly. Getting back to vegetables is not an unpleasant thing for me, but an exciting adventure. I like vegetables very much.

In this chapter I have concentrated on vegetables as main-course accompaniments. There is a strong emphasis on color. You will find greens, oranges, yellows, reds, and a purple to liven main-course plates and make them look colorful and attractive. You will also find an almost oriental preoccupation with textures and shapes. The vegetables are worked and cut into purees, chunks, clumps, slices, dices, short shreds, long shreds, rounds, squares, ovals, balls, cubes, and wholes. The amazing thing about foods, especially vegetables, is that the same one, cut and cooked in a different shape or fashion, actually *tastes* different. As a good example, try the fine-shredded, steamed carrot recipe in this section, then taste it alongside the common American dish of sliced, boiled carrots. For me, it's hard to realize that the two dishes have been made from the same vegetable. I think you are in for some pleasant surprises in this chapter.

CAULIFLOWER WITH WATERCRESS SAUCE

6 servings

This is a lovely way to serve cauliflower. The flowerets are cooked crisp-tender and served with a beautiful green-speckled sauce featuring watercress. The sauce is based on a charming old sauce that was popular years ago. I discovered it while doing research through some old cookbooks. It is called a béchamel.

I shall now stop being cute and tell you what you probably already know, that the béchamel or white sauce is most out of style at this particular moment in our culinary history, as are virtually all flour-thickened sauces. However, béchamel may be so far out that, for those who dare to be different and want to surprise and even shock, béchamel is back in. At any rate, the sauce is pretty and delicious. You will love it.

1 bunch watercress
2 Tbs. butter
2 Tbs. flour
1 cup milk (¼ L)
½ tsp. salt
White pepper
1 head cauliflower
1 to 2 Tbs. salt
2 Tbs. butter

THE WATERCRESS SAUCE I think this sauce is better made a day ahead. The watercress flavor intensifies and permeates the sauce. Be careful not to go wild on the amount of watercress. I made this once in Florida, where I found huge bunches in the market. They were so beautiful and so inexpensive that I threw in two or three times what I would normally. The sauce was so bitter that it was inedible. Have:

    1 bunch watercress

Wash and remove only the large, obvious stems. You should have approximately 2 cups packed down tight. Put on a pot of boiling water, approximately 2 quarts (2 L), then throw in the cress. Let boil for 1 minute and drain. Douse with cold water to stop the cooking, then drain again and reserve. Into a saucepan put:

    2 Tbs. butter

Heat to melt, then add:

    2 Tbs. flour

Whisk this *roux* to mix. Let foam up for 30 to 60 seconds, but do not allow to color. Remove it from the heat and add:

    1 cup milk (¼ L)

Return to the heat and simmer, whisking all the time to keep smooth. Add:

    ½ tsp. salt
    White pepper

Simmer for 5 minutes, whisking occasionally. Dump into a food processor and add the blanched watercress. Process until the cress is chopped fine and the sauce looks smooth. Transfer to a bowl. (It is not necessary to film this sauce with butter as I usually do to sauces, because the watercress seems to prevent a flour skin from forming.) Refrigerate as is, but do not cover until chilled.

THE CAULIFLOWER Have:

    1 head cauliflower

Cut flowerets that have only about ¼ inch (¾ cm) of the thinner stems attached. Save the core for another use. Wash the flowerets and reserve until serving time.

TO COOK AND SERVE At serving time, reheat the sauce. Pour 3 to 4 quarts (2¾ to 3¾ L) water into a pot and bring to a boil. Add:

    1 to 2 Tbs. salt

Add the cauliflower and cook for approximately 5 minutes or until barely tender. Meanwhile, taste the sauce and add salt and pepper if necessary. If too thick, add a little milk or water, enough to make it flow nicely. If you like, just before serving, whisk into the sauce:

2 Tbs. butter

Drain the cauliflower well and divide onto dinner plates. Spoon over some sauce. Serve at once.

PARSLEYED CUCUMBERS WITH PEARL ONIONS

6 servings

This wonderful vegetable dish comes across as light and refreshing—something that can't be said about too many vegetable dishes. The cucumber pieces turn a beautiful translucent green after cooking. The lovely jade-like pieces combined with the parsley and the small translucent white onions make an entrancing balance of greens and whites, of crunchy and soft textures, and of light and delicate flavors. There is a feeling that everything is warm and gentle and full of water.

3 cucumbers (10 to 12 oz. or 285 to 340 grams), or 2 long hothouse variety cucumbers

10 oz. pearl onions (285 grams)

½ stick butter (4 Tbs. or 60 grams)

½ cup chopped parsley

Salt and pepper

THE CUCUMBERS Have:

3 cucumbers (10 to 12 oz. or 285 to 340 grams), or 2 of the long, almost seedless hothouse variety

If you are one who doesn't like cucumbers because you burp and belch for hours after eating them, rejoice. This dish will fill you with nothing but a song. The skin and seeds are what cause all the brouhaha, and they both will be removed.

Peel the cucumbers, then cut in half lengthwise. Scoop out the seeds with a small spoon. Cut the boat-shaped pieces crosswise into 1-inch (2½-cm) sections. Cut each section into three or four little rectangles measuring about ½ × 1 inch (1½ × 2½ cm). You should have 3 to 4 cups of cucumber pieces. Refrigerate until serving time. This can be done up to a day ahead.

THE PEARL ONIONS Buy:

10 oz. pearl onions (285 grams)

To help peel and to precook the onions, have a pot with 3 quarts (2¾ L) of boiling water. Dump in the

unpeeled onions and boil for exactly 3 minutes.
Drain and plunge into cold water to stop the
cooking. Drain again. Cut off the root and sprout
ends of each, cutting off as little onion as possible.
Grab the skin between your thumb and the point of
a small knife. Pull. You should be able to peel the
onions fairly quickly this way and end with the
required amount—about 2 cups. Reserve in the
refrigerator up to a day ahead.

TO COOK AND SERVE Five minutes before serving,
have a pot containing 3 quarts (2¾ L) of boiling
water. Add:

>   2 to 3 tsp. salt

Stir, then add the raw cucumber pieces and cooked
onions. Boil for 3 minutes or until the cucumber
pieces are barely tender. Do not overcook. Drain in
a colander. Return the drained vegetables to the
pot. Add:

>   ½ stick butter (4 Tbs. or 60 grams) cut into
>   pieces, at room temperature
>   ½ cup chopped parsley

Stir until the butter melts and the vegetables are
nicely coated with the butter and parsley. Taste and
add if necessary:

>   Salt and pepper

(I don't use pepper in this, but you can.) Serve.

MY GRANDFATHER'S
NEW ENGLAND SUCCOTASH

10 to 12 servings

*My grandfather, my mother's father, was born in Connecticut and grew up there. His
name was Henry Alvord. As a young man, he settled, practiced law, and raised his
family in Vineland, New Jersey. They were rich folks, it seems to me now. They had a
big house, stables, a cook, maids, a tennis court, and an area where Grandpa grew
vegetables and berries. He grew all sorts of things, but for some reason the ones I seem to
remember are rhubarb, corn, and raspberries.*

*I have an odd assortment of sweet and bittersweet childhood memories of the old
house. I remember getting stung by bees; climbing on an old weathervane; getting sick
from eating blackberries that grew around the bottom of it; having to go view the casket of
whichever relative had just died, open in the living room in front of the fireplace; eating
Nana's chicken and dumplings, creamed sweetbreads, and at Christmas her gingerbread
and Dover cake.*

Grandpa, being a New Englander, loved baked beans, brown bread, and succotash. He taught Nana to make the succotash that he loved so much, a soupy combination of corn, lima beans, and salt pork cooked a long time. It is thickened with flour and slightly sweetened with sugar. Mother says that, when she was a kid, they used to have succotash meals—succotash in soup bowls with bread and butter on the side. That was the meal. (Mother, as you may read elsehwere in this book, is the inventor of the nothing-but-shortcake meal, another simple summer delight.)

When I was a child—in the summer at the shore when corn and lima beans were in— we would have succotash. It's a bit of trouble to make and it's rich, so Mother didn't make it often. When she did, though, she made a ton of it. We'd eat succotash every day for a week. I loved every day of it then and still do. That's why this recipe makes a lot, enough for ten or twelve people on one day or for two people all through one summer week.

¼ lb. salt pork (115 grams)

6 cups water (1½ L)

2 cups baby or regular lima beans (frozen are fine)

3 cups corn cut from the cob (approximately 6 ears)

3 Tbs. flour

6 Tbs. water

2 Tbs. (or more) sugar

THE SALT PORK Have:

    ¼ lb. salt pork (115 grams)

I just use regular, very fatty salt pork, but Mother always specifies that you should have sugar-cured salt pork. It is important that the pork be very, very fatty—pure fat if possible. Lean streaks, even after long cooking, are stringy and hard, impossible to chew. Leave the chunk in one piece with the rind on. Don't rinse. Put into a 2½-quart (2½ L) or larger heavy saucepan and add:

    6 cups water (1½ L)

The pork will float. Bring to a boil, cover, and simmer for 3 to 4 hours or until the fat is very soft. You expect it to melt away but it doesn't. Measure the water left and add water if necessary to bring the total back to 4 cups (1 L) of very flavorful liquid.

THE SUCCOTASH Add:

    2 cups baby or regular lima beans (frozen are fine)

Boil until the limas are tender. Frozen baby limas take only 3 or 4 minutes. Fresh can take longer, up to 10 or 15 minutes. Add:

    3 cups corn cut from the cob (approximately 6 ears)

Get the freshest corn possible. Cut the kernels off with a sharp knife. There are various techniques for this. Some people just slice off the kernels. Others—my mother among them—make a very shallow cut down the outside of the corn, just enough to slice off the tops of the kernels; then they scrape out the creamy insides with a knife and leave most of the skin behind. If you're a fiber lover, however, better use a third method. Make a series of cuts down the center of each row, cut off the kernels at the base, then scrape to get anything you missed. Also there are gadgets you can buy to remove corn from the cob.

However you arrive at 3 cups of kernels, add the corn to the limas and cook for 1 or 2 minutes. Into a small bowl put:

3 Tbs. flour
3 Tbs. cold water

Whisk until smooth. Add:

3 Tbs. more water

and whisk again until smooth. Add a cupful of hot succotash to this mixture, then stir. Dump this into the rest of the succotash, stirring continuously with a wire whisk. Return to the boil so the flour will thicken. Add:

2 Tbs. sugar (or more; we used to have this quite sweet)

Remove the salt pork chunk and cut into slices less than ¼ inch (¾ cm), then cut into ¾-inch (2-cm) pieces. Return to the succotash and stir to distribute. The dish may be served freshly made. Or refrigerate uncovered until chilled through, then cover and keep one or two days. To serve, reheat until hot and bubbly, stirring occasionally to make sure nothing sticks to the bottom of the pan.

Note: There is a mystery to the consistency of this succotash. Freshly cooked, it is very soupy and needs to be presented in individual bowls to keep it from running all over the plates. If you make it ahead, however, and refrigerate overnight, it is nowhere near as soupy and can be served on the plate along with the other foods. You may even want to thin it a bit with water.

Does it get thicker because the starch in the corn expands? Or because liquid evaporates as all cools? I leave these tantalizing questions to the food chemists among you who care to delve into the mystery further.

SUMMER VEGETABLE CHUNKS WITH BLACK OLIVES

6 servings

This good summer vegetable dish might be called a chunky ratatouille. *Cubes of eggplant and yellow crookneck squash are floured, fried, and presented in a sauce of onion and chopped fresh tomatoes. Black olives are the garnish. The first time I prepared this dish, its resemblance to* ratatouille *surprised me. The cooking procedure is quite different. It seems that whenever you combine three or four summer vegetables, you end up with* ratatouille *whether you want to or not.*

If you're an eggplant lover, you can double the eggplant and leave out the squash. If you're a garlic lover, you can add the object of your affection, mincing it and incorporating it during the last two minutes of sautéing the onions.

---

1 lb. eggplant (450 grams)
1 lb. yellow crookneck squash (450 grams)
Salt
Flour
About 1 cup olive oil (¼ L)
1 lb. tomatoes (450 grams)
⅓ cup olive oil (¾ dL)
1 large onion, minced
½ tsp. salt
1½ tsp. chopped fresh basil or ½ tsp. dried (or oregano)
2 cups (1 pint or ½ L) black olives (or less)
¼ cup (½ dL) chicken broth (optional)
Salt and pepper
4 Tbs. chopped parsley

THE EGGPLANT AND SQUASH Have:
    1 lb. eggplant (450 grams)
Pick a dark one with a good, green stem. Cut off the green top and also remove a thin slice from the bottom, which will be mostly skin. Cut into 1-inch (2½-cm) cubes. Have:
    1 lb. yellow crookneck squash (450 grams)
Cut into cubes as close to 1 inch (2½ cm) as you can. Sprinkle the vegetable cubes with:
    Salt
and then with:
    Flour
Shake off the excess flour. Into a large frying pan pour:
    ¼ inch olive oil (about ½ cup or 1 dL)
Get the oil hot enough so that a vegetable cube added will sizzle and bubble, but not so hot that it smokes. Put in the pan only as many floured vegetables as will fit in one layer. I crowd the pan, but keep the heat high enough so everything bubbles. If you do this right, the oil will stay in the pan and will not be all sucked up by the vegetable cubes. But don't worry if it disappears. It will come out later. As the cubes brown, turn them to color all surfaces without skin. I use two forks to turn the pieces individually. Figure on about 1 minute per side.

When the cubes are browned and tender, remove to paper towels, at which time they will give up most of the oil they swallowed. Before frying a second batch, add:
    More olive oil

to bring the level back to ¼ inch (¾ cm). Reheat and do the squash in the same fashion. (Or combine the squash and eggplant in the pan together.) When all is cooked, set aside to cool.

THE TOMATOES AND ONIONS Have:

1 lb. tomatoes (450 grams)

Peel by first putting in boiling water for 10 seconds, then stripping off the skin. Cut in half through the sides. Squeeze each half and flick out the seeds into the sink. Don't fuss with this. Just do it quickly to get rid of the worst of the seeds and the tomato liquid. Chop the pulp into ¼-inch (¾-cm) pieces. Reserve. Into a sauté pan or frying pan put:

⅓ cup olive oil (¾ dL)

1 large onion, minced

Cook over medium heat for 5 minutes or until the onion is soft and translucent but not beginning to brown. Add the chopped tomato pulp and:

½ tsp. salt

1½ tsp. chopped fresh basil or ½ tsp. dried (or oregano)

Pepper

Cook over medium heat for 5 minutes, stirring occasionally. Remove to a dish and let cool. Mix this "tomato sauce" with the eggplant and squash cubes already cooked. Refrigerate uncovered until chilled through. This can be done a day ahead.

THE OLIVES Use:

2 cups (1 pint or ½ L) black olives (or less)

Finding the right olives can be a problem. You can use those American canned ripe olives that are tasteless, but they won't do much for the dish except make it look "interesting." Once I used some Greek black olives (the wrinkled kind you buy in delicatessens) that were so bitter and so strong that each person ate only one and pushed the rest aside.

Throughout the Mediterranean area where black olives are sold in olive oil (not brine), asking to taste the olives before buying is traditional. So do so. If the olives you can find are not tasty in the shop, get rid of some of the bitterness at home by dropping the olives into boiling water until they plump up (the bitter kind are usually very wrinkled), then drain. Taste and repeat the boiling water process if necessary. Then add a sprinkle of salt if the olives have lost too much saltiness, which they probably have not; cover with olive oil and chuck a wedge or two of lemon in the oil. A bay leaf and a clove of garlic do no harm either. Let marinate out in the room a few hours or in the refrigerator as long as you like.

The other option for sweet, tasty black olives is to buy bottles of Greek Kalamata olives. These are pointed on one end and packed in a light brine. (Don't buy the big expensive ones, just the small ones that are about the size of regular olives.) Drain off the brine and taste. If very salty, rinse quickly in water and drain. Cover with olive oil. The lemon, garlic, and bay leaf treatment also is good here. Let sit in the refrigerator at least overnight or as long as you like. The longer they marinate, the better they get.

If you go to a good Greek, Italian, or Arab deli, you probably will not be sold bitter olives.

Reserve whatever olives you decide to use in the refrigerator. Drain off any oil and add just before serving.

TO HEAT AND SERVE Add the olives to the eggplant mixture, then heat in a saucepan until bubbly and thoroughly hot. If the mixture seems dry, add:

¼ cup (½ dL) water or chicken broth (optional)
Taste and add if necessary:

Salt and pepper
Have ready on the side:

4 Tbs. chopped parsley
Stir half the parsley into the mixture and then sprinkle the rest on top of each serving.

This dish can be served warm, but most Mediterranean vegetable dishes in olive oil are served at room temperature. Since it is summertime, take your pick.

THREE COLORFUL VEGETABLE PUREES (BUTTERNUT SQUASH, STRING BEAN, BEET WITH POTATO)

6 servings

These three purees, which are meant to be served together, were chosen for their contrasting flavors and textures, but especially for their colors. The array of green, orange, and deep purple-red on the plates is stunningly beautiful.

1 butternut squash, 2½
  to 3 lbs. (1125 to
  1350 grams)
1½ lbs. string beans
  (675 grams)
2 or 3 Tbs. salt
1 lb. beets (450 grams)
½ lb. boiling potatoes
  (225 grams)
6 Tbs. butter
Salt and pepper

BUTTERNUT SQUASH PUREE Select:
    1 butternut squash, 2½ to 3 lbs. (1125 to 1350
      grams)
You can prepare this a day ahead. Preheat the oven to 425°F/220°C. Cut off the funny little stem if there is one, then somehow cut the squash in half lengthwise. It takes some strength. Scrape out the seeds and fibers. Place the halves skin side up on a baking sheet. Bake for approximately 45 minutes or until tender (poke with a fork) and until you see some oozing and caramelizing of the syrupy juices. Remove, turn the halves over, and allow to cool a little. Scrape the meat from the skin and place in the container of a food processor. (You also can do this in a blender or food mill or push through a strainer or ricer.) Using the metal blade, process until smooth. Turn the machine on and let it go for 1 or 2 minutes. Reserve in refrigerator until serving time.

STRING BEAN PUREE If you can't find fresh, tender, lovely string beans, then use the frozen ones. Buy:
    1½ lbs. string beans (675 grams)
Snap the ends from the beans. In a small stockpot have 4 to 6 quarts (liters) of boiling water. Add:
    2 or 3 Tbs. salt
Stir and add the beans. Cook approximately 7 minutes or until the beans are crisp/tender. Drain right away and run cold water over to stop the cooking and to retain the color. Cut the beans across into ¼-inch (¾-cm) pieces, then put in the container of a food processor with the metal blade in place. Run the machine, stopping to stir down the sides now and then. This takes a while to get started, but once the puree is circulating, run the machine for 3 or 4 minutes or longer. Because the

beans are not overcooked, they take a while to become smooth. Taste now and then and, when the texture is agreeable to you, stop. Refrigerate. When the puree is chilled, cover with plastic. This can be done a day ahead.

BEET PUREE WITH POTATO This also can be done a day ahead. Buy:

    1 lb. beets (450 grams)

Wash and scrub. Put in a saucepan and cover well with boiling water. Boil 40 to 60 minutes or until tender. Test with a fork. Run under cold water to cool enough that you can slip off the skins. Trim away stem or root ends. Cut into a ½-inch (1½-cm) dice. Place in a food processor (metal blade) with:

    ½ lb. boiling potatoes (225 grams), peeled and cooked until tender (approximately 25 minutes)

The pureeing is easier when the vegetables are hot. Puree until the lumps are gone and all is smooth. The beets tend to be ornery, particularly if cold. You may have to pick out the last pieces that won't puree and eat them.

TO SERVE THE PUREES You need a separate saucepan for heating each. At serving time, heat the purees until they burp and bubble. Be careful you don't get spit at. Add:

    2 Tbs. butter to *each* puree

    Salt and pepper to taste

Arrange a spoonful of each on each plate. Serve.

SAUTÉED ZUCCHINI, SNOW PEAS, AND TOMATOES

6 servings

This pretty vegetable dish may be slightly on the fussy side, but it is not difficult to prepare and is quite delicious.

The treatment of the vegetables is Chinese, but the sautéing in butter brings the dish into the French or European camp. The fussiness I mentioned comes from having to cut the zucchini and tomatoes into pieces the same size and shape as the peapods.

You'll be happy to know that the dish does not take long to cut or cook and that most work can be done ahead.

4 oz. snow peas (115 grams)

1 Tbs. salt

3 zucchini, each about 6 inches (15 cm) long (1 lb. or 450 grams or slightly less)

2 large tomatoes (8 to 10. oz. or 225 to 285 grams each), lovely and ripe

½ stick butter (2 oz. or 60 grams)

Salt and pepper

TO PREPARE AND PRECOOK THE SNOW PEAS Buy:

4 oz. snow peas (115 grams)

Choose the smaller ones or those under 3 inches (8 cm) if you have any choice at all. They will be more tender and have fewer strings. To string the pods, snip off each stem end with your fingernail and pull down to remove a string—if there is one. Dig with your fingernail slightly into the other edge of the pod to see if a string is there to remove.

To precook, have a pot with 3 quarts (2¾ L) or more of boiling water. Add:

1 Tbs. salt

Stir, add the peas, and bring the water back to the boil. Cook 1 minute only from the time you put the pods in. Fish out with a slotted spoon (save the water for cooking the zucchini) and refresh the brilliant green pods right away in cold water to stop the cooking. Drain, spread on towels, and dry. Refrigerate uncovered until chilled.

TO PREPARE AND PRECOOK THE ZUCCHINI Have:

3 zucchini, each about 6 inches (15 cm) long (1 lb. or 450 grams or slightly less)

In order to get zucchini pieces that are the same size and shape as the peapods, trim off the ends, then cut each in half so that you have two 3-inch (8-cm) pieces. Stand each piece on end and cut downward into slices about ⅛ inch (½ cm) thick. The first and last pieces should be the right (peapod) size. But cut the rest of the slice in half lengthwise so they resemble the snow peas in size.

Return the peapod cooking water to a boil. Add the zucchini, timing them for 1 minute from when you put them in, as you did for the peas. Remove, refresh, drain, spread out to cool, and pat dry. Refrigerate until serving time.

THE TOMATOES Have:

2 large tomatoes (8 to 10 oz. or 225 to 285 grams each), lovely and ripe

Dip in boiling water for 10 seconds to help make the peeling easier. Peel. Then make tomato pieces that are the same size and shape as the peapods by cutting in half through the stem end. Then cut each half into six wedges.

You will use the outside thickness (the fleshy part of the tomato) only. So cut away the inside part and seeds from the outer layer, much as you cut the good part of a melon from its rind; in this case, however, the "rind" is the part you want to use. (Save the tomato centers for a salad later.)

Now you will have twenty-four pieces of firm tomato about 3 inches (8 cm) long and ⅛ inch (½ cm) thick, essentially the same size and shape as the peapods and zucchini pieces. Wipe away any seeds or excess liquid. Refrigerate until cooking time.

TO COOK AND SERVE This must be done at the very last minute. This is not one of those dishes that you can get warm and let sit, all nice and ready. If you do, the tomato turns to mush, the zucchini goes limp, and then the peapods fall open and separate. The dish is a mess.

At the very last minute have a 10-inch (23-cm) sauté pan or frying pan ready. Add:

    ½ stick butter (2 oz. or 60 grams)

Heat over high heat, then add the zucchini and peapods. Carefully stir or toss for a few seconds. Sprinkle over:

    Salt and pepper

Cover the pan for 30 seconds and cook over fairly high heat. Remove the cover and stir again. Continue if necessary until the vegetables are hot. Add the tomato pieces and cover again for 15 to 20 seconds, just long enough to get them barely warm. Serve right away.

BAKED CUBES OF BUTTERNUT SQUASH

6 servings

I am a great fan of butternut squash. It is such a beautiful color and so sweet that it almost tastes like dessert. If you bake it absolutely plain at a high temperature, by the end of the baking time, you will see the natural sugar oozing out and caramelizing. I love it.

2 butternut squash, weighing 2 to 2½ lbs. (900 to 1125 grams) each

THE SQUASH Buy:

    2 butternut squash

Pick the larger ones weighing 2 to 2½ pounds (900 to 1125 grams). Select those with fat necks and bulbous ends as small as possible. Cut off and reserve the rounded ends for later use. (These ends are hollow and contain seeds.)

Peel the thick necks with a vegetable peeler, then cut across into 1½-inch (4-cm) thick pieces. Cut the pieces into halves or quarters, then shape and trim into more or less square shapes. Don't try to get perfect cubes unless the Queen of England is coming to dinner. They can be prepared a day ahead. Cover and refrigerate.

TO BAKE Preheat the oven to 450°F/230°C. Place the squash cubes on a baking sheet or in a baking pan. Bake uncovered 30 to 40 minutes or until tender and brown, with some oozing of a sugary syrup. Serve or keep warm in a 200°F/95°C oven.

BROCCOLI FLOWERETS

6 servings

The intense green of broccoli that is not overcooked gives a beautiful color lift to any main-course dinner plate. Save the stems for supper the next night. To cook the stems, peel away the worst of the tough skin, then cut the tender insides into ¼-inch (¾-cm) diagonal slices; boil for about 5 minutes or until barely tender.

1 large bunch broccoli (or 2 smaller)
1 Tbs. salt
¾ stick (3 oz. or 85 grams) melted butter (optional)

BROCCOLI FLOWERETS You won't be serving a lot, perhaps only one clump about 2 inches (5 cm) in diameter on each plate. Buy:

1 large bunch broccoli (or 2 smaller)

Cut off and use the tender top flowerets with stems only about 2 inches (5 cm) long. Divide into six clumps. Refrigerate until serving time.

TO COOK Cooked broccoli flowerets lose their heat faster than any food I can think of, so prepare them at the very last moment. Have a saucepan ready with 3 to 4 quarts (2¾ to 3¾ L) of water. At serving time, bring to a boil and add:

1 Tbs. salt

Stir, then add the broccoli. Return to a not-too-mad boil for 4 or 5 minutes or until the broccoli is barely tender. Drain. You can serve as is or toss (carefully) in:

¾ stick (3 oz. or 85 grams) melted butter (optional)
A sprinkling of salt

Serve right away.

SHREDDED CABBAGE WITH GRATED BANANA SQUASH

6 servings

This is a delicious combination of vegetables which I like to serve separate but together, that is, by laying down a bed of shredded cabbage on individual plates and placing a small mound of the sautéed squash on top. It involves a little last-minute work, but the dividend in the appearance of the dish makes the effort worthwhile.

1 head cabbage, 1 to 1½ lbs. (450 to 675 grams)

1½ lbs. banana squash (675 grams)

1 stick butter (8 Tbs. or 120 grams)

Salt and pepper

THE CABBAGE You can shred this 5 or 6 hours before time to eat. Have:

   1 head cabbage, 1 to 1½ lbs. (450 to 675 grams)

Trim away any wilted outer leaves, then slice with a large knife into slivers as thin as you can possibly cut. There are shredders for this purpose; use a type that gives you long shreds, not a pile of sawdust. Reserve the shredded cabbage until serving time.

THE SQUASH You also can grate the squash 5 or 6 hours before serving. Have:

   1½ lbs. banana squash (675 grams)

This is a sweet, nice-tasting squash, my favorite after butternut among the pumpkin types. You buy it in big chunks cut from a gigantic squash the size of a huge watermelon. Cut the squash piece into smaller pieces that will fit down through the feed tube of a food processor. Remove the peel with a vegetable peeler, then push the pieces down the chute and shred them, using the shredding disk. You also can do this with a hand shredder. Reserve, covered, in the refrigerator until serving time.

TO SAUTÉ AND SERVE First cook the cabbage. Use a 10-inch (23-cm) sauté pan with a lid. Just before serving, set the heat to medium/high. Into the sauté pan put:

   ½ stick butter (4 Tbs. or 60 grams), cut into pieces

Heat the butter just to melt, then add the grated cabbage. Let cook without stirring for 15 seconds, then give it a stir, attempting to turn it over. Cover and let cook 15 seconds more. Remove the lid and stir again. Add:

   Salt and pepper

Keep cooking, stirring, and heating until the cabbage looks shiny, is darker green and wilted. This should take no longer than 2 or 3 minutes total. Do not overcook. Dump the cabbage into a heated bowl and cover to keep warm. Wipe out the sauté pan and cook the squash. Add to the pan:

½ stick butter (4 Tbs. or 60 grams), cut into pieces

Melt, then add the grated squash. Cook over medium/high heat without the lid. Let cook without stirring for 10 to 15 seconds, then stir and let sit another 10 to 15 seconds, and so on. The squash cooks more quickly than the cabbage and will be done in only 1 or 2 minutes total. Do not overcook. Add:

Salt

Quickly make small beds of cabbage on the plates and put spoonfuls of the squash on top.

STEAMED CARROT SHREDS

6 servings

This is the best carrot recipe of all the ones I know. There is a sweetness and an intensity of flavor that is unmatched in any other carrot dish. As you might have suspected, it is the simplest of all preparations: no salt, no pepper, no butter, just carrots and steam.

1 lb. carrots, the freshest you can find (450 grams)

TO SHRED THE CARROTS Have:

1 lb. carrots, the freshest you can find (450 grams)

If you can find them with the green tops still on, then buy them, because at least you'll know that they haven't been out of the ground for more than a week.

There's always a rub to a good, easy recipe, and the rub in this one is that you need to find a certain grater. It is imperative for this dish that you use a very fine grater. I have a four-sided standing metal grater at home that has one side that is the perfect grater for these carrots. It consists of rows of tiny round holes, a little over 1/16 inch (¼ cm) in diameter, with a small outward dent under each hole. Using this grater produces a very fine shred that is the key to the unusual character of this dish. If you can't find this same grater, go with one that has the smallest holes you can find. The special, fine, food-processor grating disk will do, but put little or no pressure on the carrots as they go down the feed tube so that they shred as slowly as possible.

Peel the carrots with a vegetable peeler. If you are shredding and cooking them right away, you don't have to peel, but if you do them ahead and do not peel, they turn dark. Shred the carrots and reserve until serving time. They can be prepared several hours ahead and refrigerated.

TO STEAM AND SERVE Place the shredded carrots in a saucepan. Add:

⅓ cup water (¾ dL)

Cover and cook over medium/high heat for 2 or 3 minutes, stirring once after a minute or so. When the carrots are steaming hot, serve.

CUCUMBER "NOODLES"

6 servings

This is perhaps the most unusual of all the recipes in this book. Cucumbers are peeled and the white pulp is sliced in noodle-like strips, with the seeds left behind. The strips are then boiled as you would boil noodles. They turn a lovely green color and make this dish one of the most different and intriguing vegetable dishes I know of.

The cucumber "noodles" would be very nice served as a separate course sauced with any of the traditional Italian pasta sauces—tomato, clam, carbonara, Alfredo, etc. My favorite way to serve them is in the simple "buttered noodles" style, as a vegetable accompaniment to a roast.

7 medium cucumbers (4 to 5 lbs. or 1¾ to 2¼ kg)
1 stick butter (4 oz. or 115 grams)
Salt and pepper
Finely chopped parsley (optional)

TO PREPARE THE "NOODLES" Since you will need one medium-sized cucumber per serving plus one for the pot, buy:

7 medium cucumbers (4 to 5 lbs. or 1¾ to 2¼ kg)

Peel the cucumbers and cut off the two ends. You will need some kind of slicing tool. I use a simple slotted-blade cheese slicer, also called a cheese

paragus, Beurre Blanc, with Green Pineapple (Pages 2–5)

Oysters on Saffron Bean Threads (Pages 8–10)

Mixed Greens with Red Bell Peppers and Toasted Hazelnuts (Pages 22–24)

Eggplant Cubes with Chopped Tomatoes and Chives (Pages 20–2

Mixed Seafood Soup with Wild Rice and Vegetables (Pages 88–92)

Double-Thick Sirloin Steak with Mustard (Pages 71–72)

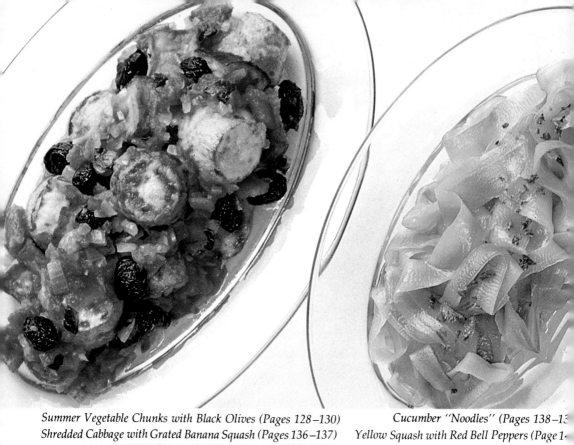

Summer Vegetable Chunks with Black Olives (Pages 128–130)   *Cucumber ''Noodles'' (Pages 138–13*
Shredded Cabbage with Grated Banana Squash (Pages 136–137)   *Yellow Squash with Red Bell Peppers (Page 1*

Crème Caramel with Small Raisins in Rum (Pages 178–181)

Spiced Apple and Pear Cobbler (Pages 209–210)

Fresh Summer Fruits with Watermelon Ice (Pages 194–197)

Blueberry Tart (Pages 217–22?

Viennese Torte with Carrots and Almonds (Pages 227–230)

Chocolate Whipped-Cream Truffle Cake (Pages 235–239)

plane. Scrape it the length of the cucumber, rotating the cucumber slightly after each scrape. Keep your fingers out of the way so that you don't scrape your knuckles. The noodles produced will vary anywhere from ⅝ inch to 1 inch (1½ to 2½ cm) wide and about ¹⁄₁₆ inch (¼ cm) thick and will be as long as the cucumber. The rotating of the cucumber should keep the noodles from getting too wide. When you come to the seeds, scrape away the pulp in smaller pieces, then discard the center, seedy core, which is hard on the digestion, anyway.

When the cucumbers are all sliced, cover with plastic and refrigerate. Bring out and uncover 1 or 2 hours before cooking to allow to come to room temperature.

TO COOK AND SERVE Have on the side:

    1 stick butter (4 oz. or 115 grams), room
        temperature or melted

In a large stock pot or spaghetti pot boil 8 to 10 quarts (liters) of water or as much water as your largest pot will hold. Have a colander in the sink. Into the boiling water put:

    1 or 2 Tbs. salt

Stir. When the water is boiling vigorously, add the cucumber in two or three batches, allowing 5 to 10 seconds between additions so that the water does not cool off too much. Start timing as soon as all the cucumbers are in. Cook 2 to 4 minutes or until the cucumber strips are barely crisp/tender. Do not overcook or the noodle strips begin to fall apart. Dump right away into the colander. Shake and stir to get rid of excess water. The water seems to drip forever. I finally place the cucumbers in the colander over a bowl to catch the water while I add the butter and stir carefully. Some of the butter goes through the holes and is lost, but that's life. Sprinkle over:

    Salt and pepper

Stir again, then taste and add more salt if necessary. Sprinkle over just a bit of:

    Chopped parsley, chopped fairly fine (optional)

Serve.

SLICED CARROTS AND
YELLOW SUMMER SQUASH

6 servings

This vegetable has a Chinese style to it, not in the taste, which is French or American, but in the looks. In the market, select carrots and squash that are close to the same diameter so that the yellow and orange oval slices will be somewhat the same size.

---

1 lb. carrots, similar in size to squash (450 grams)

1 lb. yellow crookneck squash, similar in size to the carrots (450 grams)

4 Tbs. butter

Salt and pepper

THE CARROTS Buy:

1 lb. carrots, similar in size to squash (450 grams)

Scrape or peel the carrots. If you care more about food value than about looks, then don't peel or scrape. For company, I peel or scrape. Slice the carrots on the diagonal about ⅛ inch (½ cm) thick. Reserve in the refrigerator until serving time.

THE SQUASH Buy:

1 lb. yellow crookneck squash, similar in size to carrots (450 grams)

Get the smaller squash if possible and try to match the carrots to the body, not to the skinny neck. Do not peel the squash. Wash it, then slice into ⅛-inch (½-cm) diagonal slices to match the carrot slices as best you can. Reserve in the refrigerator until serving time.

TO COOK AND SERVE Just before serving, have a large saucepan with 3 or 4 quarts (liters) of boiling water. Add:

1 or 2 Tbs. salt

Stir, then add the carrots and squash. Cook over high heat for 1 or 2 minutes only, or until the squash and carrot pieces are barely crisp/tender. Drain in a colander, then return to the saucepan. Carefully stir in:

4 Tbs. butter (or more or less) at room temperature

Salt and pepper

Serve right away.

DICED FENNEL
WITH PARSLEY

6 servings

This is an unusual and very nice vegetable dish. It goes very well with many dishes, particularly fish or chicken dishes.

For any of you who are not familiar with fennel, or finocchio as my Italian father used to call it, it is a crisp, celery-like bulb with an anise flavor. We at home used to eat it raw, cut into wedges, dipped in vinaigrette sauce. As kids, we considered it a real treat and I still consider it one. If you have never eaten it cooked, you will be pleasantly surprised.

---

1 lb. fennel (anise) (450 grams)
4 Tbs. butter
Salt and pepper
4 Tbs. chopped parsley

TO PREPARE THE FENNEL Buy:

1 lb. fennel (anise) (450 grams)

Wash, then trim off the stalks almost even with the bulb. If the stalks are tender, eat them for a little snack. If not, discard. Cut the bulb into a ½-inch (1½-cm) dice by first cutting into ½-inch slices, then cutting the slices into ½-inch fingers, and then cutting the fingers into a ½-inch dice. Cover with plastic and refrigerate. This can be done a day ahead.

TO COOK THE FENNEL AND SERVE Into a frying pan put:

2 Tbs. butter

Heat, then add the fennel. Cook, stirring now and then, over medium heat for 5 minutes or until crisp/tender. Stir in:

2 Tbs. butter
Salt and pepper
4 Tbs. chopped parsley

Serve.

WILTED LETTUCE LEAVES

Lettuce, cooked just until wilted, makes a lovely green vegetable resembling a nice, mild spinach, but with a little extra crunch coming from the ribs of the leaves. Don't use the darker green outer leaves. They may be loaded with vitamins, but they're bitter when cooked and not very pleasant to eat.

---

3 heads butter lettuce
  (also called Boston
  or garden lettuce)
⅔ stick butter (6 Tbs.
  or 90 grams)
2 Tbs. salt

THE LETTUCE Have:
  3 heads butter lettuce (also called Boston or
    garden lettuce)
Separate the leaves from the heads, keeping the
leaves whole, by trimming off and cutting out the
white core from underneath. Wash well, drain, and
reserve.
TO COOK AND SERVE In a small pan melt:
  ⅔ stick butter (6 Tbs. or 90 grams)
Reserve. In an 8-quart (8-L) pot or larger, bring
water to a boil. Just before serving, add to the pot:
  2 Tbs. salt
  Lettuce leaves
Push the leaves down into the water. Count 5
seconds and that is all. The lettuce is just to be
quickly wilted and not really cooked. Right away
pour the contents of the pot into a colander in the
sink. Toss the lettuce to get rid of excess water,
then put into a bowl and add the melted butter.
Sprinkle lightly with salt. Serve at once.

STRING BEANS WITH MINCED GARLIC

6 servings

*Few things in the vegetable kingdom are as nice or lovely as fresh young string beans
briefly cooked, tossed in butter, sprinkled with salt, and eaten as is. For the garlic lover,
minced garlic is marinated in the butter in which the beans are tossed just before serving.*

1½ lbs. string beans
  (675 grams)
1 stick butter (4 oz. or
  115 grams)
2, 3, or more large
  cloves garlic, minced
4 or 5 quarts water (3¾
  to 4¾ L)
1 to 2 Tbs. salt

THE BEANS You need:
  1½ lbs. string beans (675 grams)
Buy them the day of the dinner so they will be the
freshest possible. Take the trouble to pick out the
smallest beans. I stand in the market like an idiot,
picking up one bean at a time, to get the smallest of
the lot. Because the little ones are lovely and
tender, it is well worth the time to do this.
However, you may have to put up with a few dirty
looks from some shop owners. If you are lucky,
you will find a variety of bean called Blue Lake.
This bean appears briefly in the summer. The Blue
Lake is thinner, greener, and more rounded than

the very common Kentucky Wonder. I don't know whether the taste is necessarily any better, but the tenderness is. All beans are good when they are young and small, but for some reason beans seem to be getting more monstrous every year.

Snap or cut off the ends of the beans and leave them whole. (Unless they are great big, in which case I don't know what I'd do. I don't think I'd buy them. I'd have spinach instead.) Reserve until serving time.

MELTED BUTTER WITH GARLIC This should be prepared several hours ahead or even the day before so the garlic can flavor the butter. Into a small saucepan put:

1 stick butter (4 oz. or 115 grams)

Heat until melted, then add:

2, 3, or more large cloves garlic, minced

(You can do the mincing in the food processor by dropping the peeled cloves down the feed tube into the whirling metal blade.) Let the garlic sit in the butter overnight in the refrigerator. If you plan to use the butter within 4 or 5 hours, let it sit out in the room.

TO COOK AND SERVE THE BEANS At serving time, pour into a large saucepan:

4 or 5 quarts water (3¾ to 4¾ L)

Just before cooking, bring to a boil and add:

1 to 2 Tbs. salt

Stir, then add beans. Heat the minced garlic butter in a little pan. Cook the beans for 6 to 7 minutes or until crisp/tender. Drain *well,* then dump beans back into their cooking pot. Pour in the garlic butter and toss. Taste and add salt if necessary. Serve.

SHREDDED YELLOW SQUASH WITH RED BELL PEPPER

6 servings

This is a particularly beautiful vegetable dish with a very fresh taste. If you can't find red bell peppers, use green bell peppers or grated carrots.

1 lb. small yellow
  crookneck squash
  (450 grams)
1 lb. red bell peppers
  (2 big ones) (450
  grams)
Salt and pepper
2 Tbs. butter

THE SQUASH AND RED BELL PEPPER Buy:
  1 lb. small yellow crookneck squash (450 grams)
You get more yellow from the smaller ones. Snip off any stem ends, then grate or shred with a hand shredder or with the shredding disk of a food processor. Have:
  1 lb. red bell peppers (2 big ones) (450 grams)
Cut off the stem and top section. Remove the seeds and inner ribs. I haven't had much luck using the hand shredder or the food processor disk with this. The pepper skins are too tough. So I cut the pepper into ¾-inch (2-cm) strips, then cut across with a knife into ¹⁄₁₆-inch (¼-cm) shreds. If you can figure out an easier way to do it, let me know. Mix the squash and the pepper in a bowl. Reserve in the refrigerator until serving time.

TO HEAT AND SERVE These vegetables need practically no cooking time. They are just heated and served. Put them in a saucepan, add 2 tablespoons of water, cover tight, and steam 1 or 2 minutes over high heat, stirring once or twice or until they are hot. Add:
  Salt, pepper, some butter
and serve. *Or* cook them this way, which I prefer. Into a sauté pan put:
  2 Tbs. butter (or more)
Add the squash and peppers. Cook over high heat about 1 minute or until heated through, stirring now and then. Add:
  Salt and pepper
Serve.

SAUTÉED PLUM TOMATOES

Often in the late summer and early fall, beautiful red, good-tasting plum (Italian) tomatoes are on the market. If you happen to see some, buy them. If not, look for some good cherry tomatoes. They are almost always around.

2 or 3 plum tomatoes per person (smaller size)
3 Tbs. butter
Salt and pepper

THE TOMATOES Buy:
  2 or 3 plum tomatoes per person (select the smaller ones)
Use a frying pan that the tomatoes will just fit into in one layer. In the pan put:
  3 Tbs. butter
Melt over low heat. Add the tomatoes, which should be room temperature, not cold. Heat in the butter, stirring now and then, for 1 or 2 minutes only or until just warmed through. If you get them too hot or cook them too long, the skins will pop and they will not look very pretty. Sprinkle over:
  Salt and pepper
Serve right away.

RICE, GRAINS, AND LEGUMES, MISC.

Fresh Black-eyed Peas with Pesto

Fresh Chestnut Puree

Cornmeal Polenta Swiss-Style with Gruyère

*Brown Rice with Toasted Pine Nuts

*Bulgur and Barley Pilaf

*Steamed Millet with Onions and Oregano

Mushrooms with Peanuts and Garlic

*Special quick dishes

T his section might be subtitled "Potato and White Rice Substitutes." In truth, that's what these dishes come down to. They offer new and different foods you can serve in place of the overused potato or white rice. Try some of these unusual dishes to add new interest and variety to main-course dinner plates.

In this section you will notice that each recipe represents a whole different category of food. There is just one dish for each area of the following food groups: beans, cornmeal, chestnuts, brown rice, wheat, barley, millet, and peanuts. These are fascinating and wonderful foods to serve and will give your meals new textures and flavors and an exciting creativity.

Let me hasten to assure you that I have nothing against potatoes or white rice. I love them and eat them almost every day of my life, but I do think we have been overdoing them a bit, so to speak. For entertaining and even for daily eating, it is time we gave these other wonderful foods a chance.

FRESH BLACK-EYED PEAS WITH PESTO

6 servings

Here is an amusing and amazingly good combination of two things not usually combined: fresh black-eyed peas, which are available with increasing frequency in all parts of the country these days, and the Italian fresh-basil sauce, pesto.

Fresh black-eyed peas are around in July and August, sometimes a little bit earlier or later. They are packaged in plastic bags and displayed in the produce department. Frozen black-eyed peas also are excellent. Once cooked, they are so similar that I can't tell the difference. Fresh or frozen black-eyed peas, even though they are really beans, are extremely light in effect and quite different from the dried version, which must be cooked for some time.

Pesto is a paste of fresh basil leaves, oil, and cheese. This wonderfully aromatic sauce is simple to make, is good on many things, and keeps for months in the refrigerator. The only problem is that you somehow must find fresh basil. A suggestion follows for making the sauce with dried basil and spinach. It is not the same, but is good and well worth doing. In some markets you may find frozen pesto, *which is not as good as freshly made but good enough.*

2 cups (packed down well) fresh basil leaves
About 2 cloves garlic
1 cup olive oil (¼ L)
Salt and pepper
2 to 4 Tbs. pine nuts (optional)
½ cup grated Parmesan cheese (or half Parmesan and half Romano cheese)
3 to 4 Tbs. olive oil
2 packages (11 oz. or 312 grams each) fresh black-eyed peas or 1 package (1 lb. 4 oz. or 566 grams) frozen
1 to 2 tsp. salt
1 cup pesto (¼ L)
¼ cup pea-cooking water (½ dL)
Grated Parmesan cheese (optional)
2 cups fresh spinach leaves
2 Tbs. dried basil

THE PESTO This recipe makes about 2 cups, considerably more than you need for this dish. But *pesto* is so good and stores so well that, if you find fresh basil, you should make this amount to keep on hand.

This recipe calls for four or five small bunches of fresh basil, made up of five or six branches each. Occasionally you will find bunches twice that big, especially in Italian markets. If you buy basil ahead, stick the stems in a glass of water and wrap in paper or plastic, just as if they were bouquets of violets that you wanted to keep fresh. Do not wash until just before using or the leaves can turn black. Basil bouquets will keep for days in the refrigerator.

When ready to make the *pesto*, pick off the leaves and discard the stems. Wash the leaves and dry. Into the container of a food processor put:

   2 cups (packed down well) fresh basil leaves
   2 cloves garlic (or more or less)
   1 cup olive oil (¼ L)
   1 tsp. salt
   Pepper
   2 to 4 Tbs. pine nuts (optional)

(I don't usually add the traditional pine nuts. They're expensive, and when I leave them out, I don't miss them at all.) Process to paste consistency. Add:

   ½ cup grated Parmesan cheese (or half Parmesan and half Romano if you like that gutsy Romano flavor)

Process again quickly just to mix. Right away transfer to a sturdy drinking glass (metal can turn *pesto* black). Carefully pour over the top to seal the pesto from the air:

   3 to 4 Tbs. olive oil (or other oil)

Cover and refrigerate. It will keep for months. To use, pour off or scrape off the oil, which probably has congealed. Use the amount of *pesto* needed, then level off what remains. Warm the oil slightly, just until it flows again, then pour back over the *pesto*. Refrigerate again.

THE BLACK-EYED PEAS Buy:

   2 packages (11 oz. or 312 grams each) fresh black-eyed peas or 1 package (1 lb. 4 oz. or 566 grams) frozen

About 20 minutes before serving, have a saucepan with:

>3 to 4 quarts boiling water (2¾ to 3¾ L)
>1 to 2 tsp. salt

Stir, then add the fresh or frozen peas, breaking up as many clumps of the frozen ones as you can. Adjust the heat to just a little higher than a simmer, then cook 12 to 15 minutes or until eating one proves they are tender. You might check after 8 to 10 minutes just in case, but lately the fresh have been taking about 12 minutes and the frozen about 15 minutes to get as tender as I like. When the peas are almost tender, into a tiny saucepan put:

>1 cup *pesto* (¼ L)

Add:

>¼ cup pea-cooking water (½ dL)

Heat to be slightly warm when the peas are done, but don't let the *pesto* really cook. When the peas are tender, drain and return to the saucepan. Dump in the *pesto*, mix well, and serve right away. You can sprinkle over more:

>Grated Parmesan cheese (optional)

or pass it around at the table.

Note: These reheat well in a saucepan. Add 2 or 3 tablespoons of water, cover, and cook over low heat, stirring occasionally, until heated through.

A surprise note: These black-eyed peas are delicious served as a first-course appetizer. Present them at room temperature on lettuce leaves that have been tossed in vinaigrette. Serve as is or garnish with a few tomato slices or whatever.

If you can't find fresh basil: Try this version. For the 2 cups of basil leaves in the *pesto* recipe, substitute:

>2 cups washed, destemmed, packed-down
>   fresh spinach leaves
>2 Tbs. dried basil

Make the same way.

FRESH CHESTNUT PUREE

6 servings

There is nothing more wonderfully seasonal than mashed fresh chestnuts. Fresh chestnuts are fall and winter and Christmas. If you have never used them not from a can, then you should try them. They require a little bit of work; but if you will follow the method described here and don't invite fifty people for dinner, you will be amazed at how quickly you can get done. If you really must, you can buy peeled chestnuts in cans, packed in water (not syrup). Mash, season, reheat, and butter them the same as you would the fresh chestnuts in the following recipe.

1½ lbs. chestnuts (675 grams)
2 cups chicken stock (½ L) (homemade or canned) or milk
½ cup chestnut cooking liquid (1 dL)
3 to 4 Tbs. butter

PEELING THE CHESTNUTS This, of course, is what takes all the time. But thanks to a tip from a former student of mine named Barbara Scavullo and thanks to another idea from Charlotte Combe, who used to teach at my school in San Francisco, you can shell and peel 1½ pounds of chestnuts in only 15 minutes, without burned fingertips. Read on. Into a saucepan put:

    1½ lbs. chestnuts (675 grams)

(The larger the chestnuts, the fewer to peel.) Do not slit the chestnuts. It's not necessary. Add cold water to the chestnuts to cover, plus an inch or so more. Bring to a boil over heat that is low enough so that the water takes 8 to 10 minutes to boil. Have a small bowl of cold water handy, a spoon, a chopping board, and a heavy, sharp knife. When the water is boiling, turn it down to a very low simmer. Fish out a chestnut with the spoon and plop it into the cold water. (The cold water was Charlotte's idea.) Right away remove the chestnut with your hand and cut it in half (the chestnut, that is) so that you butterfly it and end up with two thin halves. Pop the chestnut meat out of each half with your thumbs. It should leave the skin and shell behind and come out quickly and clean. (The cutting in half and the popping out were Barbara's idea.) Continue until all the chestnuts are peeled. TO COOK THE CHESTNUTS The last chestnuts to be peeled will be tender already, but I cook them all. In a saucepan bring to a boil:

    2 cups chicken stock (½ L), homemade or canned

(You can use water or milk instead.) Add the

peeled chestnuts. Return to a boil and simmer for
20 to 25 minutes or until the chestnuts are tender.
Drain, saving the broth. You will use some here,
and the rest will make a delicious soup base. Pass
the chestnuts through a ricer or food mill, or push
through a strainer, or puree in a food processor.
Somehow get them mashed. Add:
    ½ cup chestnut cooking liquid (1 dL)
Stir, then reserve until serving. If cooked a day
ahead, refrigerate uncovered until chilled, then
cover.
TO SERVE Heat in a saucepan until hot and bubbly.
Correct the consistency if necessary by adding more
of the cooking liquid. It shouldn't be too stiff, but
more or less like creamy mashed potatoes. Just
before serving, remove from the heat and add:
    3 to 4 Tbs. butter, cut into pieces, at room
        temperature
Whisk until butter melts. Check the seasoning.
Serve hot. I can hardly read this recipe without
salivating. This stuff is really good.

CORNMEAL POLENTA SWISS-STYLE WITH GRUYÈRE

6 servings

*This wonderful, hearty "vegetable" dish, almost a meal in itself, is very easy to make
and people really love it. The recipe comes from Stanley Warmbrodt, a good friend who
worked with me for several years at my cooking school in San Francisco.*

4 cups milk (1 L)
1 cup yellow cornmeal
1 tsp. salt
1 cup whipping cream
    (¼ L)
4 oz. shredded
    Gruyère or Swiss
    cheese (120 grams)

THE CASSEROLE Into a heavy saucepan put:
    4 cups milk (1 L)
    1 cup yellow cornmeal
    1 tsp. salt
Mix, then bring to a boil, stirring or whisking all
the time. Adjust the heat to medium/low and let
the mixture bubble and burp away for 7 minutes,
stirring and beating occasionally with a wooden
spoon to keep it smooth. Stir in:
    1 cup whipping cream (¼ L)
Butter an 8 × 8 × 2-inch (20 × 20 × 5-cm) glass or

ceramic baking dish, then pour in slightly less than half the polenta. Over this place:

    2 oz. shredded Gruyère or Swiss cheese
      (60 grams)

Pour in the rest of the polenta, then add another:

    2 oz. shredded Gruyère or Swiss cheese
      (60 grams)

The dish may be done to here a day ahead. Refrigerate uncovered until chilled through, then cover with plastic.

TO BAKE AND SERVE Bake in a preheated 400°F/205°C oven for 40 minutes. Let sit 10 minutes before serving, to cool a bit and to firm.

Note: If you would like to double this recipe to serve more people, use an 8 × 13 × 2-inch (20 × 33 × 5-cm) glass baking dish or another with a 3-quart capacity. Double all of the ingredients except the milk. Use only 6½ cups (1½ L) of milk instead of doubling to 8 cups.

BROWN RICE WITH TOASTED PINE NUTS

8 servings

This is a dish that I have served again and again. It goes with almost everything and guests really love it. The brown rice is a pleasant change from white rice. It has a little more character, and combined with the toasted pine nuts, it is something really special.

Pine nuts are not nuts at all, but seeds that actually come from large pine cones. They are, unfortunately, a little on the expensive side and can be hard to find. You can substitute slivered almonds and save a little money and a little searching time.

---

4 oz. (more or less) (115 grams) pine nuts
2½ cups water (6 dL)
1 tsp. salt
1½ Tbs. butter
1½ cups brown rice (long grain or short)

THE PINE NUTS Preheat the oven to 350°F/180°C. Spread out on a baking sheet:

    4 oz. (or more or less) (115 grams) pine nuts,
    also called pignoli

Bake for 15 minutes or until the pine nuts are nicely browned. They are better a little darker than too light. Cool and reserve in plastic. Can be done a day or more ahead.

THE RICE Start cooking the rice 1½ hours before you plan to serve it, to allow enough time to really do it right. It will take 45 to 50 minutes to steam and another 30 to 45 minutes to sit and swell and fluff.

I prefer using a heavy saucepan for cooking rice. You can use a lighter pan, but if you do, you must be very careful to keep the heat low or the rice may burn on the bottom. Into a heavy 2½-quart (2½-L) saucepan put:

2½ cups water (6 dL)
1 tsp. salt
1½ Tbs. butter

Bring to a boil. Add:

1½ cups brown rice (long grain or short; long grain is fluffier)

Return to a boil. Stir once to level the rice, then cover and simmer over low heat for 45 minutes. When the heat level is correct, faint puffs of steam will be seen escaping from under the pot lid. When the 45 minutes is up, check to see if all the water has been absorbed. Tilt the pan 90° to see if any water is left. If there is still some, cover the pan again and cook 5 or 10 minutes longer. When all the water is gone, cover the pan and set aside for 30 to 40 minutes to fluff and dry further. At serving time, put back over very low heat for 5 minutes to warm up again. Be careful, the drier it is, the faster it burns. Stir in the toasted pine nuts. Taste and add more:

Salt and butter

if you like.

Serve. This reheats fairly well the next day. Add a little water, cover, and steam until hot.

BULGUR AND BARLEY PILAF

6 servings

This is a delicious pilaf. The bulgur, which is coarse, cracked, processed wheat, gives a marvelous flavor. The barley's chewiness gives a wonderful character. A side benefit of this pilaf, some claim, is that it is good diet food. Even though not particularly low in calories (an individual serving contains around 200), the pilaf has a high fiber content. The fiber, as the theory goes, pushes and shoves everything through so fast that your body doesn't have time to grab all the calories as they go rushing by. Intriguing, n'est-ce pas? Sounds great to me.

1 cup unrefined barley
2 or 3 Tbs. butter
2 Tbs. olive oil (or any oil, or all butter)
1 onion, minced
1 cup bulgur
2 cups chicken stock, beef stock, fish broth, or vegetable water (½ L)
Salt

TO PRECOOK THE BARLEY Soak:

> 1 cup unrefined barley (don't use pearl barley, which has had the bran removed)

in cold water for ½ hour. Drain, then place the barley in a saucepan. Cover, plus 2 inches, with cold water. Bring to a boil, then simmer uncovered for 20 minutes. While this is cooking, prepare the following.

THE BULGUR Into a heavy saucepan put:

> 2 Tbs. butter
> 2 Tbs. olive oil (or any oil, or all butter)

Heat, then add:

> 1 onion, minced

Stir, then let soften, but not color, over low heat for 5 minutes. Add:

> 1 cup bulgur

Stir until the grains are well coated and glistening. Cook over low heat for 10 minutes, stirring occasionally. Add:

> 2 cups liquid (chicken stock, beef stock, fish broth, vegetable water, or plain water) (½ L)
> Salt (See below)

(Note: Canned stock is all right, but taste it first and dilute with half water if salty or strong. If the liquid you use is plain water, add 1 teaspoon of salt, but if you use stock that is already seasoned, add little or no salt; you can always add more at the end.) Bring the liquid to a boil, then simmer covered for 20 minutes. Tilt the pan to see whether the liquid has been absorbed. If not, cook another 10 minutes over very low heat. (There is danger at the end that the pilaf will stick and burn, so be very cautious of the heat during the last moments.) When the liquid is all absorbed, remove from the heat, then let sit covered for 10 minutes. The grains will separate more and become drier. Mix the barley and bulgur together. Either serve right away or remove cover, cool, and refrigerate until chilled, then cover. Reserve.

TO REHEAT AND SERVE Add to a saucepan containing the barley and bulgur:

> ¼ cup water (½ dL)

Cover, then cook over low heat for 5 minutes or until the pilaf is heated through. Taste and, if you wish, add more:

> Butter and/or salt

Stir, then serve.

STEAMED MILLET WITH ONIONS AND OREGANO

6 servings

Millet is a grain of the grass family that has been grown since ancient times and still is cultivated in parts of India and Africa. Mild and very pleasant, millet somewhat resembles white rice. You can buy it in health food stores with the husks removed. What you see left are tiny (1/16 inch) yellow balls. In Africa today, millet is made into a kind of porridge with milk, similar to our breakfast oatmeal.

For this dish, I steam the millet the same way I do white rice. Adding onions and oregano fried in olive oil turns the millet into a very acceptable conversation piece. People will both talk about the dish and eat it.

---

3 Tbs. olive oil
1 onion, minced fine
½ tsp. crumbled dried oregano, or 1 to 1½ tsp. chopped fresh oregano
2 cups water (½ L)
1 tsp. salt
1 cup millet

THE ONIONS Into a frying pan put:
    3 Tbs. olive oil
Heat, then add:
    1 onion, minced fine
Cook 5 minutes over low heat, then add:
    ½ tsp. crumbled dried oregano or 1 to 1½ tsp.
    chopped fresh oregano
Mix, then cook another 5 minutes. The onions will still have a little crunch. Reserve in a saucer until serving time. This can be done a day ahead and refrigerated.

THE MILLET Cook about 1 hour before serving. Into a saucepan put:
    2 cups water (½ L)
    1 tsp. salt
Bring to a boil and add:
    1 cup millet
Cover and cook over low heat for 20 minutes. Adjust the heat as you would for rice. Look for a little bit of steam coming out from under the lid during the cooking. When the 20 minutes are up, remove the saucepan from the heat, leave covered, and let sit for 30 minutes.

TO SERVE Warm the onion mixture in a small pan. Just before serving, add to the millet and stir well.

Note: One cup of millet expands to six ample servings. However, if you want seconds to be available, increase the recipe by half.

Another note: You can do the whole dish a day ahead, including stirring in the onions. At serving time, add 2 to 3 tablespoons of water, cover, and reheat over low/medium heat for about 10 minutes. Stir with a fork before serving.

MUSHROOMS WITH PEANUTS AND GARLIC

This interesting, moist, and delicious side dish is half Chinese and half French. The peanuts give it a Chinese character. The olive oil and garlic whisk it away to southern France. The taste is transformed by the addition of Madeira. You can substitute sherry or dry vermouth, but don't leave out some form of aromatic alcohol. This dish can be completely cooked ahead, then quickly reheated just before serving.

4 oz. shelled peanuts (115 grams; approximately 1 cup), or 6 oz. before shelling (180 grams)

1 lb. mushrooms (450 grams)

3 Tbs. olive oil (or other oil or butter)

4 to 5 large cloves garlic

Salt and pepper

3 Tbs. dry Madeira, sherry, or vermouth

THE PEANUTS You have a choice of peanuts to use. My order of preference is (1) raw peanuts, the type you find in Chinese grocery stores or American health food stores; (2) peanuts in their shells, either roasted or not, bought as fresh as possible; or (3) shelled, salted peanuts that have been cooked in oil, the kind you buy in plastic bags or tins. The problem with the last type is essentially the rancidity of the oils used in processing the nuts. Rancid oil doesn't taste particularly good and I understand it's not good for the body. In any case, have:

    4 oz. shelled peanuts (115 grams; approximately
        1 cup) or 6 oz. before shelling (180 grams)
Reserve.

THE MUSHROOMS Have:
    1 lb. mushrooms (450 grams)
Wash in three changes of water, swooshing them in and out quickly so that they absorb as little as possible. If still dirty, wipe them with a damp sponge. Cut into a ¾-inch dice. Reserve. Proceed right away with the preparation of the dish or the mushrooms can darken.

TO COOK THE DISH Into a frying pan or sauté pan put:
    3 Tbs. olive oil (or other oil or butter)
Heat the oil (if using butter, cut down a little on the heat because butter burns), then add:
    4 to 5 large cloves garlic, peeled and sliced thin
Cook over high heat for 2 or 3 minutes or until the garlic slices are light brown. Turn them over in the oil from time to time. Remove the garlic and discard.

    Add the peanuts. Cook over high heat for 20 to 30 seconds or until you see the very first slight signs of color. Do not overcook or they will get too dark later. Add the mushrooms. Cook over high heat for 2 or 3 minutes, stirring often but not constantly. As the dish progresses, you may want to lower the heat. Add:

Salt

Pepper (optional)

When the mushrooms start to look cooked and the peanuts are browning nicely, add:

3 Tbs. Madeira (Sercial or Rainwater, the drier types) or dry sherry or dry vermouth

Continue tossing the mushrooms and peanuts for 30 to 60 seconds or until some of the excess Madeira has cooked off. Transfer the contents of the pan to a plate and spread to cool. Refrigerate until serving time. Cover as soon as chilled.

TO REHEAT AND SERVE Put the mushroom-peanut mixture in a saucepan. Add:

1 Tbs. water

Cover, then place over medium heat for 2 or 3 minutes or until hot. Taste and, if you like, add:

1 or 2 tsp. additional Madeira

Serve.

BREADS, CRACKERS, AND
A PANCAKE

Whole Wheat Baguettes

Whole Wheat Bread with Scotch Oats

Whole Wheat–Rye Molasses Bread with Dill

Rolled Oat Crackers with Peanuts and Sesame Seeds

*Pumpernickel Crackers with Wheat Flakes
and Caraway Seeds*

*Green Pea Bread

A Fat, Broiled Pancake with Pecans

*Special quick bread

You will notice that this section contains mostly whole grain breads. That seems to be the way the cookie is crumbling these days. According to current thinking, whole grain breads seem to be better for the human body, and because of the fiber and the natural nutritional elements they contain, they are not so unjustifiably fattening as "white" bread.

Commercial breads have improved so much in the last ten to fifteen years that it is almost not worth the time and effort to make your own bread. There are two reasons, however, that justify continuing to do it. The first is if you have some kind of wheat-grinding mechanism or appliance attachment that allows you to grind your own wheat. There is something mysteriously good about bread made from freshly ground flour that makes it different and really incomparable. If you have never ground your own flour, I urge you to give it a try.

The second reason for making bread these days is that you can create combinations that are not available commercially. The breads, crackers, and pancake in this section certainly are not available anywhere I know of, and they are all delightful and delicious.

One of my favorite ways to use bread for entertaining is with a soup-salad-homemade-bread-and-dessert meal. The following lunch or dinner, for example, is my idea of a really wonderful one to serve for guests.

Mixed Greens with Red Bell Peppers and Toasted Hazelnuts

Mixed Seafood Soup with Wild Rice and Vegetables

Whole Wheat Bread with Scotch Oats

Spiced Apple and Pear Cobbler

WHOLE WHEAT BAGUETTES

Makes 6 loaves

This wonderful bread is no more trouble to make than any ordinary loaf. You can make it with the whole wheat flour you buy, but it is even better made with wheat you grind yourself right before the baking.

A few years ago a friend named Bill Kuretich introduced me to grinding wheat. Bill has a fine-kitchenware shop in Torrance, California, called What's Cooking. One day while I was there teaching classes, Bill and I went out and bought some wheat. We returned to the shop, where we ground it in an attachment for a Kenwood mixer. We mixed the wheat with one-third white flour to make the bread. The proportions were ones that the lady in the (Mormon) shop had suggested. I chose to bake the bread in a baguette shape because that long, skinny shape produces lots of the crust I like. The bread we baked (the same bread for which I give the recipe here) was divine. We ate like a couple of kids, or maybe I should say pigs. In an hour we devoured almost all we had made.

By the way, did you know that baguette *is the French word for "wand," as in a fairy's wand? Here's another little gem of information: the French call chopsticks* baguettes. *If that doesn't make your day, at least I tried.*

This recipe makes six loaves. The instructions call for using an electric mixer, but you can mix the dough in a bowl with a wooden spoon and do the kneading by hand.

2¾ cups warm water (6½ dL)

2 envelopes dry yeast (or 2 cakes fresh, crumbled)

4½ cups whole wheat flour (about 1 lb. 5 oz. or 600 grams)

2½ cups unbleached all-purpose white flour (10½ oz. or 300 grams)

1 Tbs. salt

MAKING THE DOUGH AND THE FIRST RISING Into a small bowl put:

> ½ cup barely warm water (1 dL)
> 2 envelopes dry yeast (or 2 cakes fresh, crumbled)

Stir occasionally to dissolve the yeast. Into the bowl of an electric mixer put:

> 4½ cups whole wheat flour (about 1 lb. 5 oz. or 600 grams)

(Use about 3¼ cups wheat kernels if you grind your own flour. Use the finest-grind setting on the machine.) Also add:

> 2½ cups unbleached all-purpose white flour (10½ oz. or 300 grams)
> 1 Tbs. salt

Mix well. Give the yeast another stir to dissolve and add it to the flours with:

> 2¼ cups barely warm water

Stir, then fit your mixer with a paddle beater. Turn the mixer on the lowest speed and mix for 1 minute. Let rest 5 minutes. Switch to a dough hook and run the machine, still on the lowest speed, for 2 minutes more.

Turn the dough out on a floured board and work it with your hands a little to see whether it is wet or dry. I prefer it a little on the sticky side. If the dough is impossibly wet, work or knead more flour in. If too dry, dip your fingers into water and poke them into the dough.

Put the dough in a bowl, greased if you like; cover with plastic wrap and towels, a board, or something to shut out light. Allow to rise until tripled in volume. In a chilly kitchen rising may take up to 6 hours, but it can take 3 hours or less if your kitchen is warm. Don't let the dough over rise or the bread will ferment and develop too yeasty a taste.

THE SECOND RISING When dough has tripled properly, turn out on a floured counter. Using a rolling pin or your hands, flatten the dough to get rid of the major gas bubbles. Fold three or four times into a small package, then place in a clean bowl. Cover as before and let rise again, but just to twice the volume. If you like, you can let this second rising take place overnight in the refrigerator.

FORMING THE LOAVES After the second rising, turn the dough out onto the counter and flatten into a rectangle. Cut into six long pieces as equal in size as possible. Fold each in half so that it is half as long; let rest 5 minutes. Using your hands or a rolling pin, flatten each piece, pushing it out to as long as possible. Make a furrow the length of the strip, then fold in half on this line. Pinch the edges together, place the pinched edge to the side, flatten the dough again, and make another furrow. Fold, then pinch together again. All this folding builds surface tension to make a pretty top on each loaf.

Place three loaves on a baking sheet that has been slightly greased (don't use butter—it burns). You can sprinkle the sheet with cornmeal if you like. Cover the loaves with towels and allow to double. This should not take more than an hour. Don't let bread rise too much or you will get too light a bread and too fat a loaf. Typical French baguettes are long and skinny

TO BAKE Preheat the oven to 500°F/260°C. Allow a good half hour for preheating so it is really good and hot all the way through and around. Prepare a pan with 1 or 2 inches of boiling water. Just before putting the bread in the oven, slash the tops with four or five diagonal slashes, using a very sharp razor blade (or use the steel blade from a food processor). The slashes open during baking and look pretty.

I think the crusts are harder and better if you bake only three loaves at a time. Therefore, put three loaves in on the top oven shelf and right away put the pan of boiling water on the shelf underneath. Put the water pan in a little bit sloppily so you spill a little onto the oven floor and cause some steam to form. (It is all right to do this in a gas oven but not in an electric one.) Close the oven door quickly. Bake the bread for 8 minutes, then remove the pan of water. Continue baking another 12 minutes. Remove the bread and cool on racks. Prepare more boiling water and bake the other three loaves.

These loaves freeze well. Reheat the thawed bread for 5 minutes in a 350°F/180°C oven to reharden the crust.

WHOLE WHEAT BREAD WITH SCOTCH OATS

Makes 4 loaves

Scotch oats or steel-cut oats are hulled oat groats or berries that have been cut into coarse pieces at an angular ⅛-inch dice. They look a lot like cracked wheat. They are different from the rolled oats we use for oatmeal, which are whole oat groats softened by steaming, then flattened between heavy rollers. In bread, Scotch oats become firm little lumps that give your teeth something to chew on. This is a good, hearty, important bread.

4 cups water (1 L)

½ cup sugar (100 grams), honey, or dark molasses

2 Tbs. butter

2 cups Scotch oats

Salt

6 cups whole wheat flour (approximately 1½ lbs. or 675 grams)

¼ cup warm water (½ dL)

2 envelopes dry yeast (or 2 cakes fresh yeast)

3 cups all-purpose white flour (360 grams)

THE BREAD Have four loaf tins, each approximately 2¼ × 3⅝ × 7¾ inches (6 × 9½ × 20 cm), or two tins, each 2¾ × 5 × 9 (6¾ × 12½ × 22½ cm), if you like gigantic loaves. Rub the tins with oil, leaving just a light coating. Into a saucepan put:

    4 cups water (1 L)

    ½ cup sugar (100 grams), honey, or dark molasses

    2 Tbs. butter

Heat, stirring occasionally to dissolve the sugar and butter. I am lazy and use an electric mixer for mixing and kneading, but you can do both by hand if you prefer. Into the bowl of an electric mixer (or into a large mixing bowl) put:

    2 cups Scotch oats

    3 to 4 tsp. salt

    6 cups whole wheat flour (approximately 1½ Tbs. or 675 grams)

(I grind my own wheat with an attachment that fits on my Kenwood electric mixer.) Mix these together. When the water-sugar-butter mixture boils and the sugar has dissolved, add it to the oats and flour in the bowl. Mix just enough to form dough. Let cool 10 minutes. Into a saucer put:

    ¼ cup warm water (½ dL)

(If using fresh yeast, have water lukewarm.) Sprinkle over:

    2 envelopes dry yeast or 2 crumbled cakes fresh yeast

Mix to wet the yeast, then let sit, stirring occasionally to help dissolve. When the flour mixture has cooled for 10 minutes, add to it the yeast plus:

    3 cups all-purpose white flour (360 grams)

Mix. Knead with the dough hook of an electric mixer or by hand. If using the machine, set at the lowest speed and let it run for 3 or 4 minutes. Knead by hand for 8 to 10 minutes. The dough should be somewhat tacky, but if it is a sticky nightmare and impossible to knead, add more whole wheat or white flour.

THE FIRST RISING Place the dough in a bowl, cover with plastic, and let rise until doubled. (I put it in a turned-off gas oven to let it rise because the heat of the pilot light keeps the oven slightly warm. This warmth speeds things up—the dough is doubled in about 2 hours.)

SHAPING THE LOAVES AND THE SECOND RISING Turn the dough out on a table. Divide into four equal pieces. Flour a little if very sticky. Flatten each piece.

Fold each piece in half and pinch the seams together; then fold in half another way and pinch the seams again. Fold another time or two if necessary to get a nice sausage shape that fits the pan. With your hands, push down on both ends and tuck the resulting flaps under so the ends are rounded and neat. Place the loaf in an oiled tin. Do the rest of the loaves. Each tin will be almost full of dough.

Place the tins in a warm place away from drafts to let the dough rise to half again its volume, not double. (I put the tins back in the turned-off gas oven. In about 45 minutes when the dough has risen, I remove the tins and preheat the oven.)

THE BAKING Bake the loaves in a preheated 375°F/190°C oven for 45 minutes or until nicely browned. Remove from the tins and thump or tap the bottoms if that seems like fun to you. Some people can tell from the sound whether the bread is done or not. I can't. I follow the time given in this recipe and leave the rest in the hands of the kitchen gods.

Let the bread cool on racks at least ½ hour before eating. This allows some nasty gases time to get out of the bread and therefore makes it more digestible.

Note: I love this bread at any stage. But it seems to me to taste better and to have a better texture when allowed to cool thoroughly. In fact, I think it tastes better a day old. It freezes very well. Or just let it cool completely, slice, seal in a plastic bag, and use as you like. It is delicious toasted.

WHOLE WHEAT–RYE MOLASSES BREAD WITH DILL

Makes 3 loaves

This is one of the best-textured, finest-tasting, hearty, peasant-type breads I have eaten. The butter in it is part of the reason. Another is the combination of flours—one-third each of whole wheat, rye, and white. Finally, the combination of dill seed and dill weed has something to do with the wonderful, pleasant, but not overbearing dill flavor of the loaf. I'm not too crazy about the crust on this bread, but you can't have everything. The recipe makes three loaves.

½ cup warm water
(1 dL)
2 packages dry yeast
3 cups rye flour (350
grams)
2 cups white flour (240
grams)
1 stick unsalted butter
(120 grams), melted
2 cups lukewarm
water (½ L)
1 Tbs. salt
¼ cup molasses (½ dL)
2 Tbs. dill seed
1 Tbs. dill weed
3 cups whole wheat
flour (350 grams)
1 cup white flour (120
grams)

THE YEAST DOUGH Into a saucer put:
   ½ cup warm water (bathtub temperature)
      (1 dL)
   2 packages dry yeast
Mix, then let the yeast dissolve, stirring occasionally. Into the bowl of an electric mixer (or regular bowl) put:
   3 cups rye flour (350 grams)
   2 cups white flour (240 grams)
   1 stick unsalted butter (120 grams), melted
   2 cups lukewarm water (½ L)
   1 Tbs. salt
   ¼ cup molasses (½ dL)
   2 Tbs. dill seed
   1 Tbs. dill weed
Mix, then beat with an electric mixer (or with a wooden spoon) at medium speed for 5 minutes. Add the yeast dissolved in water and:
   3 cups whole wheat flour (350 grams)
Mix as best you can, then either knead in a mixer with the dough hook or dump out onto a countertop and knead 5 to 10 minutes by hand while adding another:
   1 cup white flour (120 grams)
as you need it as you knead it. The dough should not get too dry but remain slightly tacky. If it does get dry, add more water by wetting your fingers and poking them into the dough. Shape into a ball.
THE FIRST RISING Butter a bowl. Smear the top of the dough ball with butter by rubbing in the bowl, then leave in the bowl buttered side up. This is the lazy way of buttering the top of the dough to keep a dry skin from forming. Cover the bowl with plastic, then with a couple of thicknesses of towels.

Let the dough rise in a warm place until doubled in size or a little more. For a warm place try (1) a turned-off gas oven kept slightly warm by the heat of a pilot light; (2) setting the bowl in another bowl of bathtub-temperature water and changing the water as it cools; or (3) if it's a sunny day, putting the bowl in your car, which probably will be warm. Forced this way, the dough should double in 2 hours or less.

TO SHAPE DOUGH The last time I baked this bread, I made two round loaves and one loaf-tin loaf. I love the look of the round loaves, although I prefer the more normal-shaped slices from a rectangular one. To do this combination, use the bottoms of two 8-inch (20-cm) cake tins and one 7¾ × 3⅝ × 2¼-inch (20 × 9½ × 6-cm) loaf tin. Grease the loaf tin and cake tin bottoms. Divide the dough into three equal parts. Shape two parts into nice balls with smooth tops, then put to rise on the cake-tin bottoms. Shape the third piece and put to rise in the loaf tin. Cover with plastic and towels and return to a warm place if you like, but keep an eye on the bread, which will rise faster this time. I think it is somewhat critical that you do not allow overrising the final time. When the dough looks somewhat blown up and feels soft and swollen, bake it. If allowed to rise too much, the bread doesn't seem to rise further in the oven. It will still be good, though, so don't lose sleep over this.

TO BAKE THE BREAD Preheat the oven to 400°F/205°C. Before baking, you can slash the tops of the loaves if you like, but I think they look prettier unslashed. Place the loaves in the oven quickly. The first burst of heat is very important and, if you take too long to get the loaves in, the oven will be cold. Bake the loaves for 40 minutes, but after 30 minutes take a quick peek at the bottoms and, if they are getting too dark, place a piece of parchment or brown paper bag between the loaves and the pan bottoms. Continue cooking the full 40 minutes. If the tops get too dark, cover them with a loose sheet of foil. Don't be tempted to think the bread is done before 40 minutes are up because that much time is needed to cook the centers. Some people can tell if bread is done by the sound made when tapping on it. I used to think

I could, but I got fooled. Now all I listen for is the sound of the timer going off.

After 40 minutes, cool the loaves on racks. This bread will stay fresh three days or longer because of the butter in the dough. It freezes well, but is better if eaten those first few days, not frozen.

ROLLED OAT CRACKERS WITH PEANUTS AND SESAME SEEDS

Makes about 150 crackers

Crackers require a little fussing, but essentially they're easy to do. These oat-wheat-peanut-sesame ones (whew!) are so delicious that it's difficult to stop eating them. If you want to be a little classier, you may be tempted to substitute filberts, almonds, or pine nuts for the peanuts, but don't do it. After all, even though peanuts are common, we really shouldn't hold that against them. In these crackers, they are uncommonly good.

3 cups rolled oats (10 oz. or 285 grams)
2 cups whole wheat flour (8 oz. or 225 grams)
¾ cup peanuts (4 oz. or 115 grams)
1 tsp. salt
2 sticks butter (8 oz. or 225 grams)
1 cup cold water (¼ L)
Beaten egg
Sesame seeds (3 oz. or 85 grams)

THE CRACKERS Preheat the oven to 350°F/180°C. Butter two 17 × 14-inch (43 × 35-cm) baking sheets, preferably with a nonstick finish. Into a large mixing bowl put:

   3 cups rolled oats (10 oz. or 285 grams)
   2 cups whole wheat flour (8 oz. or 225 grams)
   ¾ cup peanuts (4 oz. or 115 grams), salted ones are okay, skinned or not, chopped into ⅛-inch (½-cm) pieces
   1 tsp. salt

Mix together well. In a small saucepan melt:

   1½ sticks butter (6 oz. or 180 grams)

Add:

   1 cup cold water (¼ L)

Mix the butter and water briefly, then dump in the oat mixture. Stir quickly with a fork, just enough to bring the dough together. Turn out on a counter and knead just a few strokes until the dough seems a little smoother. Divide the dough in half, then place each half on one of the prepared baking sheets. Flatten with your hand to get started, then place a sheet of plastic wrap or waxed paper over the dough and roll out until the dough covers the

baking sheet. I use an empty quart mayonnaise
bottle to do the rolling. Next brush the dough with:
    Beaten egg
Sprinkle with salt, then sprinkle over:
    Sesame seeds, approximately ½ cup (3 oz. or
        85 grams)
Use approximately 4 tablespoons of seeds per sheet
of dough. Place the plastic back over the dough,
then roll well to push the sesame seeds down into
the dough so that they will stick after baking. Then
use a ravioli wheel to cut into 1½ × 2-inch (4 × 5-
cm) rectangles. Bake in the upper third of a
350°F/180°C oven for 25 to 30 minutes or until you
can see that they are browning. When done,
remove from the oven and brush right away with:
    Melted butter
Taste one of the crackers and, if you think
necessary, sprinkle on more salt. Let cool on a rack,
then right away place in plastic bags to retain the
crispness. These crackers can be made at least a
week ahead.

   Note: If you want delicate, thinner crackers, use
one-third of the dough instead of one-half on each
baking sheet. The thin crackers are very elegant
and very nice, but for some reason I prefer the
fatter ones.

PUMPERNICKEL CRACKERS WITH
WHEAT FLAKES AND CARAWAY SEEDS

Makes about 200 crackers

Here is a cracker with a crunchy texture and a lot of character that people like very much. The crackers are made of rye flour and wheat flakes. Wheat flakes are like rolled oats, only they are rolled wheat. (To make them, the manufacturers steam wheat soft and then roll it.)

   So that these crackers will be a darker pumpernickel, I have added bitter chocolate and dark molasses. Both are there for the color. I really can't say that I can taste either one in the finished cracker. I can taste the caraway seeds, however. Without them the crackers are dull. If you don't like caraway, substitute dill or aniseed or pumpkin seeds or pine nuts or nut nuts.

3 cups wheat flakes (360 grams)

3 cups rye flour (360 grams)

½ oz. unsweetened baking chocolate (15 grams)

⅔ cup oil (corn oil or whatever) (1½ dL)

1 cup lukewarm water (¼ L)

1 Tbs. dark molasses

1 tsp. salt

2 Tbs. caraway seeds

Beaten whole egg

¾ stick butter (3 oz. or 85 grams), melted

THE CRACKERS Preheat the oven to 350°F/180°C. Into a bowl put:

    3 cups wheat flakes (360 grams)

    3 cups rye flour (360 grams)

(The package of wheat flakes may say old-fashioned wheat flake cereal. You can also use rolled oats. I grind my own rye flour in a wheat-grinding attachment for my electric mixer; this is terribly "snob.") Mix well. Into a small saucepan put:

    ½ oz. unsweetened baking chocolate, chopped or shaved (15 grams)

    ⅔ cup oil (corn oil or whatever) (1½ dL)

Heat, stirring, until the chocolate melts and the mixture is smooth. Remove from heat and add:

    1 cup lukewarm water (¼ L)

    1 Tbs. dark molasses

    1 tsp. salt

Whisk together well until the salt dissolves. Dump into the flour mixture. Stir until all the dry flour is moistened. The mixture will be a coarse, heavy, crumbly dough. Dump it out onto a counter and divide into two equal parts. Shape by pushing into two mounds. Lightly grease two 17 × 14-inch (43 × 35-cm) baking sheets. Place one mound of dough on each. First roll out the dough on one and put it in to bake while you work on the second. Flatten the dough with your hands, then roll out however you can, using a sheet of waxed paper on top and a rolling pin or empty mayonnaise jar, whichever works better. If the dough crumbles and breaks, just patch things up and keep going. If the dough is an absurdly crumbly nightmare, knead in 1 or 2 tablespoons water. Make sure to roll all the way out to the edges of the pans, because the dough has to be thin. It is important that it be no more than ⅛ inch (½ cm) thick all over. The crackers are not nearly so good if they are too thick. They aren't as crispy and crunchy. Place on a countertop or board:

    2 Tbs. caraway seeds (you will use 1 Tbs. per sheet)

Roll firmly with a rolling pin to crush a bit. Brush the whole surface of the dough with:

    Beaten whole egg

Sprinkle over:

    Salt

Then sprinkle half the crushed caraway seeds over

each sheet of dough. Place a piece of waxed paper on top and roll to push the seeds into the dough. Using a sharp knife, cut the dough into strips about 1¼ inches (3 cm) wide, then cut in the other direction in 2-inch (5-cm) strips to make rectangular crackers. Push down hard in a "guillotine" cut or else you will get ragged edges. If the dough sticks, wet the knife.

Bake in the upper third of a 350°F/180°C oven for 25 to 30 minutes or until done. It's not a bad idea to reverse the pans in the oven after 20 minutes, but do it quickly so the oven doesn't cool off. These crackers are fairly dark and you really can't tell by looking whether they are done or not. I remove several crackers, let cool a minute on a rack, then taste. As long as they have dried out enough to get crisp as they cool, they are done. They get a nasty bitter taste when burned, so don't overbake. Once done, remove and right away brush with:

> Melted butter, approximately ¾ stick (3 oz. or 85 grams) for both sheets

Sprinkle over:

> Salt

Remove the crackers from the pan while still warm. You may have to scrape them off with a large, sharp knife. Allow to cool on racks, then store airtight in plastic or a tin. They will keep for weeks. If not as crisp as you want on the day you serve them, dry them out for 10 minutes in a 350°F/180°C oven. Cool again on racks.

GREEN PEA BREAD

Makes 2 loaves

When I first mentioned to a friend that I had made a loaf of bread with fresh green peas in it, he looked at me as if I were some kind of weirdo. On tasting the bread, he loved it and decided that I wasn't so strange after all. The bread is basically a white loaf with pea puree replacing about 20 percent of the flour. I love white bread but have trouble justifying eating very much of it because of its nutritional deficiencies. By adding peas, you add vitamins and an unusual flavor as well.

The bread rises to a wonderful shape, the slices are a lovely green color, and the texture is marvelously moist and dense without being heavy.

The miracle of this bread is that it is a yeast bread but a quick one. If you move along—and I don't mean that you have to bust your derriere—about 40 minutes pass from the time you walk into the kitchen until the time the bread goes into the oven. This is due to a technique I invented called "dumping tons of yeast into the bread." I use three packages of dried yeast instead of one. Because everything is kept warm along the way and the kneading is done in the food processor, the rising time is only 10 minutes.

The only trouble I have had with this bread is its sticking to the pans, even the nonstick kind. So I use a band of parchment across the sides and the bottom of the pan. Then the bread comes out just fine.

Baking parchment (or
brown paper)
1 (10-oz. or 285-gram)
package frozen peas,
or 2 to 3 lbs. fresh
shelled peas (900 to
1350 grams)
½ cup water (1 dL)
3 packages dried yeast
or crumbled fresh
yeast cakes
1 cup whipping cream
or milk (¼ L)
2 Tbs. sugar
2 tsp. salt
2 Tbs. butter
About 5 cups flour
(540 grams)

THE DOUGH Oil two loaf tins about 2¼ × 3⅝ × 7⅜ inches (6 × 9½ × 20 cm). Run baking parchment or brown paper across the bottoms and up the long sides. Oil the paper lightly.

At this point it is a little early, but sometime along the way (15 to 20 minutes before baking), preheat the oven to 425°F/220°C.

Have:
    1 package (10 oz. or 285 grams) frozen peas or
        2 to 3 lbs. fresh peas before shelling (900 to
        1350 grams)
Put the peas in a saucepan with:
    ½ cup water (1 dL)
Do not add salt because this water is used later for soaking the yeast. Cover, bring to a boil, and cook for 5 to 7 minutes or until the peas are tender. Drain off the cooking liquid into a 1-cup measure and add enough cold water to make ¾ cup (1¾ dL). The liquid should be warm, but not hot. Pour it into a small bowl. Sprinkle over:
    3 packages dried yeast or crumbled fresh yeast
        cakes
Stir to mix, then set aside. Into a saucepan put:
    1 cup whipping cream or milk (¼ L)
    2 Tbs. sugar
    2 tsp. salt
    2 Tbs. butter
Heat, stirring just until everything dissolves. Do not get this mixture too hot; it is not necessary to boil the cream or milk because the rising time is short. Set aside.

Into a food processor put the cooked, drained peas. Process to start the pureeing, then add 2 tablespoons of the warm cream mixture and process some more. Continue processing, adding the cream mixture until all is in and the puree is smooth. Fluff into the cup, level off to measure, and add to the puree, along with the *yeast mixture:*

    3 cups flour (360 grams)

Process for 1 minute to knead the flour. Then add:

    1½ cups more flour (180 grams)

Process for just a few seconds or until the flour is worked in. Dump out onto the counter. Knead for a few seconds, adding a little more flour (up to ½ cup) if you think it is necessary. The dough should still be a little sticky, however.

Divide the dough in half and shape each into a loaf by doing a little folding and pinching to get some surface tension on the smooth top.

Place the loaves in the prepared pans. Cover with plastic, then with some folded dish towels. Let rise for 10 minutes.

TO BAKE Bake the loaves in a preheated 425°F/220°C oven for 10 minutes. Then reduce the heat to 400°F/ 205°C and bake for 40 minutes more. About 10 minutes before the baking time is up, check the tops of the loaves. If they are pretty and brown, cover loosely with a sheet of foil to prevent overbrowning. When the time is up, remove the bread from the tins, cutting down to free the two ends if necessary. Cool on racks.

I think this bread tastes much better if it is allowed to cool completely before being sliced and eaten. The wrapped loaves keep well for two or three days stored in the room. To keep longer, slice the bread, wrap well, and freeze.

A FAT, BROILED PANCAKE WITH PECANS

8 servings

Here's an odd thing that's easy and delicious. It's one fat pancake about 1 inch (2½ cm) thick, loaded with pecans, that is broiled in the oven in a frying pan. When you serve it, you slice it in wedges like a cake.

The batter is the traditional one, but made with half whole wheat flour and with extra eggs. I increase the eggs and beat them like crazy to eliminate the need for baking powder, which seems to me the granddaddy of all chemical food additives.

¾ **cup white flour (90 grams)**

¾ **cup whole wheat flour (90 grams)**

1 tsp. salt

¾ **cup nonfat milk (1¾ dL)**

¼ **cup cream (½ dL)**

3 Tbs. butter

10 oz. pecans (285 grams) whole or pieces

4 eggs

1 Tbs. sugar

Maple, blackberry or any syrup; or any good jam

THE PANCAKE This is enough batter for two big pancakes that serve eight people. Start the preparation several hours ahead. Into a bowl put:

> ¾ cup white flour (90 grams)
> ¾ cup whole wheat flour (90 grams)
> 1 tsp. salt

Mix well. Into a saucepan put:

> ¾ cup nonfat milk (1¾ dL)
> ¼ cup cream (½ dL)
> 3 Tbs. butter

Warm just enough to get the milk to body temperature so that, as it sits, the butter will melt. Have on the side:

> 10 oz. pecans (285 grams), whole or pieces (approximately 2 cups)

Divide the pecans into four equal piles; you will use two for each pancake.

THE FINAL ASSEMBLY Preheat the broiler for at least 10 minutes. Just before serving, add the milk mixture to the flour mixture all at once and stir with a wire whisk until completely mixed and smooth. Separate:

> 4 eggs

Beat the yolks (I use a small electric mixer) for about 3 minutes or until they are thick and light and make a ribbon. (This means that when you dribble a snake of batter over the surface, the tracks remain for at least 3 seconds.) Rinse off the beaters, then beat the whites to soft peaks. Sprinkle over:

> 1 Tbs. sugar

Continue beating until the whites are stiff, but do not overbeat. They should just arrive at the stage where they do not fall out of the bowl when you turn it over. Fold the yolks into the flour batter, then fold in the whites. With a paper towel rub a little cooking oil over the bottom of a regular black-iron frying pan with a bottom measuring about 9 inches (28 cm) in diameter. Heat the pan on the stovetop until hot enough that drops of water flicked over the surface skip about and sizzle. Sprinkle one-fourth of the pecans in an even layer over the bottom of the pan. Add half the pancake batter (approximately 2½ cups or 6 dL), pouring it over the pecans so as not to disturb them. Even out the top with a spatula. Sprinkle over the top another one-fourth of the pecans.

Right away put the pan under the broiler, 7 or 8 inches from the heat. I do this in a gas oven with the door closed. As soon as the top is nicely browned, in about 4 minutes, remove the pan from the oven. Loosen the pancake all around the edge, then turn over with a spatula. This is not difficult because the pancake will be very firm. Return the pan to the broiler to brown the top. Caution! It will take only about 1 minute. Turn the pancake onto a serving plate. Cover with a towel to keep warm while you repeat the procedure to make the second pancake. Serve with:

Maple, blackberry, or any syrup; or any
good jam
These are good cold, even the next day, spread with butter and sprinkled with powdered sugar.

DESSERTS

CREAMS, MOUSSES, AND JELLIES

Crème Caramel with Small Raisins in Rum

Lemon Mousse with Candied Peel

Marquise au Chocolat, Chartreuse Cream

Pomegranate Creams

*Raspberry Jelly

*Sauternes Jelly

FRUITS AND ICES

Fresh Summer Fruits with Watermelon Ice

Strawberries Three

*Truffled Pears

*Sliced Mangoes with Mango Cream

ICES

*Crenshaw Melon Ice

*Blueberry Ice

*Fresh Fig Ice

*Grapefruit Ice

*Special quick dishes

D esserts and pastry desserts are my first love and there is not much use trying to hide this fact. From the very first days that I discovered cooking in 1953, when entertaining I would start by selecting the dessert and design the meal around it.

By my calculation I was conceived in mid-July while my parents were living in south Jersey, a great fruit- and vegetable-growing area. Mother must have eaten berries and fruits galore that summer, because these are the things that have always been a very pleasant obsession in my life. Even as I write this, it is the middle of summer, and upstairs in my kitchen there are fresh figs, blueberries, pears, plums, bananas, and a mango and they will be gone in two days, just from my eating them, not from practicing recipes. Fruits, desserts, pastries, high cakes, cookies, candies, and sugarplums are the things my dreams are made of.

The three categories of desserts in this section probably contain the most beloved desserts in the world. Within these categories you will find interesting variations of universal favorites. The Marquise au Chocolat is a chocolate mousse with twice the normal amount of chocolate. The Crème Caramel is the classic one, but with the addition of some small raisins that have soaked in rum. The Lemon Mousse and the Pomegranate Creams are Bavarian cream variations, and the balance of the jellies, fruits, and ices are interesting and different combinations of the wonderful fruits that you can find in any town or city if you search a little to get the best quality and choose fruits in their seasons.

CRÈME CARAMEL WITH SMALL RAISINS IN RUM

6 servings

Here is an interesting variation on one of the world's most beloved desserts, a truly international dish. In Spanish-speaking countries it is called flan. *In America we call it baked custard. The French caramelize the mold and call it* Crème renversée au caramel, *or upside-down cream with caramel. I have added some rum-soaked zante currants plus brown sugar. They make the dessert appropriate to the fall season and to winter holidays, although it is good in any season. Zante currants, by the way, are not currants at all, but tiny raisins. Don't ask me why they are called currants.*

4 cups water (1 L)
¼ cup zante currants
  (½ dL)
2 Tbs. dark rum (or
  light)
⅓ cup dark brown
  sugar
2 Tbs. water
2½ cups milk (6 dL)
½ cup dark brown
  sugar
4 eggs
1 tsp. vanilla
1 tsp. dark rum (or
  light)

THE CURRANTS Bring to a boil in a small saucepan:
  4 cups water (1 L)
Add:
  ¼ cup zante currants (½ dL)
Return to a boil, then remove from the heat. Let the currants soak for 30 seconds and drain. Place them in a small dish, then add:
  2 Tbs. dark rum (or light)
Let sit 1 hour. I leave it uncovered because it makes the kitchen smell so good. Cheap entertainment for the cook.

TO CARAMELIZE THE MOLD This is going to be a brown sugar caramel. For a regular caramel you watch the color to decide when it is done. When the white sugar turns caramel-colored, it is caramel. When using brown sugar, which is already so dark, you have to look for smoke. Have a pan with 1 inch of boiling water in it. I use a 9 × 12-inch (23 × 30-cm) baking pan. Place it on top of the stove and regulate the heat so that it simmers. Also have a 4-cup (1-L) charlotte mold sitting in the boiling water to heat it. Have two oven mitts or potholders ready. Into a small saucepan put:
  ⅓ cup dark brown sugar
  2 Tbs. water
Stir together, then put the saucepan over low heat and bring to a boil, stirring now and then to dissolve the sugar. When the mixture starts to boil, remove from the heat and check to make sure that the sugar has completely dissolved. Do not stir anymore or you can have problems. Return the pan to the heat and turn to high. With a brush and a small glass of cold water, wash down the sides of the pan one time. Let the sugar cook over high heat until you see quite a bit of smoke coming from the pot as if the sugar were starting to burn. Remove from the heat and right away dump the caramel into the warmed charlotte mold. Put the oven mitts on and pick up the mold. Tilt slowly all around to try to get the caramel to coat about 2 inches up the side of the mold. Once the mold is lined, I dip the

bottom in cold water to help make the caramel stop running.

Don't worry about this coating too much. If it is uneven or if it sets when you're halfway around, it doesn't matter. The finished dessert will work fine and it will probably look the same no matter how you think you've messed it up. The caramel slides down anyway as it bakes. Place the caramelized mold on a rack to finish cooling.

THE CUSTARD Preheat the oven to 350°F/180°C. Into a saucepan put:

    2½ cups milk (6 dL)
    ½ cup dark brown sugar

Heat and stir until the sugar is completely dissolved. When the mixture just starts to be too hot to touch, remove from the heat. Into another mixing bowl put:

    4 eggs at room temperature

Beat the eggs just enough to mix them together but not to cause froth. Add to the eggs:

    1 tsp. vanilla

Drain the rum from the currants and add it to the eggs. Mix well. Sprinkle 1 tablespoon of the currants into the bottom of the mold. Add the hot milk mixture to the eggs in a slow stream, beating it in so that the eggs do not get cooked by too fast an addition of the hot milk. Pour the custard into the mold by pouring it onto a spoon aimed toward the side of the mold, so that it does not mess up your arrangement of currants. Place the custard in the oven in its pan of boiling water. Cover with a loose sheet of foil so the top won't skin and the currants you add later will sink in.

Bake for 15 minutes, then quickly open the oven a crack and toss a few currants on top of the custard. If they stay there or seem to sink very slowly, then distribute the rest of the currants evenly around the top. Put the sheet of foil over the mold again to keep the currants from drying out. Do all this very quickly so that you don't have the oven door open too long.

Bake the custard another 10 minutes or until a cake tester inserted halfway between the middle and the outside comes out clean. Do not overbake or the custard can turn watery. When done, remove the mold from the pan of water. Place on a rack to let the cooking finish and to cool, about 1 hour. Refrigerate uncovered until completely chilled. I like to make this a day ahead so that the custard has a chance to really set, but it must have a minimum of 5 to 6 hours in the refrigerator.

TO UNMOLD AND SERVE Unmold just before serving. Insert a knife down ⅛ inch (½ cm) or so and run all around the edge of the custard. Use a serving dish that is curved enough to hold a little trench of caramel sauce all around the dessert. Place the serving dish on top of the mold, then turn everything upside down. Give the plate and the mold a little bit of a flick and the dessert will drop down. Remove the mold and into it put:

1 tsp. dark rum (or light)

Stir around well with a rubber spatula to dissolve any caramel remaining. Pour this sauce in the trench around the dessert. Serve the custard in wedges, cutting all the way down to the plate so that people get some of the currants on the bottom. Spoon a little of the rum-caramel sauce over each portion.

LEMON MOUSSE WITH CANDIED PEEL

6 servings

This lovely lemon mousse is a perfect dessert for a light luncheon. The frothy, pale yellow cream topped with syrup-glazed lemon-peel shreds is especially attractive served in stemmed glasses. It is a kind of softly set Bavarian cream, similar to the true Bavarian mixture consisting of English custard (crème anglaise), gelatin, and whipped cream. This version, however, contains no gelatin and incorporates lemonade thickened with egg yolk instead of English custard.

When it comes to lemon desserts, people are divided in how they feel about sweet and tart. You can adjust the sweetness of this mousse to suit yourself. Taste it at the very end and, if it seems sweeter than you like, add lemon juice until it is just right.

3 or 4 lemons
½ cup sugar (100 grams)
¼ cup water (½ dL)
Grated zest of 2 medium lemons
½ cup lemon juice (1 dL)
¾ cup sugar (150 grams)
¼ cup water (½ dL)
6 egg yolks
2 cups whipping cream (1 pint or ½ L)
Lemon juice (optional)

THE CANDIED LEMON-PEEL GARNISH The garnish isn't a must, but it really makes the dish. Using a vegetable peeler or knife, remove thin strips of zest (just the yellow part) from:

> 3 or 4 lemons (allow zest from ½ medium lemon per guest)

Cut the zest into a fine julienne—long, skinny shreds about ¹⁄₁₆ inch (¼ cm) wide. Simmer the shreds in boiling water for 10 minutes or until tender. Pour into a sieve, discard the water, and rinse the shreds well with cold water. Reserve while you prepare a syrup. Into a small saucepan put:

> ½ cup sugar (100 grams)
> ¼ cup water (½ dL)

Bring just to a boil, stirring to make sure all the sugar dissolves. Remove from the heat, add the lemon shreds, and stir to mix. Pour into a small dish and allow to cool, then chill in the refrigerator up to one or two days ahead.

Note: The lemons can be saved for the juice needed in the mousse.

THE LEMON MOUSSE Be sure to grate the lemon zest before you squeeze the juice. Into a heavy saucepan, preferably not of uncoated aluminum, put:

> Grated zest of 2 medium lemons (or less or more if you like)
> ½ cup lemon juice (1 dL) (2 to 4 lemons depending on size and juiciness)
> ¾ cup sugar (150 grams)
> ¼ cup water (½ dL)

Bring this lemonade to a boil, stirring occasionally to help melt the sugar. Into a small mixing bowl put:

> 6 egg yolks

Mix the yolks just enough to break them. When the lemon mixture is boiling, remove from the heat and add one-third to the yolks while whisking briskly. Dump the yolk mixture into the hot lemonade, then place over low/medium heat. Cook, whisking rapidly all the time, until the mixture comes just *barely* to the boil. You will have to stop whisking for a few seconds now and then to check.

When you see the first signs of a boil, immediately pour the mixture into a bowl to stop the cooking. Refrigerate uncovered to get cold or hurry the cooling by putting the bowl into a larger bowl containing half ice cubes and half water. Stir now and then while cooling. When the mixture is chilled, whisk it to get it smooth again and add:

> 2 cups whipping cream (1 pint or ½ L),
>   whipped stiff

Fold thoroughly. If the mixture seems lumpy with pockets of whipped cream, whisk until smooth. Taste, then add more:

> Lemon juice (optional)

Add a tablespoon of juice at a time, mix, and taste again. When the tartness is nice, spoon the mixture into stemmed glasses or individual dessert saucers or into one attractive serving bowl. Refrigerate up to a day ahead of the dinner or lunch.

Warning: Dishes containing egg yolks are very perishable. They must be kept refrigerated and should be eaten within two to three days.

At serving time, lift the lemon-peel garnish out of the syrup with a fork, leaving most of the syrup behind. Place a small mound of peel over each individual portion or scatter the peels attractively over the bowl of mousse. Serve cold.

MARQUISE AU CHOCOLAT, CHARTREUSE CREAM

6 servings

Of the many chocolate desserts I know, this is the one with the most appeal to really hard-core chocolate lovers. I mean this is really it. Even people who do not particularly like chocolate (yes, there are a few) seem to smile guiltily upon tasting this dessert. The recipe for it came from my days at the Cordon Bleu in Paris. It is the classic chocolate mousse recipe, but with double the quantity of chocolate.

8 oz. semisweet chocolate (225 grams)

¾ stick butter (3 oz. or 85 grams)

3 Tbs. sugar

1 tsp. rum (or Chartreuse)

½ tsp. vanilla

4 eggs (4 yolks and 3 whites)

1 cup whipping cream (¼ L)

2 Tbs. powdered sugar

2 Tbs. Chartreuse liqueur (green or yellow)

2 Tbs. angelica, minced

1 or 2 tsp. Chartreuse

THE MARQUISE This dessert can be served in an attractive dish and spooned out at the table, or it can be presented in individual dessert glasses or saucers. For this recipe, it will be chilled in a 4-cup (1-L) charlotte mold, then unmolded and sliced into wedges (not terribly neat ones) at the table.

Place a waxed paper circle in the bottom of a 3- or 4-cup charlotte (or other) mold. Line the sides of the mold with waxed paper. A few small spots of butter here and there in the mold will hold the paper up. Lining the tin is a pain in the neck, but you will be thankful when you unmold the marquise. Into a mixing bowl put:

> 8 oz. semisweet chocolate (225 grams), cut into small pieces
> ¾ stick butter (3 oz. or 85 grams) at room temperature

Heat in the top of a double boiler (the water not quite boiling) or in a 170°F/77°C oven, stirring occasionally, until the butter and chocolate are melted and the mixture is smooth. Add:

> 2 Tbs. sugar
> 1 tsp. rum (you could use Chartreuse)
> ½ tsp. vanilla

Stir together well until smooth. Allow to cool for 5 minutes. Add one by one:

> 4 egg yolks

Beat about 30 seconds with an electric mixer after each yolk is added. Into a small bowl put:

> 3 egg whites

Beat as for a soufflé. When the whites form soft peaks, sprinkle over:

> 1 Tbs. sugar

Beat until stiff peaks form, then fold right away into the chocolate mixture. Pour into the prepared mold and level. Chill in the refrigerator for 4 or 5 hours or overnight. Several hours before serving, unmold onto a serving dish, tugging gently on the paper with the mold upside down. Peel off and discard the paper, then return the marquise to the refrigerator.

CHARTREUSE CREAM This touch did not come from the Cordon Bleu. They used *crème anglaise*. I prefer serving the marquise either with plain, sweetened whipped cream or with this Chartreuse cream. The recipe makes more than you will need. You could probably get away with half, which would just about make it. You can prepare it the morning of the dinner. Into a bowl put:

    1 cup whipping cream (¼ L)

Beat until starting to thicken, then add:

    2 Tbs. powdered sugar

    2 Tbs. Chartreuse liqueur (green or yellow)

Mix, then beat until stiff, but do not overbeat. Reserve in the refrigerator until you are ready to use it.

OPTIONAL GARNISH If you can find angelica, it would be interesting to add, but it's not important, so don't knock yourself out searching for it. Have:

    A small amount of angelica (about 2 Tbs.),
        minced

Angelica is the candied stalk of a plant that looks like green celery. You buy it in a jar and you may or may not find it in shops that sell candied violets. The leaves of the angelica plant are one of the ingredients used in making Chartreuse, so it seems like a logical garnish for this cream. If you can't find angelica, citron will do, or candied orange or lemon peel or nothing.

    Place the minced, candied garnish in a small saucer and add:

    1 or 2 tsp. Chartreuse

Stir, then let sit until serving time.

TO SERVE Whether serving unmolded or not, you must decide whether to: (1) beat the cream stiff and decorate the marquise by piping the cream out of a pastry bag and spooning on the angelica at the table as you serve; or (2) cut wedges or spoonfuls of the marquise, place a blob of the softly whipped Chartreuse cream on each, and top with a teaspoon of the minced angelica. Serve small portions. It is *really* rich.

    Note: You can leave the liqueur out of this recipe altogether. It will still send chocoholics into rapture.

    Warning: This dessert contains uncooked eggs. Keep it refrigerated and, to be on the safe side, eat it within two or three days.

POMEGRANATE CREAMS

6 servings

Turn the lights up a bit for this because the colors are fascinating: pale pink on a kind of mauve. The mauve is a very soft-textured pomegranate Bavarian cream. The pink is lightly sweetened pomegranate whipped cream. The total effect is one of an ethereal, refined, elegant dessert of the type that Alice B. Toklas would have adored.

---

4 large pomegranates (approximately 2 lbs. or 900 grams) or 5 or 6 smaller ones (2½ lbs. or 1125 grams)

Pomegranate juice

1 rounded tsp. plain gelatin

5 to 6 *level* Tbs. sugar

2 egg yolks

1 cup whipping cream (¼ L)

½ cup whipping cream (1 dL)

2 Tbs. powdered sugar

¼ cup pomegranate juice (½ dL)

POMEGRANATE JUICE To save yourself work, buy the pure juice in a bottle. Look for it in health-food stores. Desserts made with this bottled juice are amazingly close to ones made with the juice that you squeeze yourself from the fruit. However, I think it is worth the trouble to juice the pomegranates yourself, especially since I am about to tell you a very simple way to do it.

I learned this easy method from one of my students. Simply cut each pomegranate into halves, cutting *across* the fruit. Separate out and reserve 6 teaspoons of pretty, perfect seeds that you will refrigerate, then use at the last minute as a garnish. Squeeze the pomegranate halves using any orange-juice squeezer, proceeding as if you were squeezing oranges. It is fast, easy and works like a charm.

For this recipe you will need:

4 large pomegranates (approximately 2 lbs. or 900 grams) or 5 or 6 smaller ones (2½ lbs. or 1125 grams)

Store the juice in a glass beaker or bowl. The acid in pomegranate juice acts on metal so don't let it be in contact with metals except for brief moments.

POMEGRANATE BAVARIAN CREAM The amount of sugar in this recipe is based on pomegranate juice that tastes fairly pleasant, mildly sweet and mildly tart. As I worked out this recipe, I was very much repelled when I used more sugar. Into a small saucer put:

1 Tbs. pomegranate juice

Sprinkle over:

1 rounded tsp. plain gelatin

Stir if necessary to make sure all the gelatin is moistened by the juice. Let soften. Next make a kind of pomegranate *crème anglaise*. Into a small heavy saucepan (use Calphalon or enameled iron if possible) put:

    1 cup pomegranate juice (¼ L)

    5 to 6 *level* Tbs. sugar

Bring to a boil, stirring occasionally. Into a small bowl put:

    2 egg yolks

When the pomegranate juice has come to a boil, pour it slowly into the yolks, whisking constantly. Return to the saucepan and place over medium/low heat. Whisking all the time, heat until you see the first signs of a boil. You will have to pause now and then, of course, to check. Five seconds after the boil starts, pour the hot cream into a glass bowl.

Right away add the gelatin and stir well to help it dissolve. Put two trays of ice cubes into a large bowl. Add cold water to come halfway up the ice cube level. Into a small bowl put:

    1 cup whipping cream (¼ L)

Beat the cream over the ice until it is stiff. Set aside. Place the glass bowl containing the pomegranate cream in the ice and stir it slowly until very chilled. It will thicken. If this seems to take forever in the glass bowl, transfer the mixture to a stainless steel bowl and stir over the ice. When the pomegranate cream is chilled and thick, fold in the whipped cream. You can stop folding if you like while there is still a ribbony swirl of the two unmixed colors. Pour approximately ⅓ cup (¾ dL) of the cream into each of six serving glasses, preferably attractive stemmed ones. One-third cup may not seem very much, but it is plenty. This is not the sort of dish you eat a lot of. (The addition of the Pomegranate Whipped Cream will help it look as though there's more in the glass.) You can make this recipe a day ahead. Cover each glass with plastic and reserve in the refrigerator.

POMEGRANATE WHIPPED CREAM You may prepare this the morning of the dinner, but don't add it to the desserts until the last minute. The pomegranate juice tends to separate out of the cream after it sits for a while, but you can beat it back together just before spooning the cream over the desserts. Into a mixing bowl put:

½ cup whipping cream (1 dL)

Beat until starting to get stiff, then add:

2 Tbs. powdered sugar

Continue beating until stiff, but don't turn it into butter. If it should suddenly look overbeaten and curdly, stir in a tablespoonful of new cream. Fold in:

¼ cup pomegranate juice (½ dL)

If the cream seems to be a little runny, beat it stiff again by hand or with an electric mixer. Even with the pomegranate juice, the cream will beat stiff, although only to a kind of "soft" stiffness. Put a generous blob of the cream over each dessert. Sprinkle 1 tsp. reserved pomegranate seeds over each dessert. Stand back and look at the lovely colors. Serve. It is very nice to serve this dessert with small, crunchy cookies.

RASPBERRY JELLY

6 servings

Fruit gelatins made from real fruit are delicious but very scorned as desserts today. They were immensely popular years ago, but in the thirties and forties virtually disappeared due to the rise in popularity of those awful, artificially colored and flavored powders that take up acres of space on supermarket shelves.

A sparkling natural gelatin dessert of pure lime, lemon, or true red raspberry is a beautiful thing to present to guests and tastes marvelous.

3 boxes (10 oz. or 285 grams each) or 3 bags (12 oz. or 340 grams each) frozen raspberries
1 envelope unflavored gelatin (2 rounded tsp.)
Sugar (optional)
½ cup water (1 dL)
½ cup whipping cream (1 dL)
Powdered sugar to taste (optional)

THE FROZEN RASPBERRIES For notes on using canned or fresh berries, see the end of recipe. Buy:
3 boxes (10 oz. or 285 grams each) or 3 bags (12 oz. or 340 grams each) frozen raspberries
The boxed berries usually contain some sugar and water and therefore must be defrosted so you can pick out six of the prettiest berries for garnishing. The bagged berries usually are just separately frozen berries; finding six beauties for the decorating can be done without defrosting first. Reserve the garnish berries in the freezer, separated so they won't stick together.
Be sure to save all the juices if you defrost the berries or empty them from their bags.
THE RASPBERRY JELLY This can be made one to two days ahead. Into a saucer put:
2 Tbs. cold water
Sprinkle over:
1 envelope unflavored gelatin (2 rounded tsp.)
Mix, then let stand. Into a saucepan, preferably not uncoated aluminum, put the defrosted or frozen raspberries, including all the juices, plus:
½ cup water (1 dL)
Bring to a boil, stirring now and then, and let simmer uncovered for 1 minute. Pour into a sieve over a bowl. Let the juices go through and push with a rubber spatula to strain through 1 or 2 Tbs. of raspberry puree. This will cloud the jelly (bad), but it will add much desired flavor (good).
Place the sieve containing the remaining pulp over another bowl and let it rest a second while you complete the jelly. Do not let it sit too long unless the sieve is stainless steel or plastic, or it can

turn blue. Right away add the softened gelatin to the hot raspberry juices. Stir to dissolve, then taste and decide whether or not to add:

Sugar (optional)

If using frozen berries already containing sugar, you probably will not need to add more. If using berries from plastic bags, you may want to add some because the berries often are unsugared. If you add sugar, add 1 tablespoon at a time, stir to dissolve, and taste. Be sure not to oversweeten. Most people prefer the jelly somewhat tart.

You should end with a total of 3 cups (¾ L) raspberry juice. If short, add water to get that quantity, but the full measurement isn't necessary. Taste and decide whether you want to dilute.

Pour the jelly mixture into six individual serving glasses or cups. Refrigerate for a minimum of 4 to 5 hours.

Then return to the raspberries in the sieve. Using a rubber spatula, push the raspberries through the sieve to puree them and strain out the seeds. Discard the seeds and refrigerate the puree, which will be used for the whipped cream topping. This much can be prepared one to two days ahead.

THE RASPBERRY WHIPPED CREAM TOPPING Make this the morning of the dinner. Into a bowl put:

½ cup whipping cream (1 dL)

Beat until starting to set, then add 4 to 6 tablespoons of the reserved raspberry puree and:

Powdered sugar to taste (optional)

If using sweetened berries, you may not need any sugar. For unsweetened berries, sugar probably will be necessary. Add 1 tablespoon of the powdered sugar at a time, stir, taste, and add more only if needed. Refrigerate until serving time.

TO SERVE Stir the raspberry whipped cream to make sure it has not separated. If it seems too thin, you can beat it stiffer again. Spoon over the desserts. Place one of the reserved frozen berries for garnish on top of each dessert. Serve.

TO USE CANNED BERRIES Buy three cans (16 oz. or 450 grams each) red raspberries. Drain off the syrup and, where the recipe calls for ½ cup (1 dL) water, use ½ cup of this syrup instead. Use the rest of the drained syrup for another purpose. Then follow the same procedure described in the recipe. Remember to pick out and freeze six of the best berries for garnish.

TO USE FRESH BERRIES Frankly, I have not made this dessert with fresh berries and I do not intend to. However, if you should find tons of cheap, good raspberries someday, before you make them into jelly, give me a call and I'll come over and help you eat them.

I would guess that you need four to five half-pint boxes of fresh berries and that you could follow the same procedure for the unsugared frozen berries in a bag.

SAUTERNES JELLY

6 servings

This dessert greatly appeals to wine lovers. It is a simple gelatin made with wine and topped with whipped cream flavored with wine, either a good French Sauternes or a good California late-harvest dessert wine. You will like the refined and lovely quality of this dessert very much, especially if you like French Sauternes.

This jelly is a variation of the wine jelly very popular some years ago, which was based on a dry white or red table wine to which brandy and lemon juice were added. That wine jelly still makes a very nice dessert, but it lacks the simple purity of this Sauternes Jelly, which has no extra flavors added.

The jelly is very pretty served individually in wineglasses, although footed compotes, sherbet glasses, cups, or saucers will do fine. It is very dramatic made in one large ring mold. However, in order to succeed in the unmolding, you must add extra gelatin, which makes the texture slightly firmer and, I believe, less desirable.

1 bottle French Sauternes, Barsac, or Preignac; or a sweet California dessert wine

THE SAUTERNES Have:

1 bottle French Sauternes, Barsac, or Preignac; or a sweet California dessert wine

Please don't feel that you have to buy a bottle of Château d'Yquem or one of the expensive first-

1 *level* **Tbs. unflavored gelatin (about 1½ envelopes)**
½ to 1 cup sugar (100 to 200 grams)
½ cup chilled whipping cream (1 dL)
1 Tbs. powdered sugar

growth French Sauternes. A second-growth Sauternes, Barsac, or Preignac does nicely. If you deal with a wine merchant who knows his stock, he may be able to recommend a bottle that is good but not quite so expensive. Don't expect to get off too cheaply, though. This is not an inexpensive dessert.

If you spot a late-harvest white (or occasionally red) wine from one of the reputable California vintners, give it a try. It will be sweet, considered a dessert wine. Some possibilities are: Freemark Abbey Johannisberg Riesling, Sweet Select; Château St. Jean Johannisberg Riesling, Individually Selected Late Harvest; or Mirassou Fleuri Blanc, Monterey White Wine, Rich and Semi-sweet.

Important note: Don't confuse a California Sauterne (no "s" on the end) with a French Sauternes. The two are nothing alike. A California Sauterne will not do because it is not a sweet, rich dessert wine—just a slightly sweet "drinking" wine designed for those people who don't like their wines dry.

THE WINE JELLY Be sure to measure 2 tablespoons of the wine, pour into a cup, cover, and refrigerate; it will be used for flavoring the whipped cream topping. (If molding the jelly in a ring mold, measure 4 tablespoons because you probably will want to make a double batch of whipped cream.)

Also measure ¼ cup (½ dL) Sauternes into a small saucer and sprinkle over it:

    1 *level* Tbs. unflavored gelatin (about 1½ envelopes)

Note: If using a ring mold, increase the gelatin to 2 envelopes or 4 rounded teaspoons. Let the gelatin soften for a minute or two. Into a saucepan put 1½ cups (3½ dL) *more* Sauternes and:

    ½ to 1 cup sugar (100 to 200 grams)

Taste the wine to determine how much sugar to use. If it seems really sweet, take a chance with ½ cup. If not, go with ¾ cup or 1 cup. Any decision is a gamble until you have experience with a particular wine.

Heat the wine, stirring to help dissolve the sugar. When the mixture is almost boiling and the sugar has completely dissolved, remove from the heat. Add the softened gelatin and stir until dissolved. Also add the rest of the bottle of Sauternes (about 1¾ cups or 4 dL) and stir well.

Pour into six individual serving glasses. Or, if you like, squeeze out eight servings. This jelly is fairly robust and, just like a good Sauternes, a little goes a long way. If you are using a ring mold, use a 4-cup (1-L) size and oil it very, very lightly with vegetable oil before pouring in the gelatin.

Chill 4 to 5 hours or overnight. Cover with plastic once the jelly has set to keep refrigerator odors from contaminating the delicate flavor.

THE WINE WHIPPED CREAM Into a small bowl put:

½ cup chilled whipping cream (1 dL)

Whip the cream (over ice if you like) until starting to set. Add:

1 Tbs. powdered sugar

plus 1 tablespoon of the Sauternes that was reserved and chilled in the refrigerator. Taste and then decide whether to add the remaining tablespoon. Beat until nicely fluffy and softly set. Reserve until serving time. This can be done the morning of the dinner.

Important note: If you have molded the jelly in a ring mold, I would suggest that you prepare a double batch of the wine whipped cream and beat it very stiff. You need more cream to fill the center hole and to decorate the rim.

TO SERVE THE WINE JELLY If the cream has separated, whip it back to fluffy consistency. Place dollops (what an awful word) over the individual desserts. Serve very cold.

If you made a ring mold, unmold onto an attractive serving dish. You should be able to do this without dipping the mold in hot water if you first loosen the jelly around the rim with a knife, only going down about ¼ inch (¾ cm), then tilt the mold sideways and tap or shake to get an air space between the jelly and the mold. Carefully tip over onto the dish. Beat the whipped cream (preferably the double batch suggested) back to very stiff. Fill the center hole with cream, then decorate the rim, and even make some fancy swirls on the center top.

FRESH SUMMER FRUITS WITH WATERMELON ICE

6 servings

Sweet summer "stone" fruits (plums, peaches, nectarines, and apricots) combined with summer berries (strawberries, raspberries, and blueberries) make an ambrosial dessert. The fruits for this dessert are lightly sugared and moistened with just a touch of apricot liqueur. A small ball of homemade watermelon ice is added. The result is as fine a summer dessert as can be concocted.

2 large peaches
2 large nectarines
4 soft and ripe plums
4 apricots
1 pint blueberries
1 pint strawberries
4 Tbs. plus 2 tsp. sugar
4 Tbs. plus 2 tsp. apricot liqueur or cordial
1 cup raspberries
Mint sprigs (optional)
5-lb. piece (2¼ kg) of watermelon, beautiful, deep-red, ripe, and sweet
4 to 5 Tbs. sugar (I would put in 5)
1 Tbs. lime or lemon juice

THE FRUITS AND BERRIES Before buying, make a little study of market conditions. If you can buy ripe fruit, sweet and ready to eat, then get it the last day or two before the dinner. If you can't, then buy three or four days ahead and let sit in the room in paper bags until properly ripe. I don't peel any of the fruits because I like the textures and flavors of the skins, but you can peel if you like. I don't wash fruits or berries either; but I do rub the fruits with paper towels, which at least gets rid of the fuzz from the peaches. Am I crazy? Will I die of some ghastly insecticide poisoning? Does washing with water get rid of those nasty chemicals? Wash if you must, but dry well immediately afterward. Strawberries can spoil soon after being washed, but you can wipe them with a wet towel. I hear that some people wash fruits in dry white wine, but I have never met anyone who does. The people I know are the kind who wash them *down* with dry white wine.

Four or 5 hours before serving, prepare the following fruits or use any combination you like. Put into a mixing bowl:

2 large peaches, sliced
2 large nectarines, sliced
4 soft and ripe plums, each cut into 6 slices (Santa Rosa, which are round and very dark blue, if available)
4 apricots, each cut into 6 or 8 slices (If you can't find ripe ones or those that ripen in 3 or 4 days, then don't use apricots. Don't worry if apricots develop mushy spots because they will taste better.)
1 pint blueberries
1 pint strawberries, hulled and cut in halves or, if large, in quarters

Sprinkle over the fruit in the bowl:

   4 Tbs. sugar (more or less)

The sugar helps keep the peaches and nectarines from turning dark. It also sweetens things ever so lightly, brings out natural sweetness, and gives an attractive glazed appearance. Mix carefully, then add:

   4 Tbs. apricot liqueur or cordial (more or less)

(I like Marie Brizzard Apry. You also can use orange liqueur or brandy such as Grand Marnier, Cointreau, Triple Sec, Curaçao, or any fruit liqueur, cordial, or brandy that you happen to have around.) Stir, then refrigerate. Have ready:

   1 cup raspberries

These will be added to the servings at the last minute. You don't dare mix them with the rest because they will get crushed and mutilated by the weight of the other fruits. Put the raspberries in a small bowl and sprinkle with:

   1 to 2 tsp. sugar
   1 to 2 tsp. fruit liqueur

Mix carefully. Refrigerate until serving time. (If the raspberries are sweet and perfect, you can forget the sugar and liqueur.)

TO SERVE Decide whether you want to serve the fruits right from the refrigerator or whether you want to remove them ½ hour ahead so they are not quite so cold. The weather may help you with that awful decision. Spoon the fruit into saucers or compotes. Sprinkle raspberries around the sides, then place a ball of watermelon ice in the center of each serving (see recipe below). Add:

   Fresh mint sprigs (optional)

Serve.

ABOUT FRUIT ICES I have had very good luck making fruit ices just by freezing pure fruit purees (my goodness, try saying those last three words three times fast) with a minimum of sugar and a few teaspoons of lemon or lime juice. There's no need for an ice cream maker. I work the frozen puree in the food processor until smooth.

   Some ices will hold a fairly smooth consistency for days and therefore can be done ahead. Others turn rock hard and must be worked again an hour or two before serving. The watermelon ice that follows and melon ices in general can be done ahead. They seem to benefit, as do all fruit ices, from being brought out into the room at least ½ hour before serving to soften a bit and become wetter, slushier, more delicious.

The most important consideration affecting the quality of any fruit ice (you know what's coming, don't you?) is the quality of the fruit. First find good fruit, then decide which ice you are going to make. The formula for watermelon ice works equally well for other melons and for most fruits and berries that are pleasant to eat as they are. If you can't find great watermelon but can find really sweet ordinary or exotic melon of another kind, use that instead.

The basic proportions for fruit ice are: for each cup of fruit puree, add 1 tablespoon sugar and 1 teaspoon lemon or lime juice. The sugar can be increased if you like; I tend to prefer 4 tablespoons sugar per 3 cups (¾ L) fruit puree.

Here are a few more principles I have observed about fruit ices:

1. Peaches, nectarines, and apricots need to be handled slightly differently or they will turn brown and be ugly.

2. Certain berries take on deeper, richer flavors if cooked very briefly before being made into ices. Blueberries definitely are improved by a short cooking. I haven't made up my mind completely, but two other candidates for brief cooking are strawberries and kiwi.

3. Why add sugar if the fruit or berries are perfectly sweet? Every once in a while I try leaving sugar out. The last time was with a watermelon ice. The puree was so sweet and perfect with natural sugar that I thought it would be a shame to add anything. I froze it as was, but the ice was awful. The sweetness was gone and a slightly unpleasant freezer taste had taken its place. Apparently some sugar and some citrus are needed to preserve the fruit flavor. Even after I let that watermelon ice melt, the puree still was not pleasant as it had been before.

4. Some purees are so thick with natural pulp (blueberries with their skins and figs with their seeds) that they need thinning with water. I add about 1 or 2 tablespoons water per 1 quart (3¾ L) of puree. Also, sometimes 1 tablespoon whipping

cream does something magic in smoothing out and softening the flavor.

WATERMELON ICE This recipe makes 1 quart (3¾ L). Prepare it at least one day ahead to allow time for freezing. Buy:

> 5-lb. piece (2¼ kg) of beautiful, deep-red, ripe, sweet watermelon

Cut and use only the red part. Slice into small, thin pieces so you can remove all the seeds. Once I tried removing the seeds by pushing the pulp through a strainer, but too much pulp was lost and the flavor was affected.

Put the pulp in a food processor and process until smooth and lump free. You may have to stop and stir to get rid of the lumps. You can always eat the last few. Stop when you have 4 cups puree. Pour into a bowl and add:

> 4 to 5 Tbs. sugar (I would put in 5)
> 1 Tbs. lime or lemon juice

Stir until the sugar dissolves. This may take a while. Taste and add more sugar if necessary. The puree must be really sweet because, as I mentioned above, it becomes considerably less sweet when frozen. Put the bowl of puree in a plastic bag, seal, and freeze at least 5 or 6 hours or overnight.

TO PROCESS THE ICE Chop the puree into pieces, then dump into the food processor. Process 2 or 3 minutes, stopping now and then to stir and fold. Eventually, all will be smooth. Return to the freezer. If you do this 4 or 5 hours before serving, the ice will be almost the perfect consistency to serve right from the freezer. If you do it one or two days ahead, bring the ice out to the room ½ hour before serving. Stir to smooth it out a bit before serving.

STRAWBERRIES THREE

6 servings

This refreshing and elegant dessert is the reddest dessert you will ever see in your life. Make it when you find really great strawberries. The "three" in the title refers to the three red parts involved: sliced strawberries, strawberry ice, and strawberry sauce.

**2 pints strawberries,
    ripe and delicious
2 to 4 Tbs. sugar
1 to 2 Tbs. lemon juice
1 pint strawberries
2 Tbs. sugar (or more
    or less or none)
1 pint strawberries
Candied lilacs or
    violets (optional)**

THE STRAWBERRY ICE Make this at least one day ahead so that the ice will have time to set. Buy:

2 pints strawberries, ripe and delicious

Brush the berries if necessary to clean (I don't wash them) and hull. If you must wash the berries, get them in and out of the water as fast as you can and dry in a lettuce (salad) whirler. Place the berries in a food processor fitted with the steel blade. Process until liquid and completely lump free. You will get about 2½ cups (6 dL) of puree. Add:

2 to 4 Tbs. sugar, or to taste

The amount of sugar depends on the quality of the berries, but you must add *some* for the preservation of the natural sweetness of the fruit. Process to help dissolve the sugar. Taste and, if it has little or no character, add:

1 to 2 Tbs. lemon juice

Frankly, I hate to add lemon, but sometimes it is unavoidable. Whatever you do, don't add so much that you taste the lemon; otherwise, it just becomes red lemon ice. Pour the puree into a bowl, cover, and freeze.

THE STRAWBERRY SAUCE Buy:

1 pint strawberries, ripe and delicious

Brush, then hull. Process to a smooth, liquid puree (about 1 cup or ¼ L). Pour into a small saucepan and bring just to the boil. Taste, then add:

Sugar (2 Tbs. or more or less or none)

Let cool, then chill. This can be done a day ahead.

THE SLICED STRAWBERRIES Buy:

1 pint strawberries

Hull. I normally leave these out at room temperature and slice them just before serving. But if you're not the last-minute type, slice no more than 3 or 4 hours before serving, sugar lightly, and refrigerate.

TO ASSEMBLE AND SERVE Five to 10 minutes before you are going to serve the dessert, remove the strawberry ice from the freezer. Cut it into ½-inch (1½-cm) cubes and put in a food processor fitted with the metal blade. Process to break up the cubes, then let sit 5 minutes or so to warm slightly. Process again and keep trying if necessary for the next few minutes until the ice gets wetter and very red.

Use small elegant dessert saucers, sherbet

glasses, or wineglasses for serving. Put some sliced strawberries in each, then a small scoop of the strawberry ice on top. I use a small ice cream scoop about 2 inches (5 cm) in diameter. Spoon some sauce over the berries, around the base of the ice. Place on the top in the center:

> Candied lilacs (the purple ones are prettier than the pink ones) or candied violets (optional)

Serve.

TRUFFLED PEARS

6 servings

This is a very pretty dessert, an easy one, and a pleasure for the legions of chocolate lovers in our midst. Two poached pear halves (canned, of course, since this is a quick dish, remember?) are sandwiched together with an easy chocolate ganache filling. The filling is the rich mixture used for making chocolate truffles. Each pear pair is decorated with whipped cream and a single chocolate curl, much as if it were an ornate Easter egg. The dessert is very impressive, as well as incredibly simple and good.

2 large cans pear halves (29 oz. or 820 grams each)

6 oz. semisweet chocolate (180 grams)

½ stick butter (4 Tbs. or 60 grams)

4 Tbs. powdered sugar

½ cup whipping cream (1 dL)

1 square semisweet chocolate (1 oz. or 30 grams)

½ cup whipping cream (1 dL)

1 Tbs. powdered sugar

THE PEARS Buy:

> 2 large cans pear halves (29 oz. or 820 grams each)

I like to use the larger pears for this dessert, but you can use the smaller ones that come in the smaller 1-pound cans. For reasons known only to the canners, 29-ounce cans usually contain about seven huge-to-large pear halves and 1-pound cans usually contain about seven small-to-tiny ones. Sometimes you can get a very odd assortment of sizes in the same can, which may have some relationship to the price.

Drain the pears and lay on plates, cut sides up. Blot dry with a paper towel. Place uncovered in the refrigerator to chill and to dry. Don't be upset if the pear halves are different sizes. For the pairs, you can place larger halves on the bottom and smaller ones on top. After you finish the decorating, no one can see the difference.

THE CHOCOLATE GANACHE FILLING Into a saucepan put:

> 6 oz. semisweet chocolate (180 grams), chopped into pieces
>
> ½ stick butter (4 Tbs. or 60 grams), cut into pieces
>
> 4 Tbs. powdered sugar
>
> ½ cup whipping cream (1 dL)

Heat the mixture to slightly warm, stirring until everything is melted and smooth. Spread the filling over the bottom of a large mixing bowl, metal if possible, and refrigerate for 1 hour or until set to the consistency of creamy peanut butter. If the filling sets too firm for spreading or piping, work it a little until it softens.

TO FILL THE PEARS You can spread and mound the filling with a knife and spoon or you can pipe it from a pastry bag fitted with a ½-inch (1½-cm) plain tip.

Place six of the largest pear halves together in a group, cut sides up. Spread or pipe a ³⁄₁₆-inch layer of filling on the pear edges and ends. Also make a ball of filling in the center of each, large enough to fill the core holes when the two pear halves are placed together. Use all the filling on the pears or almost all. It's good stuff.

Place six smaller or equal-size pear halves on top of the six halves prepared with filling; place cut sides down to re-form a whole pear shape more or less. Push down a little to make sure the halves stick together. The filling will ooze out a little but will be hidden later with whipped cream. Refrigerate until serving time.

CHOCOLATE CURLS FOR GARNISH These can be prepared ahead. Have:

> 1 square semisweet chocolate (1 oz. or 30 grams)

On a warm day the chocolate will soften slightly to the right consistency. If the weather is cool, warm the chocolate slightly by holding for a minute in your hands or by setting it in the sun for 1 or 2 minutes or by putting in a 200°F/95°C oven for a few seconds.

Using a vegetable peeler, scrape off some strips

from one of the sides of the chocolate square. The peelings will curl if the chocolate is the right temperature. If they don't, simply use the flat strips or whatever you get. You can always sprinkle a little powdered sugar over anything that's too ugly. Ideally, you want six curly pieces. Reserve until serving time.

THE WHIPPED CREAM This can be done a few hours ahead. Beat until thick:

½ cup whipping cream (1 dL)

(This amount should be enough, although just barely enough.) Add:

1 Tbs. powdered sugar

Whip until fairly stiff, but don't overdo the beating. Reserve in the refrigerator.

THE FINAL ASSEMBLY At serving time, fit a pastry bag with a medium-size decorative tip. I like Ateco 4-B in the pastry series or their no. 2 open-star tip. Give the whipped cream a final beating to get it stiff enough to pipe out well and to hold firm edges. Fill the bag, then pipe out rows of rosettes to cover the area all around the pears where the top and bottom halves are joined. Pipe a single rosette on the top of each "whole" pear. Place one chocolate curl on top of each single rosette. Serve.

ICE CREAM NOTE If you want to go a little wild, you can serve these pears on vanilla ice cream pedestals. Put a scoop of ice cream on each chilled serving plate. Flatten the ice cream down to a pedestal about ½ inch (1½ cm) high, then place a decorated pear on top. This pedestal, in addition to being good to eat, serves the practical function of keeping the pear from sliding around on the plate.

SLICED MANGOES WITH MANGO CREAM

6 servings

This is probably the easiest dessert in the book and one of the best tasting. It is simply a plate of sliced fresh mangoes with a sauce of softly whipped cream blended with ripe mango puree. The success of the dish depends on finding sweet mangoes. Be on the lookout for mangoes in the summer, any time after mid-June. Whenever you see any, investigate. Squeeze them and, if they are soft but not mushily so, get excited. You can be almost positive that they are sweet. Buy four or five large ones, rush home, get on the phone, and invite some people for dinner. Ripe mangoes can be kept in the refrigerator for a couple of days, so your friends don't have to come over that very night.

Another way to proceed is to schedule your dinner first and go in search of mangoes four or five days in advance. Buy them firm if soft ones aren't available, leave them in a warm place in a paper bag for three or four days, and hope they will get ripe. Go to a good produce seller who can assure you that the mangoes were not picked so green that they will never ripen.

---

4 or 5 mangoes (8 to 10 oz. or 225 to 285 grams each)

½ cup whipping cream (1 dL)

1 to 2 Tbs. powdered sugar (optional)

THE MANGOES Buy:

    4 or 5 mangoes (8 to 10 oz. or 225 to 285 grams each)

On the day of the dinner, set one mango aside to use for the cream. Peel the rest. (Peeling can be done a day ahead if you want to save precious last minutes.) Slice the flesh lengthwise off the long, flat, skinny seed. Cut as close to the seed as possible and try to get pieces that look as pretty and neat as possible. Use a sharp knife and do your slicing on a board. Mango flesh has hairy fibers near the seed that don't affect the flavor, but you must cut with a certain authority to get through them. If you don't, instead of lovely mango slices, you will have a mangled mango mess.

    The slices do not need to be sprinkled with sugar or lemon. They will not turn dark or do anything untoward. Cover them and keep refrigerated until time to eat. You can bring them out a little ahead so they are not ice cold, but they are good a little bit chilled.

THE MANGO CREAM This can be made the morning of the dinner or a day ahead. Use the reserved mango. Peel and cut the pulp from the seed. Put the pulp in the container of a food processor. Process to a smooth puree. Beat:

    ½ cup whipping cream (1 dL)

just until starting to set. Stir in the mango puree. Taste and add if it seems desirable:

    1 to 2 Tbs. powdered sugar (optional)

The cream should be smooth and somewhat runny, more like a sauce than a blob. Refrigerate until serving time.

TO SERVE Arrange the mango slices in dessert saucers or footed compotes. Give the mango cream a final stir. If it is too stiff and doesn't flow like a sauce, add 1 to 2 tablespoons more cream or water. Spoon over the mango slices. Serve.

CRENSHAW MELON ICE

6 servings

In the summer of 1979, during one of the week-long courses at my cooking school, we made five rather unusual ices from fresh fruits. On the last day of the course we tasted them all. I saved the few brief notes that I made about them that day:

Fig Ice. *Interesting; would be better with* great *figs.*

Peach Ice. *This was delicious! The peaches were sweet and good.*

Blueberry Ice. *This is good! Perhaps a bit too sweet.* (Note: *We had used 4 Tbs. sugar for 1 pint blueberries.)*

Papaya Ice. *O.K. (That's all I wrote.)*

Crenshaw Melon Ice. *This was the most delightful—very light and very lovely. The melon was a sensational one.*

I still remember the Crenshaw Melon Ice very well. It was the overwhelming favorite of us all. It is interesting to note my comment about the sensational melon. There's a lesson there somewhere.

In case you're not familiar with Crenshaw melon, it is a cross between a Persian melon and a casaba. It is one of the really great melons. Crenshaws are in season all summer, but are most plentiful in August and September. If you have trouble finding one, substitute any other "sensational" melon. See also the recipe for Watermelon Ice.

---

1 Crenshaw melon (the size of a human head)

2 Tbs. lime or lemon juice

4 Tbs. sugar

THE CRENSHAW MELON ICE MIXTURE Have:

1 Crenshaw melon (the size of a human head)

Cut open, remove the seeds, and scoop out the pulp. Place the pulp in a food processor fitted with the steel blade and process until smooth and lump free. Measure 3½ cups (⅘ L) melon (now a juice). Add:

2 Tbs. lime juice (or lemon if you can't find limes)

4 Tbs. sugar

Stir until the sugar dissolves. This may take a while. If you taste the mixture at this point, you may think it is too sweet, but don't be concerned. Ices and sherbet mixtures lose sweetness when frozen. For further notes on ice making and more comments on melon ices, see the recipe for Summer Fruits with Watermelon Ice.

Put the bowl containing the melon puree in a plastic bag to keep the mixture from picking up refrigerator flavors. Seal and freeze at least 5 or 6 hours or overnight.

TO PROCESS THE ICE Chop the puree into pieces, then dump into a food processor fitted with the steel blade. Process 2 to 3 minutes, stopping now and then to stir and fold. Eventually all will be smooth.

Return to the freezer. If you process the ice 4 to 5 hours before serving, it will be almost the perfect consistency to use right from the freezer. If you process it one to two days ahead, bring the ice out to the room ½ hour before serving. Stir to smooth it out a bit. If it still is not a good consistency, process again until smooth.

BLUEBERRY ICE

6 servings

Blueberries are magic for me, all mixed up in my mind with childhood, my grandmother and grandfather, pies, pastry squares, muffins, and things from long ago. So, with nostalgia, I approached making this blueberry ice. It, like all blueberry things, is special and something I like very much.

Calling this an ice is a little strange because it has cream in it, which means that technically it isn't an ice. But it has only a little bit of cream. It still looks and tastes like an ice, so that's what I'm calling it. Why is there cream in it? Certain ices seem to be smoothed, softened, and improved by the addition of a little cream. Cream makes the color prettier, too.

If you want to serve this ice with a little style, top each scoop with some lightly sweetened whipped cream, then garnish with a beautiful blueberry or two or three.

---

1 pint blueberries (about 2½ cups)
2 Tbs. sugar
¼ cup water (½ dL)
¼ cup whipping cream (½ dL)

THE BLUEBERRY ICE MIXTURE Into the container of a food processor fitted with the steel blade, put:
1 pint blueberries, stems and leaves removed (about 2½ cups)
Process 30 seconds, then pour into a saucepan. Add:
2 Tbs. sugar (or more depending on berries, but I once made this with 4 Tbs. sugar and it was a little too sweet)
¼ cup water (½ dL)
¼ cup whipping cream (½ dL)
Bring to a boil. Simmer 1 to 2 minutes, pour into a bowl, and let cool. Put the bowl in a plastic bag, seal, and freeze at least 5 to 6 hours or overnight.
TO PROCESS THE ICE Chop the puree into pieces, then dump into a food processor fitted with the steel blade. Process 2 to 3 minutes, stopping now

and then to stir and fold. Eventually all will be smooth. Return to the freezer.

If you process the ice 4 to 5 hours before serving, it will be almost the perfect consistency to use right from the freezer. If you process it one to two days ahead, bring the ice out to the room ½ hour before serving. Stir to smooth it out a bit before serving. If it still is not a good consistency, process again until smooth.

FIG ICE

6 servings

This has quite a fascinating flavor. It is most delicious made with really great, sweet figs.

2 cups packed-down unpeeled fresh figs (clip off hard stem ends)
2 Tbs. sugar
¼ cup water (½ dL)
3 Tbs. lime juice

THE FIG ICE Into the container of a food processor fitted with the steel blade, put:
    2 cups packed-down unpeeled fresh figs (clip off hard stem ends)
    2 Tbs. sugar
    ¼ cup water (½ dL)
    3 Tbs. lime juice (or a little less if figs are very flavorful)
Process to a smooth puree. Freeze the puree. For the final processing, follow the procedure for Blueberry Ice.

GRAPEFRUIT ICE

6 servings

Here is another of my favorite ices. When made from really delicious grapefruit, it is one of the most wonderfully refreshing ices of all.

3 cups fresh grapefruit juice (¾ L), about 3 or 4 12-oz. (340-gram) grapefruit
⅓ cup sugar (65 grams)

THE GRAPEFRUIT ICE Into a bowl put:
    3 cups fresh grapefruit juice (¾ L), about 3 or 4 12-oz. (340-gram) grapefruit
    ⅓ cup sugar (65 grams) (you could try less)
Let sit, stirring now and then, until the sugar completely dissolves. Freeze. For the final processing, follow the procedure for Blueberry Ice.

PASTRY DESSERTS

PASTRY DESSERTS WITH FRUITS

Spiced Apple and Pear Cobbler

Pear Pie

Brioche Plum Tart

*Blueberry Tart

*Strawberry-Rhubarb Shortcake with
Toasted Almond Biscuits*

*Kiwi Upside-Down Cake

CAKES AND TORTES

Viennese Torte with Carrots and Almonds

Chestnut Torte with Chocolate and Chestnut Creams

Chocolate Whipped-Cream Truffle Cake

Marie Summers's Coffee-Crunch Cake

*Special quick pastry desserts

If you've never made pastries before or if you have tried and failed and are discouraged about doing them again, I hope you will try some of the recipes in this section. I have worked very hard to give you the kind of detailed instructions you need to be successful with all of them. Start with the dishes in the first group, the pastry desserts with fruits. Three of them have very simple doughs, the kind that you just stir together and the less you work them, the better. They are the Spiced Apple and Pear Cobbler, Strawberry Rhubarb Shortcake, and Kiwi Upside-Down Cake. The other three dishes in the first group all have doughs made in the food processor, which really makes them easy to do. If you can figure out how to turn the thing on and off, and if you will read and follow the directions carefully, you should have very successful results.

When you are confident and ready to try the cakes and tortes, start with the Chocolate Whipped-Cream Truffle Cake. The cake, which is the only difficult part, is made 100 percent in the food processor. Baking powder does the work of the rising, so all you have to do is to dump the stuff into the processor and follow the instructions. I feel certain that even without experience you will be able to assemble a pretty good version of this wonderful cake. If there is one item in this entire cookbook that I am proudest of, it is this Chocolate Whipped-Cream Truffle Cake. A slice of it on a plate is truly a beautiful sight, and the cake is one of the best-tasting things I have ever eaten.

Some of my other personal favorites are the cobbler, the shortcake, the blueberry tart, and the chestnut torte. Everything in here is good, however, and well worth the time and effort it takes to make them. The easiest pastries are probably the cobbler and the upside-down cake. The most difficult one, at least the one I find the hardest to do perfectly, is the coffee-crunch cake, but it is *fabulous*.

SPICED APPLE AND PEAR COBBLER

9 servings

This really good dessert is the kind you dream of finding in some little country inn way off the beaten path somewhere. I call it a cobbler for want of a better name, although the top dough is not a biscuit dough. Maybe a better name for it would be a Right-Side-Up Upside-Down Cake.

This "cobbler" is a deep-dish apple and pear affair with a cake-like crust of whole wheat flour, pecans, and lots of butter. The nice thing about "hearty" or "country" desserts is that you don't have to prove anything about them to anyone. All they have to be is good, and no one asks any questions about their lineage. This one is delicious.

3 Tbs. butter
3 to 5 Tbs. sugar
3 medium apples (1 lb. or 450 grams)
3 medium pears (1 lb. or 450 grams)
1 Tbs. flour or quick-cooking tapioca
¾ tsp. cinnamon
1 to 2 Tbs. lemon or lime juice
1 stick butter (4 oz. or 115 grams), melted
½ cup cream or milk (1 dL)
1 egg
½ cup whole wheat flour (50 grams)
½ cup white flour (60 grams)
¾ cup sugar (75 grams)
1½ tsp. baking powder
¼ tsp. salt
½ cup pecans (approximately 2 oz. or 60 grams)

THE FRUIT Use an $8 \times 8 \times 2$-inch ($20 \times 20 \times 5$-cm) baking pan. It will yield nine squares, about right for six people if half have seconds. If you're inviting a crowd, double the recipe and bake in an $8 \times 13 \times 2$-inch ($20 \times 33 \times 5$-cm) pan. Into a large sauté pan or frying pan put:

    3 Tbs. butter
    1 to 2 Tbs. sugar (depending on tartness of apples)
    3 medium apples (1 lb. or 450 grams), not peeled, but cored and sliced into ½-inch (1½-cm) wedges (I use Pippins, as green as possible)
    3 medium pears (1 lb. or 450 grams), not peeled, but cored, halved, and sliced across into ½-inch (1½-cm) slices (use Bosc or any pear just starting to be ripe enough to eat)

Don't use more than these weights or, when assembled later, the pan will be too full and the pastry topping will run over. Cook the apples and pears over high heat for 5 minutes, stirring occasionally. The purpose is to get the fruit started cooking and also to evaporate some of its moisture. After 5 minutes, remove from the heat. In a small bowl mix:

    2 to 3 Tbs. sugar
    1 Tbs. flour or quick-cooking tapioca (to absorb pan juices)
    ¾ tsp. cinnamon

Sprinkle over apples and pears; stir to mix well. Add:

    1 to 2 Tbs. lemon or lime juice

Stir again, then dump into the baking pan. Make sure to scrape all the good stuff from the sauté pan with a rubber spatula; don't leave any behind. Pack down and level the fruit.

THE CAKE TOPPING In a bowl mix:

>   1 stick butter (4 oz. or 115 grams), melted
>   ½ cup cream or milk (1 dL) warmed
>   1 egg

Beat with a whisk or an electric mixer until the egg is well mixed. In another bowl put:

>   ½ cup whole wheat flour (50 grams)
>   ½ cup white flour (60 grams)
>   ¾ cup (75 grams) sugar (you can use half brown sugar)
>   1½ tsp. baking powder
>   ¼ tsp. salt

Mix well, then dump into the cream mixture. Stir until smooth. Pour over the fruit and spread to distribute evenly. Sprinkle over:

>   ½ cup pecans (approximately 2 oz. or 60 grams), chopped coarse in ¼-inch (¾-cm) pieces

Place the pan on a baking sheet in case it drips over. Bake in a preheated 375°F/190°C oven for 45 to 50 minutes or until the top is a good, deep brown. Cool on a rack at least an hour before serving. The cobbler can be baked a day ahead and served at room temperature.

PEAR PIE

6 servings

This pie was first served to me by a friend and former student, Jean Vannucci. Jean is an excellent cook. Her pie has an appealing country look and tastes wonderful. One of the key factors in bringing off this pie successfully is the proper ripeness of the pears.

1 cup flour (120 grams)
1 stick *frozen* butter (4
    oz. or 115 grams)
3 Tbs. cold water
¼ tsp. salt
¾ cup sugar (75 grams)
½ stick butter (2 oz. or
    60 grams) at room
    temperature
¼ cup flour (30 grams)
⅓ cup almonds
    (approximately 2 oz.
    or 60 grams),
    blanched or not
2 eggs at room
    temperature
1 tsp. vanilla
2½ to 3 lbs. barely ripe
    pears (1125 to 1230
    grams) (5 large or 6
    to 7 smaller ones)
1 lemon

THE CRUST This is not Jean's crust but an unusual food-processor dough discovered by another friend and former student, Barbara Power. Barbara runs a gourmet cookware shop in San Jose called The Kitchen Scene and is an accomplished cook. I think of her dough as kind of an instant puff paste. You get a certain rise from the dough without the traditional turning and folding. The ingredients don't seem like anything special, but the results are. The cooked dough has a mysterious crunch unlike that of any other I know. The critical points are the *frozen* butter and the size of the lumps of butter when you add the water. Notice that the equal weights of flour and butter are the same as for puff paste.

Have ready a 9-inch (23-cm) metal or glass pie pan. Into the container of a food processor fitted with the metal blade, put:

    1 cup flour (120 grams)
    1 stick *frozen* butter (4 oz. or 115 grams), cut
        into ½-inch (1½-cm) dice

Give the machine a couple of quick on-and-off movements, then put it on for 15 seconds steady. That should be enough to reduce the butter into lumps no larger than small peas. Do not take this to the coarse-meal stage or you will change the texture of the dough. In a small bowl put:

    3 Tbs. cold water (full tablespoons; don't
        skimp)
    ¼ tsp. salt

Stir to dissolve the salt. Turn the processor back on and immediately pour the water in a stream through the feeding tube into the flour. Process the dough for 15 seconds, dump it out onto a countertop, and gather and push it together into a disk. Flouring lightly, roll the dough into a round that just nicely fits the pie pan. Line the pan with the dough. Trim off any dough hanging over. Crimp the edge to make it attractive, then refrigerate.

THE FILLING You can do this with a hand or electric beater, but it's a little faster using the food processor. Into the container put:

    ¾ cup sugar (75 grams) (you can decrease to ½
        cup or increase to 1 cup, depending on
        sweetness of pears)

½ stick butter (2 oz. or 60 grams) at room
temperature

¼ cup flour (30 grams)

⅓ cup almonds (approximately 2 oz. or 60
grams), blanched or not

2 eggs at room temperature

1 tsp. vanilla

Process the filling until it is mixed and smooth by
letting the machine run for 1 or 2 minutes. The
almonds can be a little chunky.

THE PEARS Preheat the oven to 450°F/230°C. Have:

2½ to 3 lbs. pears (1125 to 1350 grams) (5 large
or 6 or 7 smaller ones)

Bosc and Bartlett are good, but I think any pear will
do. The pears should be just barely ripe. If they are
too hard, they will not have enough sweetness and
also will not be tender by the time the crust and
filling have finished cooking. Of course, they
cannot be overly ripe or they will become mushy.
The ideal is that stage when they are just barely
ready to eat. The flesh of the pear will just yield to
very firm pressure from your thumb. Have:

1 lemon

I like to rub the outside of the pears with lemon
juice just as they are peeled to keep them from
turning dark. Peel all the pears first, rubbing with
lemon. Cut each in half and scoop out the core with
a melon-ball scoop or spoon. Cut the halves in half,
then trim off any fibers or ends. When all are cored
and trimmed, place a layer of the quarters on the
bottom of the pie shell in a neat circle, with the
hole sides up and the rounded, fat ends toward the
rim of the pan. If the pears are too large, trim the
narrow ends to V-shaped points to make them fit
properly. Pour in about one-third of the filling.

Make a ring of pear quarters on top, this time
with the rounded sides up; stagger so that the top
pears do not fit right on top of the pears on the
bottom layer. You should end with a neat rosette
pattern. If necessary, trim the pears to make them
fit. If space remains in the center, cut a round pear
piece and fit it into the center to make the pie look
pretty. Pour the rest of the filling over the middle
of the pears and let it run down and into the
cracks. As the filling cooks, it will first become

runnier and will fill in the cracks even more. Bake at once.

TO BAKE Place the pie on a baking sheet, then bake in the preheated 450°F/230°C oven for 30 minutes. Lower the heat to 350°F/180°C and bake another 30 minutes. The pears should be tender and the crust and filling should be nicely browned.

TO SERVE This pie is best served warm, about 2 hours out of the oven, but it is fine served at room temperature. It also is very good the day after baking. Because the filling has egg in it, it must be refrigerated. The next day, either serve at room temperature or let come to room temperature and rewarm in a 350°F/180°C oven for 10 or 15 minutes.

   Note: You will get a crack in the top of the pie all around the rosette where the pears meet the filling because the pears cool and shrink. I know of no way to avoid this. If it really bothers you, you could puree some poached or canned pears and pipe the mixture into the cracks. Or, if you are serving the pie at room temperature, cover the crack with a ribbon of whipped cream.

BRIOCHE PLUM TART

6 servings

This is a kind of plum pizza. It is a big, beautiful tart loaded with plums, all glazed and shining and luscious-looking. The crust is made with brioche dough. Brioche is a yeast dough of whole eggs and butter, related in texture and taste to Jewish challah. The dough is covered with slightly underripe plums, then buttered, sugared, baked, and glazed. The finished tart has a slightly acid quality reminiscent of desserts made with tart apples.

   At summer buffets at my cooking school in San Francisco, when a plum tart is among the many beautiful, elaborately decorated cakes and pastries, it is one of the most popular and invariably disappears first. This is one of those desserts that does taste as good as it looks.

   Brioche dough used to require a lot of time and skill to make. Julie Dannenbaum, a wonderful lady and well-known cooking teacher from Philadelphia, first gave me the idea of making this dough with an electric mixer, and I have incorporated her technique. I can't imagine a better-tasting crust, even if made the classic French way by hand. (A food processor version is given at the end of this recipe.)

½ cup barely warm
   water (1 dL)
1 package dry yeast or
   1 cake fresh yeast
3 sticks unsalted
   butter (¾ lb. or 340
   grams)
¼ cup sugar (50 grams)
6 eggs at room
   temperature
2 tsp. salt
4½ cups flour
12 or more plums, not
   quite ripe
2 to 3 Tbs. butter
4 Tbs. sugar
Currant jelly
Whipped cream or
   crème fraîche
1 cup whipping cream
   (¼ L)
1 tsp. buttermilk
¾ cup warm water
   (1¾ dL)
2 envelopes dry yeast
4½ cups flour (540
   grams)
3 sticks butter (¾ lb.
   or about 340 grams)
   at room temperature
¼ cup sugar (50 grams)
2 tsp. salt
5 eggs at room
   temperature

THE BRIOCHE DOUGH Into a small bowl put:
   ½ cup barely warm water (1 dL)
   1 package dry yeast or 1 cake fresh yeast
Let stand for 5 minutes, stirring occasionally to
dissolve. Into the bowl of an electric mixer put:
   3 sticks unsalted butter (¾ lb. or 340 grams)
Beat the butter with the paddle beater, carefully
heating the bowl now and then in a bigger bowl of
warm water and working the butter until it is the
consistency of mayonnaise. Add to the bowl:
   ¼ cup sugar (50 grams)
   6 eggs at room temperature
   2 tsp. salt
   3 cups flour (400 grams), measured by dipping
      cup in and scraping level with knife
and the yeast mixture just prepared. Stir right away
with a spatula to mix in the flour a little, then beat
at medium speed for 4 minutes. Add and stir in:
   1½ cups flour (approximately 180 grams)
Beat at slow speed for 2 minutes. The dough tends
to collect around the paddle, but don't worry.

Transfer the rather sticky dough to a clean bowl.
Smooth out as best you can. Cover with plastic
wrap and let rise until doubled. Cover the bowl
with towels or something to keep out the light. The
rising may take 2 hours, even 4 if the room is cool.
I sometimes cheat and put the bowl in a warm
turned-off gas oven, but rising still seems to take 2
hours.

When the dough has doubled, work it down
with a rubber spatula. Turn out onto a floured
countertop. Flatten to get rid of the main gas
bubbles, then fold once or twice, put into a clean
bowl, and cover with plastic. Refrigerate for 2 or 3
hours or overnight.

Bring the bowl out to the room 2 hours before
using the dough, but don't let it get too warm or
the dough will be a sticky mess. If you are in a
hurry, the dough can be used right from the
refrigerator.

THE TART You can make this on a 14 × 17-inch
(35 × 43-cm) baking sheet or on a pizza pan 12
inches (30 cm) in diameter. You need only part of
the batch of brioche dough. Use one-sixth of the
dough for each elegant thin-crusted dinner dessert

or one-third for a thicker, coffee-cake version. The extra dough can be used for making brioche rolls (see any good classic French cookbook for shaping and baking method), or bake the balance of the dough as you would bake any loaf of bread.

The tart is lovely if assembled and baked about an hour before eating, but you certainly can do it 4 or 5 hours ahead, even longer if you have to.

Use either one-third or one-sixth of the brioche dough, depending on the type of crust you have decided you would like. Push with your hands or use a rolling pin to make a 12-inch (30-cm) round. You can throw the dough up and spin it in the air, the way pizza makers do, if you feel frisky. Or, once you have a 6- or 7-inch (15- or 18-cm) disk, take your rings off and try stretching the dough over the backs of your hands, also as pizza makers do.

Put the 12-inch round of dough on the baking sheet and form a little rim around the edge to hold in the plum juices while the tart cooks. Have:

12 or more plums, not quite ripe

(You also can make this tart with apricots, pears, or apples.) Preheat the oven to 375°F/190°C. Cut the plums almost, but not quite, in half, open to remove the pits, and flatten out a little. Next, cut each half almost in half again without cutting through the skin. Lay the plums all over the dough, skin sides down, crowding them in. Dot with:

2 to 3 Tbs. butter

Sprinkle over:

4 Tbs. sugar (or more or less, depending on plum tartness)

Do not let the dough rise, but bake right away.

TO BAKE THE TART Place in the 375°F/190°C oven and bake 20 to 30 minutes or until the edges of the dough have browned a little and the plums have some dark edges. Let cool to room temperature (2 or 3 hours) or, if you bake at the last minute, glaze while still somewhat warm. In a small saucepan put:

Currant jelly

and bring to a boil to melt. (Use a good brand of jelly or it may be sickeningly sweet. Also, the better

brands generally liquefy and become very smooth.
If the jelly has too much pectin, you may have to
strain it after melting to get rid of little lumps.)
Paint the top of the tart with jelly to glaze. Serve at
room temperature or warm. If you like still further
loveliness, serve with the tart:

Whipped cream or *crème fraîche*

For whipped cream, whip ½ cup (1 dL) heavy
cream and add 1 Tbs. powdered sugar and ½ tsp.
vanilla.

CRÈME FRAÎCHE To make this, place in a glass
container:

1 cup whipping cream (¼ L), warmed to just
barely take off the chill (do not allow to go
above 85°F/29°C)

1 tsp. buttermilk

You can use sour cream or yoghurt instead of
buttermilk. I generally put in more than 1 teaspoon
in the hope that it will hurry up the fermenting.

Let the room-temperature cream-buttermilk
mixture sit out overnight or until it thickens, then
refrigerate. When chilled, it will thicken even
further and will be the consistency of sour cream,
but with a milder taste.

FOOD PROCESSOR BRIOCHE DOUGH If you have one
of the larger-capacity food processors (one in which
approximately 7 cups or 1¾ L of liquid will come to
the top of the center post attached to the metal
blade), you can prepare this dough all at once. If
not, at the point when the addition of ingredients
causes the dough level to rise above the center
post, remove the dough to a bowl, mix, return half
to the processor, and finish the processing in two
batches.

Into a small bowl put:

¾ cup warm water (1¾ dL) (the temperature of
bathtub water)

Sprinkle over:

2 envelopes dry yeast

Let stand for 5 minutes, stirring occasionally to help
dissolve the yeast. Into the food processor container
put:

3 cups flour (about 360 grams)

3 sticks butter at room temperature (¾ lb. or
about 340 grams)

Process until the mixture forms a paste and the butter is free of lumps. Add:

¼ cup sugar (50 grams)

2 tsp. salt

5 eggs at room temperature

Process for 2 minutes, stopping to stir down and clean the sides of the container once, about halfway through. Add the yeast mixture and:

1½ cups more flour (about 180 grams)

At this point the processor will be awfully full. Process with a series of about twenty on-and-off turns of about 2 seconds each. If the machine starts to sound funny or if you begin to sense an electrical smell, you'd better stop and divide the dough in half. Then process each half separately.

The dough will be quite soft and quite warm. It may look a little curdly on top, but if you give it a little stir, it will get smooth again. The dough will be very sticky on your hands, but will have a kind of strange, elastic body, which you can see if you cut and lift it with a rubber spatula.

Scrape the dough out and dump into a clean bowl. Cover with plastic wrap and let rise in a warm place (not too warm or the butter will melt) until doubled, about 1½ hours. Stir with a rubber spatula to deflate, then dump into a clean bowl. Cover with plastic and refrigerate for 3 or 4 hours or until the dough is chilled through and can be handled.

BLUEBERRY TART

8 servings

This is a beautiful, elegant tart and quite an unusual one. It consists of a bottom crust similar to Scottish shortbread, made from a quick food-processor dough, topped with a layer of blueberries, and decorated with swirls of whipped cream piped around the top. Not only is it delicious and quick, but it can be done a day ahead as well.

This tart is the result of the challenge to create special quick desserts for this book. Fruit tarts have never been considered very quick, but if you leave out the traditional pastry cream layer and if you make them with a rapid food-processor base, they can squeeze into the quick category—although perhaps just barely.

Getting rid of the pastry cream, however, leaves the problem of finding something to hold the fruit together in the tart. In this recipe, some of the blueberries are pureed and stirred into the whole ones. A very small amount of gelatin is added, just enough to permit the tart to set and to be sliced neatly, but not so much as to be noticeable.

After my various experiments with this tart, I came to a conclusion that shocked me and probably will horrify you. I prefer canned berries to fresh. The reason is not a matter of fresh versus canned. Rather, I prefer a special variety of blueberries that is only available canned. It is Wyman's wild blueberries in heavy syrup, sold in supermarkets in California and, I believe, in the rest of the country as well. According to the label, the berries are packed by Jasper Wyman & Son in Milbridge, Maine (I love it already). The berries are tiny and very flavorful. Straight from the tin, they are hard and not very exciting; however, when cooked or otherwise prepared, they are unique and wonderful. A tart made with these berries is far, far superior ('Tis a far, far superior tart I make . . .) to any I have ever made using large, fresh blueberries, whether from New Jersey, Arkansas, or California.

I am, therefore, giving you this recipe calling for the canned wild blueberries, in the hope that you will be able to find them. If you can't, there is a note at the end of the recipe that tells how to use fresh blueberries. Ain't that a switch from my usual warnings about how you lose points for opening cans?

---

2 Tbs. butter
½ cup flour (60 grams)
2 Tbs. sugar (25 grams)
½ stick butter (2 oz. or 60 grams) cut into ½-inch pieces (1½-cm)
1 egg yolk
1½ tsp. cold water
1 Tbs. cold water
1 envelope unflavored gelatin (2 rounded tsp.)
3 cans (15 oz. or 425 grams each) Wyman's wild blueberries in heavy syrup
1 cup whipping cream (¼ L)
1 Tbs. powdered sugar

THE "WATERPROOFING" BUTTER Have:
     2 Tbs. butter
Cut into thin slices, spread out, and let come to room temperature. This butter will be brushed over the bottom crust later to keep it from losing its crispness when the wet layer of berries is added.
THE SHORT-DOUGH CRUST Preheat the oven to 425°F/220°C. Use an 8-inch (20-cm) springform cake tin. Cut out an 8-inch circle of baking parchment or brown paper to use for lining the bottom of the tin.
     Into the container of a food processor fitted with the steel blade put:
     ½ cup flour (60 grams)
     2 Tbs. sugar (25 grams)
     ½ stick butter (2 oz. or 60 grams) cut into
          ½-inch (1½-cm) pieces
Process for about 30 seconds or until the butter lumps disappear. Into a saucer put:
     1 egg yolk
     1½ tsp. cold water
Mix, then dribble onto the flour-sugar mixture. Process for 15 seconds or until the dough comes together into a ball.
     Put the ball of dough on waxed paper and, with floured hands, flatten into a ½-inch (1¼-cm)-thick disk. On top of the dough, lay the 8-inch

parchment circle. On top of that, invert the bottom of the springform pan. Turn the whole business over. Then, using a rolling pin, roll out the dough so it just fits the whole area of the pan bottom. Peel the waxed paper off carefully. (If the paper sticks badly, give the whole business a 10-minute shot in the freezer and try again.)

Lock the pastry-lined pan bottom into the springform frame. Prick the pastry all over with a fork. Right away, bake in the 425°F/220°C oven for 20 minutes or until the crust is lightly browned. Cool on a rack.

THE BLUEBERRY FILLING Into a saucer put:

1 Tbs. cold water

Sprinkle over:

1 envelope unflavored gelatin (2 rounded tsp.)

Note: If you can put up with a little crumbling when the tart is cut, you may reduce the gelatin to a bare minimum of 1½ teaspoons. Mix, then set aside. Have:

3 cans (15 oz. or 425 grams each) Wyman's wild blueberries in heavy syrup

Strain the syrup from one can of the berries and reserve ¼ cup (½ dL); keep this can separate. Strain the other two cans. Use the rest of the syrup for another purpose. Look through the berries and remove any stems (sometimes some really good-sized branches are left behind).

Place one can of the drained berries in the container of a food processor fitted with the steel blade and add the reserved ¼ cup syrup. Process 10 to 15 seconds or until the berries are pureed. Transfer to a saucepan. Bring to a boil. Then add the whole blueberries from the other two cans. Stir, return to a boil, and cook for 30 seconds. Remove from the heat and add the softened gelatin. Stir to dissolve the gelatin.

Transfer the hot mixture to a mixing bowl (preferably stainless steel because the mixture will be stirred later over ice). If using the Wyman berries, you should not need any more sugar. If using another brand or fresh berries, taste and add more sugar if you like. Place the bowl on a rack and let cool.

While the filling and the crust are cooling, do

something else for a half hour or longer. Do not consider this as a part of the time to make the quick tart. It definitely does not count.

TO ASSEMBLE THE TART When the crust has cooled completely, brush it all over with the room-temperature "waterproofing" butter. Lift the crust cautiously from the pan bottom. Remove and discard the parchment, then brush butter all around the edges until waterproofed too. Put the crust back on the pan bottom and lock back into the springform pan.

Nestle the bowl containing the blueberry mixture in a larger bowl containing half ice cubes and half water. Let the mixture chill, scraping the bottom now and then with a rubber spatula. Let sit until ice cold to the touch and thickened.

Pour the mixture over the buttered crust in the springform pan and shake to level. Refrigerate to set, at least 4 to 5 hours or as long as overnight.

SWEETENED WHIPPED CREAM This can be prepared the morning of the dinner. Beat until softly whipped:

1 cup whipping cream (¼ L)

Add:

1 Tbs. powdered sugar

Stir, then refrigerate until serving time.

TO UNMOLD THE TART This can also be done the morning of the dinner. Slide a knife between the blueberries and the pan rim, then open the springform and carefully remove the sides. Transfer the tart to an attractive serving platter by carefully sliding it off the pan bottom. Cover with plastic and store in the refrigerator. Bring out to the room 1 to 2 hours before serving.

TO DECORATE AND SERVE Just before serving the tart, finish whipping the cream until stiff enough for piping. Place in a pastry bag fitted with a pastry tip. The one I like to use is Ateco 8-B, which is very large and has skinny, jagged teeth. Make eight swirls of the cream, spacing them evenly around the top of the tart. Cut into eight wedges to serve.

TO USE FRESH BLUEBERRIES Buy 2 pints or about 5½ cups. If you want a garnish, set aside eight nice berries for decoration. Puree 2 cups of the berries with 2 tablespoons of sugar (instead of the syrup that is used for canned berries). Pour the puree into a saucepan, bring to a boil, remove from the heat, and add the softened gelatin called for in the recipe; stir to dissolve.

Add the remaining whole berries, but *do not cook them at all*. Taste and add more sugar if desired. Transfer to a bowl as described in the recipe and follow the rest of the recipe as for canned berries.

Use the eight whole berries for decoration by putting one berry on each whipped-cream swirl.

STRAWBERRY-RHUBARB SHORTCAKE WITH TOASTED ALMOND BISCUITS

6 servings

My mother made good shortcake. Every summer, usually on only one night of the year, Mother would make a shortcake supper. Huge portions of peach shortcake were all we had. It was the meal. We gorged ourselves and got full and happy.

The fruit she used was peaches because we always had our shortcake orgies in mid-summer, after the strawberries were gone. My father would stop at a road stand out in the country and buy a bushel of either Elberta peaches or Georgia Belles. Mother would make the shortcake with typical baking powder biscuits. We loved the shortcake dinners. I remember them fondly.

This spring shortcake uses a combination of strawberries and rhubarb. It is a combination that I love in many different pastries, but particularly in shortcake. There is something about the two reds and the two acids that makes a marvelous blending. In addition to the selection of good-quality fruit, there are two secrets to a great shortcake, I believe. One is to serve the biscuits warm so that there is a contrast between the heat of the biscuits and the cold fruit. The second is to have a certain amount of wet, crushed fruit to act as a sauce for the cake.

The biscuit dough for this shortcake is not very conventional. I have added brown sugar, whole wheat flour, extra butter, and some chopped, toasted almonds. The dough is baked as a cake in a square pan and then cut into squares because this seems simpler to me than rolling out the dough and cutting round biscuit shapes.

---

2 lbs. rhubarb (900 grams)
1 cup sugar (200 grams)
4 pints good, ripe strawberries (1 L)
¼ cup sugar (50 grams)

THE RHUBARB COMPOTE Try to find good field rhubarb, which comes in very briefly every year from mid-April to around the end of May. Although hothouse rhubarb has a prettier color, I find it more acid, its texture less pleasant, and its flavor less complex. Frozen rhubarb also can be used, but keep an eye on the baking because it may get done sooner.

2 cups rhubarb compote (½ L), including some of its syrup

4 Tbs. sugar

1 cup whipping cream (¼ L)

2 Tbs. powdered sugar

1 tsp. vanilla

½ cup blanched almonds (approximately 3 oz. or 85 grams)

1 cup whole wheat flour (100 grams)

1 cup unbleached all-purpose flour (120 grams)

1 Tbs. baking powder

1 tsp. salt

2 Tbs. brown sugar (dark or light)

1 stick frozen butter (4 oz. or 115 grams)

¾ cup milk (1¾ dL) at room temperature

This recipe will give you 4 cups of rhubarb compote, twice as much as you need for the shortcake, but I can't bear the thought of not having some left over. Preheat the oven to 350°F/180°C. Have:

2 lbs. rhubarb (900 grams)

Trim off and discard any green leafy parts. I have been told that the leaves are poisonous. I haven't tried them. Wash the stalks, cut into ¾-inch (2-cm) lengths, and place in a 9 × 13 × 2-inch (23 × 33 × 5-cm) glass baking dish. Sprinkle over:

1 cup sugar (200 grams)

Cover tightly with foil. Bake for 20 minutes, remove, stir the contents, cover again, and return to the oven. Bake another 10 minutes or until the rhubarb is tender but not cooked to shreds. Uncover and allow to cool. You can do the baking two or three days ahead. Keep covered in the refrigerator.

THE STRAWBERRIES Have:

4 pints good, ripe strawberries

Prepare the berries the day of the dinner—I think they lose something if done a day ahead. Brush the berries or wipe with a slightly damp paper towel; hull. Set aside six attractive, medium-sized berries for decoration.

Pick out 1 pint of the worst berries, worst in terms of not being very ripe, for the sauce. Puree to a liquid in the food processor, then pour the puree into a small saucepan. Add:

¼ cup sugar (50 grams)

Bring just to a boil, stirring to dissolve the sugar. Taste and add more sugar if you like. Pour into a food processor:

1 cup rhubarb compote (¼ L), including some of its syrup

Add the warm strawberry puree, then process with just a few quick ons and offs until the rhubarb chunks are broken up. This is sauce for the strawberries. Refrigerate uncovered until chilled through.

Cut the remaining 3 pints berries into ³⁄₁₆-inch slices. Place in a bowl and sprinkle over:

4 Tbs. sugar (or more or less)

Stir well to coat the berries with sugar. Add:

1 cup rhubarb compote (¼ L)

Stir, then chill in the refrigerator. When both the sauce and the sliced berries plus rhubarb compote are chilled, mix everything in one large bowl. Keep covered in the refrigerator until serving time.

THE WHIPPED CREAM Have:

> 1 cup whipping cream (¼ L)

Beat until starting to thicken. Add:

> 2 Tbs. powdered sugar
> 1 tsp. vanilla

Continue to beat until almost stiff, but still slightly flowing. (You could beat until stiff and pipe the cream on at the end, using a pastry bag with a fancy tip, but cream beaten stiff is drier and doesn't taste as good to me. I prefer to spoon it on while still a tiny bit runny.) The cream can be done hours ahead or even the day before; refrigerate. If necessary to revive the fluffiness, beat again briefly at serving time.

THE BISCUIT DOUGH You can bake this a day ahead and reheat at serving time. It keeps well because of the amount of butter in the batter. Use an 8 × 8 × 2-inch (20 × 20 × 5-cm) baking pan. Butter the pan. Place a square of parchment or brown paper in the bottom. Butter the paper. Toast:

> ½ cup blanched almonds (approximately 3 oz.
>   or 85 grams)

by spreading them on a baking sheet and baking in a preheated 350°F/180°C oven for 5 to 7 minutes or until nicely browned. Chop the nuts into ⅜-inch (1-cm) pieces. Reserve.

Preheat the oven to 450°F/230°C for baking the dough. Into the container of a food processor put:

> 1 cup whole wheat flour (100 grams)
> 1 cup unbleached all-purpose flour (120 grams)
> 1 Tbs. baking powder
> 1 tsp. salt
> 2 Tbs. brown sugar (dark or light)

Process for a few seconds to mix the dry ingredients well. Add:

> 1 stick frozen butter (4 oz. or 115 grams), cut
>   into ½-inch (1½-cm) pieces

Process until the texture of coarse meal. Add:

> ¾ cup milk at room temperature (1¾ dL)

Process until the dough comes together. Scrape out onto a floured countertop. The dough will be wet and sticky. Sprinkle the chopped, toasted almonds over the dough and knead in very briefly, just until evenly distributed, using as little flour as necessary. Transfer the dough to the baking pan. Press with floured fingers to fill the pan and build the dough slightly higher around the pan edges so it will bake level. Cover the pan tightly with foil and bake 25 minutes in the preheated 450°F/230°C oven. Remove the foil and bake another 15 minutes. Let cool 10 minutes in the pan, then turn out on a rack to cool. Leave the parchment lining in place.

TO ASSEMBLE AND SERVE Have six 8-inch (20-cm) dessert plates. Preheat the oven to 350°F/180°C. Place the biscuit dough on its parchment square back into the baking pan. Cover with foil and heat for 20 minutes or until hot. Cut into squares. I cut nine squares and serve only six, but you may want to be more generous. Split each square as you would split a biscuit. Put the bottom halves on a serving plate. (If you wish, you can butter the biscuits.)

Mix the sliced berries in berry-rhubarb sauce well, then spoon over the bottom biscuits. Place the tops on and spoon the rest of the fruit mixture over, letting it spill and run onto the plate. Place a good blob of whipped cream on each top and garnish with one of the six whole strawberries reserved for decoration. Serve right away, while the biscuits are still hot and the fruit is still cold.

KIWI UPSIDE-DOWN CAKE

6 servings

This is a good, down-home kind of dessert. It is related to the Spiced Apple and Pear Cobbler elsewhere in this chapter, but this kiwi cake is much simpler and it is served upside down. To keep this preparation quick, the kiwis are not peeled, but simply sliced and placed in the dish. Another hurry-up feature is that the cake batter is completely assembled in the food processor. By the time the oven is preheated, the cake should be ready to bake. Well, almost.

The dessert consists of a square, butter-egg-cinnamon-ground-walnut cake with baking powder added to make it easy and quick. The cake is topped with overlapping slices of kiwi fruit and the whole thing is covered with a brown-sugar glaze. The tart kiwis with the sweet brown-sugar glaze make a wonderful combination, and the whole tart is brown and luscious and very much in the country style.

Kiwi fruit has a long season because the berries (they are known in some circles as Chinese gooseberries) keep for a long time in storage and because the seasons of the two major producing areas are staggered. The New Zealand batch arrives by boat in full force in June and the California crop appears in November. One of these days I hope both places will be producing enough so that the price of the dear little things will start to drop.

1 cup dark (or light) brown sugar

½ stick butter (2 oz. or 60 grams)

5 kiwi fruit, approximately 2 inches (5 cm) in diameter and 2¼ inches (5¾ cm) long, firm and barely ripe

3 eggs

1 cup cake flour (100 grams)

1½ tsp. baking powder

½ tsp. cinnamon

½ cup walnuts (2 oz. or 60 grams)

⅔ cup sugar (135 grams)

½ stick butter (2 oz. or 60 grams)

1 tsp. vanilla

½ cup milk (1 dL) chilled or room temperature

THE GLAZE AND THE KIWIS Preheat the oven to 350°F/180°C. Have an 8 × 8 × 2-inch (20 × 20 × 5-cm) glass baking dish. Into the dish put:

1 cup dark brown sugar (you can use light)

Pour over:

½ stick butter (2 oz. or 60 grams), melted and cooled a little

Stir with a fork until the butter and sugar are mixed. Spread in an even layer over the bottom of the dish. Set aside. Have:

5 kiwi fruit, approximately 2 inches (5 cm) in diameter and 2¼ inches (5¾ cm) long, firm and barely ripe

Wash the kiwis and rub with a scratch cloth or brush to get off some of the bristly hairs. Don't spend a lot of time doing this because the hairs will soften and become edible when cooked. You may peel the kiwis if you like, but I find that, after baking, the skin is edible and even adds a certain country charm to the cake.

From the ends of each kiwi, cut a slice that is mostly skin. When cutting the ends, you will notice that there is a hard core in the center of one end. Using the point of a small knife, remove this nib. Cut each kiwi across into five equal slices. Don't eat one because you will need all twenty-five slices. Place the slices in five rows of five in the bottom of the baking dish on top of the brown sugar and butter mixture. Arrange so that the slices and the rows overlap by ¼ inch (¾ cm) and the attractive sides face down. When done, the bottom of the dish should be completely covered. Set aside.

THE FOOD PROCESSOR CAKE In a bowl place:

3 eggs (still in their shells)

Fill the bowl with hot tap water and let sit to warm the eggs. Place in a sifter:

1 cup cake flour (100 grams)

1½ tsp. baking powder

½ tsp. cinnamon

Mix, then set aside. Into the container of a food processor fitted with the steel blade, put:

½ cup walnuts (2 oz. or 60 grams)

⅔ cup sugar (135 grams)

Process for 15 seconds or until the nuts are ground fine. Add:

½ stick butter (2 oz. or 60 grams), melted and cooled a little

Process for 30 seconds, then add the 3 warmed eggs (out of the shells, of course) and:

1 tsp. vanilla

Process for 1 minute. Add:

½ cup milk (1 dL) chilled or room temperature

Process for 2 seconds. Stir, then process for 2 seconds more. Sift in the flour mixture and process 2 seconds, stir, then process 2 seconds more. Pour the batter carefully over the kiwis in the baking dish. Don't worry if some of the batter goes under the kiwi slices. Place the baking dish in the upper third of the preheated 350°F/180°C oven. Bake for 40 to 45 minutes or until the cake is golden brown and firm to the touch. You might want to slip a baking sheet on the shelf underneath the cake after 25 minutes of baking time to catch any drippings. When done, cool on a rack for 5 minutes; cut around the outside edge of cake to make sure it is free, then invert onto a serving dish.

TO SERVE Serve warm or at room temperature, alone or with sour cream or vanilla ice cream on the side. This cake can be made a day ahead. To reheat before serving, use a microwave or cover with foil and place in a 350°F/180°C oven and bake for 25 minutes. Let sit 5 minutes before serving.

VIENNESE TORTE WITH CARROTS AND ALMONDS

This is an excitingly good cake—a torte, really, because it contains no flour. The layers of ground almonds and carrots are assembled with a carrot-lime buttercream and frosted with carrot-lime whipped cream. The cake is moist and creamy, with lots of nutty texture, a beautiful finish to a meal.

The cake layers are typically Viennese. The buttercream is a variation on a French theme. The whipped-cream frosting, of Viennese style, is similar to the chestnut whipped cream elsewhere in this book, with carrots and lime juice used instead of chestnuts and rum. The combination is mine. I think it is one of the best things in this book.

The cake layers are interesting. Notice the almost equal weights of the four main ingredients: eggs, sugar, nuts, and carrots. The formula is much like that of a pound cake, with almonds in place of butter and carrots in place of flour. The result is heavy, but very moist.

You can save work by making 1½ times the recipe for the carrot whipped cream and using it both as filling and frosting (eliminating the buttercream). You can save even more by buying two bakery sponge cake layers and assembling them with the carrot-lime filling and topping.

---

12 oz. unblanched or blanched almonds (340 grams), processed until texture of cornmeal
1½ Tbs. cornstarch
1½ tsp. chopped lime or lemon rind
5 or 6 medium carrots (12 oz. or 340 grams)
6 egg yolks
1 cup sugar (200 grams)
1 Tbs. rum
2 Tbs. lime or lemon juice
6 egg whites
½ cup sugar (100 grams)
1 lb. carrots (450 grams) (6 or 7 medium)
4 Tbs. water
3 Tbs. sugar

THE CAKE LAYERS These could be made two or three days ahead. Preheat the oven to 350°F/180°C.
Liberally butter three 9-inch (23-cm) round cake tins that have 1⅞-inch (5-cm)-high sides. Put parchment or brown paper circles in the bottoms and butter the papers. Shake flour all around in the tins, then dump and tap out the excess. Into a bowl mix:

12 oz. unblanched or blanched almonds (340 grams), processed until texture of cornmeal
1½ Tbs. cornstarch
1½ tsp. chopped lime or lemon rind

(The almonds, roughly 2⅓ cups before grinding, can be prepared in a food processor. To prepare the lime or lemon rind, remove sections of the peel with a vegetable peeler, then chop fine.) Add and fold in:

5 or 6 medium carrots (12 oz. or 340 grams), grated fine

Slice the carrots, unpeeled, into coarse chunks, then process using the steel blade until fairly fine. Reserve. Into a large bowl put:

6 egg yolks
1 cup sugar (200 grams)
1 Tbs. rum
2 Tbs. lime or lemon juice

1 stick butter (4 oz. or 115 grams) at room temperature

¾ cup sifted powdered sugar (75 grams)

1 egg yolk

2 Tbs. lime juice (you could use lemon)

⅓ cup grated, cooked carrot already prepared (50 grams)

1½ cups whipping cream (3½ dL)

1 cup powdered sugar (100 grams)

4 Tbs. lime juice (you could use lemon)

1½ cups grated, cooked carrot already prepared (200 grams)

1 cup whipping cream (¼ L)

2 Tbs. powdered sugar

Beat with an electric mixer for 2 or 3 minutes (I use a hand-held mixer) until fluffy, pale, and forming a ribbon. (This means you can trace a circle on top of the mixture with the batter that falls from the beaters and the circle will remain for at least 3 seconds.) Add the carrot-almond mixture and stir together well. In another bowl beat:

6 egg whites at room temperature

to soft peaks. Sprinkle in, continuing to beat:

½ cup sugar (100 grams)

Add a tablespoon at a time, but keep adding almost without interruption. Beat to stiff peaks, which won't take long after the last sugar is in. Fold the whites into the batter, first folding in one-third of the whites to lighten the mixture. Give the remaining whites a final short beat to make creamy again before folding in. Pour equal portions of the batter into the three prepared pans and level. Bake in a preheated 350°F/180°C oven for 35 to 40 minutes or until the tops are nicely browned and the cakes feel firm. (If your finger disappears into the center of the cake and comes out wet, the cake is not done.) Remove the cakes from the oven and cool 5 minutes on a rack. Free from the sides of the pan if necessary, then unmold onto racks. Peel off the papers and turn the cakes over so that the original tops are up. Let cool. These cakes stay moist a long time if kept in plastic bags in the refrigerator.

You may assemble the cake a day ahead and finish except for the piped whipped-cream decorations.

CARROTS FOR BUTTERCREAM, WHIPPED CREAM, AND GARNISH Buy:

1 lb. carrots (450 grams) (6 or 7 medium)

Scrape or peel and cut off the ends. Select one or two medium-size or smaller carrots to use for garnish and keep them whole. Cut any really fat carrots in half in both directions; otherwise, leave all whole.

Cook the carrots in a pot of boiling water for 7 to 8 minutes or until just barely starting to get tender. Test with a fork. Drain and run under cold water to stop the cooking. Cut nine diagonal pieces about ½ inch (1½ cm) thick from the carrots earmarked for garnish. Make a quick sugar syrup.

Place in a small saucepan:
>   4 Tbs. water
>   3 Tbs. sugar

Bring to a boil, stirring occasionally to dissolve sugar. Let cool. Place the nine diagonally cut carrot pieces in the cooled syrup. Reserve in the refrigerator. Cut the rest of the carrots into ½-inch (1½-cm) pieces and process in the food processor until grated. The carrots should not be pureed to mush but should stay in somewhat firm, grated pieces. Reserve.

CARROT-LIME BUTTERCREAM This stuff is divine. You can use it as a filling and frosting for a typically French *gâteau*. It would also make a much more interesting frosting for the ubiquitous American-style carrot cake than that awful, sickeningly sweet cream cheese stuff everybody uses. Into a bowl put:

>   1 stick butter (4 oz. or 115 grams) at room
>   temperature

Beat, warming very carefully if necessary (do not let the butter melt), until fluffy or *en pommade*, as they say *en français*. This means to beat to the consistency of Vaseline, but the expression loses something in translation. Add all at once:

>   ¾ cup sifted powdered sugar (75 grams)
>   1 egg yolk
>   2 Tbs. lime juice (you could use lemon)

Stir in the sugar and the yolk and the lime, then beat 1 or 2 minutes or until fluffy. Stir in:

>   ⅓ cup grated, cooked carrot already prepared
>   (50 grams)

Reserve.

CARROT-LIME WHIPPED CREAM Beat:

>   1½ cups whipping cream (3½ dL)

until starting to thicken. Add:

>   1 cup sifted powdered sugar (100 grams)
>   4 Tbs. lime juice (you could use lemon)

Continue to beat until stiff. Fold in:

>   1½ cups grated, cooked carrot already prepared
>   (200 grams)

Refrigerate, covered with plastic.

TO ASSEMBLE THE CAKE Trim the cake layers if necessary so that they are even. Place one layer on an attractive serving dish. Spread half the carrot-lime buttercream on top. Add the second cake layer, spread over the balance of the buttercream, then add the third cake layer. Frost the top and sides with an even, smooth layer of the carrot-lime whipped cream. Film the cake with plastic wrap, with the plastic in contact with the cream on the top and sides of the cake. The cream must be kept from contact with the air. The plastic will peel off easily when you are ready to add the final decorations.

THE FINAL DECORATION You may finish the cake 3 or 4 hours before serving. Longer ahead than that, and the whipped cream frosting and decorations will pick up a funny flavor from the refrigerator. Beat:

　　1 cup whipping cream (¼ L)
until starting to thicken. Add:

　　2 Tbs. powdered sugar
(I don't use vanilla in this because it darkens the cream.) Beat until stiff. Place in a pastry bag fitted with a decorative tip. Make eight swirling rosettes, evenly spaced around the outside top edge of the cake, and one in the center. Make some rays emanating from the center, each heading toward one of the outside swirls. Make a series of rosettes or another border around the bottom edge of the cake.

　　Into each of the rosettes place one of the reserved carrot pieces with a point sticking up in the air. Refrigerate. Bring out 1 or 2 hours before serving. I think the cake is better served at room temperature or just slightly chilled.

CHESTNUT TORTE WITH CHOCOLATE AND CHESTNUT CREAMS

This is a light, cold, moist, delicious cake dessert. It is essentially Viennese but also has a little help from France and just a touch of San Francisco. There is no wheat in it. Chestnut flour is used instead.

*　　The best way to make chestnut flour is to peel, cook, and sieve your own chestnuts (see Chestnut Puree elsewhere in this book for an amazingly fast method). Or, to save time, use canned chestnuts, which are almost as good.*

500 grams (about 17 oz.) chestnuts or buy 2 10-oz. (285 grams) tins of water-packed whole chestnuts (not the kind preserved in syrup)

6 egg whites at room temperature

⅔ cup sugar (140 grams)

3 cups chestnut flour (300 grams)

4 oz. semisweet chocolate (115 grams)

1 cup heavy cream (¼ L)

2 Tbs. powdered sugar

½ cup heavy cream (1 dL)

3 Tbs. powdered sugar

100 grams (1 cup) chestnut flour

1 Tbs. rum

4 oz. good apricot jam (115 grams)

100 grams chestnut flour (1 cup)

2 oz. semisweet chocolate (60 grams), melted over hot water with 2 Tbs. butter

3 Tbs. powdered sugar

2 tsp. rum (dark preferred)

½ cup heavy cream (1 dL)

1 Tbs. powdered sugar

THE CHESTNUTS You will need a total of:

500 grams (about 17 oz.) chestnuts or buy 2 10-oz. (285 grams) tins of water-packed whole chestnuts (not the kind preserved in syrup)

Drain, rinse, and dry the chestnuts very well. You are going to turn them into flour, so they must be as dry as possible. Rub the chestnuts through a sieve by hand (not too fine a sieve or this takes forever). They are very soft and will go right through. At the end, scrape off the underside of the sieve with a knife and do not smear or push once the chestnuts go through or they will cake. Let fall lightly into a bowl. (You could use a food mill or ricer to do this.) *Note:* I measure the amounts needed later by weighing, but you can use cup measures if you are careful not to pack the chestnut flour down—keep it light and loose.

THE TORTE This is an egg-white chestnut torte that contains no egg yolks or butter. It is very light, which contributes to the lightness of the finished dessert. Preheat the oven to 325°F/165°C. Use a cake tin 9 inches (23 cm) in diameter but with sides that are 1¾ inches (4½ cm) high, which is higher than the traditional cake tin. You also can bake the cake in an 8- or 9-inch (20- or 23-cm) springform or in two regular (lower-sided) 8- or 9-inch tins. (If you decide to bake in two pans, cut 10 minutes or so from the baking time.) Butter the cake tin(s) liberally, then put a parchment or foil circle in the bottom and butter it. Flour the tin and knock out the excess thoroughly. Into a mixing bowl put:

6 egg whites at room temperature

Beat to soft peaks, then sprinkle over and beat in, a tablespoon at a time:

⅓ cup sugar (70 grams)

Beat to stiff peaks. If you are using a Kitchen Aid electric mixer, do not go above speed 6 and do not take too long to add the sugar or you can overbeat the whites. If you overbeat and they lose their creamy texture, add a fresh egg white and beat in gently with a wire whisk. Sprinkle over the whites all at once:

⅓ cup sugar (70 grams)

Cut in or fold in the sugar five or six strokes, then fold in:

300 grams (3 cups) chestnut flour just prepared in two additions. Do not fold thoroughly until the

second addition. Proper folding is critical to the success of this or any cake. Use a rubber spatula and cut down into the center of the batter. Go along the bottom of the bowl and cut up the side and come out of the batter, twisting in such a way that you flop the batter over onto itself a little. Then turn the bowl about one-third turn after each stroke so that the next fold is from a new position. This should be done quickly.

When folding is complete, dump the batter into the prepared cake tin. It is going to fill the pan to the very top, but do not be alarmed. This cake rises very little. The batter will be thick and firm like meringue. Carefully press it into the pan to eliminate any air holes. Level and smooth off the top. Place the cake tin on a baking sheet (to deflect some of the heat from the sides), then put in the upper third of a preheated 325°F/165°C oven. Bake for 50 minutes or until the top is nicely browned. The cake will shrink from the sides after about 30 minutes, but do not mistake that for its being done. It must bake further until done in the center. (Actually, this cake is good underbaked, so don't worry.) In 45 or 50 minutes, if it is pretty and brown, take it out and call it done. Let cool 5 minutes in the tin, then unmold onto a rack. Peel off the paper and turn the cake over onto another rack so that the original top is up. Let cool. The cake shrinks quite a bit. Don't be discouraged. It ends up only about ¾ inch (slightly under 2 cm) high. Place in a plastic bag and let rest overnight at room temperature.

THE CHOCOLATE CREAM Shred with a knife:

4 oz. semisweet chocolate (115 grams)

Place in a bowl and melt the chocolate over hot (not boiling) water, stirring occasionally. In a small bowl beat:

1 cup heavy cream (¼ L)

When the cream starts to thicken, add:

2 Tbs. powdered sugar

Beat until stiff. (Be careful not to overbeat, but if you do, stir in 2 to 3 tablespoons of fresh cream.) At this point the chocolate must still be warm or the shock of adding the chilled cream can cause a chocolate chip effect (actually, not all that great a disaster). So if the chocolate has cooled off, warm again over hot water. Dump in half the whipped cream and stir the chocolate and cream together in a kind of frantic, circular motion, scraping the bottom of the bowl all over to get the chocolate mixed in smooth before chips can form. When the mixture is a smooth brown color, add the rest of the cream and calmly fold or stir in until incorporated. Set this aside, but do not refrigerate or it will set. On a cool day, if it sets anyway, whisk gently over warm water until smooth again.

THE CHESTNUT CREAM Beat:

> ½ cup heavy cream (1 dL)

until starting to thicken. Add:

> 3 Tbs. powdered sugar

Continue to beat until medium stiff. Stir in:

> 100 grams (1 cup) chestnut flour already prepared
>
> 1 Tbs. rum (dark preferred)

Stir or beat until everything is incorporated. Taste. Isn't it wonderful? Add more rum if you like.

TO ASSEMBLE THE CAKE Heat and strain:

> 4 oz. good apricot jam (115 grams)

Cut the chestnut torte into two layers. Place the bottom layer on a cake cardboard or use the metal bottom of a springform or quiche tin. Brush the cake layer with the hot, strained jam. Over this spread slightly more than half the chocolate cream. Smooth into a thick, even layer. Add the second cake layer, then place all the chestnut cream over it; spread into a thick, even layer. Smooth the sides and top and make everything neat. Place the unwrapped cake in the freezer for 10 minutes, just to set the creams. Bring out, then ice the top and sides with the remaining chocolate cream. Return to the freezer for 10 minutes. Remove and wrap well in two layers of plastic wrap. The cake may be kept frozen for a week or longer.

CHOCOLATE RUM CHESTNUTS These are a little option for decoration. Into a small bowl put:

> 100 grams (1 cup) chestnut flour already prepared
>
> 2 oz. semisweet chocolate (60 grams), melted over hot water with 2 Tbs. butter
>
> 3 Tbs. powdered sugar

2 tsp. rum (dark preferred)

Stir with a rubber spatula until smooth. Give the mixture a 2-minute shot in the freezer to firm it enough to work with. Make eleven balls approximately ⅞ inch (2 cm) in diameter by pinching and working bits of the mixture and rolling into balls between your palms. They don't have to be perfect. Take each ball and flatten the bottom a little, then pinch the top with the thumb and index finger of one hand and the thumb and index finger of the other hand. Make a pinch-bottle shape, narrower at the top, to resemble the shape of a chestnut. You can make yours even more realistic if you're artistic. Chill. These can be made a week or so ahead and kept refrigerated in plastic. THE FINAL DECORATION Five or 6 hours before the cake is to be served, whip:

½ cup heavy cream (1 dL)

until starting to thicken. Add:

1 Tbs. powdered sugar

Continue beating until stiff. Remove the cake from the freezer and place on an attractive serving dish. Place the whipped cream in a pastry bag fitted with a decorative tip (I use Ateco 4-B). Make a small, attractive border around the base of the cake and ten evenly spaced, rather large rosettes around the top near the edge and one in the center. Place one chocolate-rum chestnut in each of the eleven whipped-cream rosettes. Before you begin, practice making a rosette on a table top and set a chestnut in it to get an idea of how large to make the rosettes. The dark chocolate "chestnuts" against the white rosettes against the chocolate-cream icing makes a very attractive finish to the cake. Refrigerate until serving time. Serve chilled.

CHOCOLATE WHIPPED-CREAM TRUFFLE CAKE

This cake is perhaps the most exciting creation in this book. It is actually more a dessert than a cake. Meltingly delicious, it works perfectly after any meal, at least as far as chocolate lovers are concerned, and there are a lot of us around. If you serve this cake at a dinner party, I guarantee it will be a smash.

This is a great, high cake consisting of six American-style chocolate cake layers with three whipped-cream and two chocolate-truffle fillings, all iced with sweetened whipped cream and decorated with a light scraping of semisweet chocolate. Because the decoration is fairly plain, I like to serve this cake with fresh flowers placed on the plate around the base of the cake.

The cake itself is the traditional devil's food that you will find in a thousand American cookbooks, but the amount of butter in the recipe has been doubled. At first, this extra shortening caused the cake to fall as it baked. Finally, twenty frustrating batches later, I found that, if small amounts of batter are baked in three cake tins instead of only one or two, the layers hold up well.

Start this dessert at least two or three days ahead. Bake the layers one day and let them sit overnight, then assemble the cake. Let the cake rest a third, even a fourth day. It seems to get better. If you like, bake the layers weeks ahead and freeze them.

1⅓ cups cake flour (130 grams)
1 tsp. baking soda
¼ tsp. salt
1 stick butter (4 oz. or 115 grams) at room temperature
1⅓ cups sugar (270 grams)
2 eggs at room temperature
3 oz. unsweetened baking chocolate (85 grams), melted and cooled
⅔ cup milk at room temperature (1½ dL)
1 tsp. vanilla
6 oz. semisweet chocolate (180 grams), chopped

THE CAKE LAYERS These are simple and quick and can be done 100 percent in the food processor. Butter three 8-inch (20-cm) cake tins. Place a paper circle in the bottom of each tin, then butter the paper. Flour the tins, shaking out the excess. Preheat the oven to 350°F/180°C. Mix together in a sifter:

> 1⅓ cups cake flour (130 grams)
> 1 tsp. baking soda
> ¼ tsp. salt

Set aside.

Into the container of a food processor fitted with the steel blade put:

> 1 stick butter (4 oz. or 115 grams) at room temperature
> 1⅓ cups sugar (270 grams)

Process for 1 or 2 minutes, stirring once or twice if necessary. Keep an eye on this. You do not want the butter to melt. I was making this cake in Baton Rouge one very warm evening, and because of the heat of the room, the butter was awfully soft, practically melted, before it went in. You could see

½ stick butter (2 oz. or 60 grams), cut into pieces

½ cup whipping cream (1 dL)

¼ cup sugar (50 grams)

2 cups chilled whipping cream (½ L)

4 Tbs. powdered sugar (sift if lumpy)

2 tsp. vanilla

⅓ to ½ cup crème de cacao (¾ to 1 dL) (white preferred) (optional)

3 Tbs. cold water

1½ tsp. plain gelatin

1 cup whipping cream (¼ L)

2 Tbs. powdered sugar

1 tsp. vanilla (optional)

Semisweet chocolate

Powdered sugar

the mixture collapse in the food processor as I worked it. The cake still turned out all right, but it was a little strange. Add:

    2 eggs at room temperature

Process for 2 or 3 seconds, then stir and process for 2 seconds more. Add:

    3 oz. unsweetened baking chocolate (85 grams), melted and cooled

Process for 2 seconds; stir, then process for 2 seconds more. Add:

    ⅔ cup milk at room temperature (1½ dL)

    1 tsp. vanilla

Process for 2 seconds. The mixture will be very runny now. Sift in all the prepared flour-soda-salt mixture. Process 2 seconds; stir, then process 2 seconds more.

Divide the batter equally into the three prepared tins and tilt to make as level as possible. You will not have much batter, only about ½ inch (1½ cm) per tin. While you are tilting, let the cake batter run up the sides of the tins ¼ inch (¾ cm) all around. This is *supposed* to help cakes bake level, but for this cake I'm not sure it works.

Put the tins on baking sheets (to help bake evenly; this is optional) and place in the preheated 350°F/180°C oven. Bake 25 minutes or until the cakes shrink from the sides and feel done to the touch. Do not open the oven until the 25 minutes are up. There is an exception to this rule: If smoke is pouring out of the oven, open it. In general, chocolate cakes light in flour and eggs and high in fats and liquids are delicate and can fall if they get a cold draft before completely set.

Let the cakes in their tins cool 10 minutes on racks, then unmold and let them finish cooling on the racks. The layers will be about ¾ inch (2 cm) high each. Don't worry if they are a little lopsided. You will correct this when assembling the cake. Once the layers are completely cool, put them in plastic bags and let sit out in the room overnight. Then either assemble them or freeze.

TO PREPARE THE CAKE LAYERS FOR ASSEMBLY On the day you assemble the cake, start by cutting the cake layers. This should be done before the cream and the chocolate fillings are prepared because both set firm and are difficult to spread if they sit very long. Carefully cut each layer in half to make two thinner layers of the same size. You will have six layers in all, each approximately ⅜ inch (1 cm) thick.

Here is how to make sure the layers fit together to make a level cake. Using the removable bottom from a quiche pan for moving the layers around, pile them one on top of the other, rotating each as you put it on, so you end with a more or less level cake. Make a V-shaped ¼-inch (¾-cm) notch down the side so you can remember how the layers fit together. Spread the layers out again, with the notches all facing you, and proceed with the fillings.

THE CHOCOLATE TRUFFLE FILLING This is what the French call a *ganache*. A *ganache* is a mixture of chocolate, butter, and heavy cream. You will encounter it most frequently inside French chocolates such as truffles, a popular candy rolled in cocoa powder. Incidentally, this filling gives the cake its name.

Into a saucepan put:

6 oz. semisweet chocolate (180 grams), chopped
½ stick butter (2 oz. or 60 grams), cut into pieces
½ cup whipping cream (1 dL)
¼ cup sugar (50 grams)

Heat, stirring, until everything is melted and the mixture is shiny and smooth. Do not overheat. Transfer to a bowl, preferably metal so the mixture can be stirred later over ice water to cool it faster. *Ganache* is the consistency of sauce when warm, but it sets firm when cooled. When ready to assemble the cake, stir the filling over ice water until it is no longer runny and just nicely spreadable. Set aside for the moment.

THE WHIPPED-CREAM FILLING Into a bowl put:

2 cups chilled whipping cream (½ L)

Beat until starting to thicken. Add:

4 Tbs. powdered sugar (sift if lumpy)
2 tsp. vanilla
⅓ to ½ cup crème de cacao (¾ to 1 dL) (white preferred) (optional)

(You can substitute Grand Marnier, but use less; try 3 or 4 tablespoons. I like the crème de cacao better.) Continue beating until stiff, but do not overbeat. Set aside for 10 minutes in the room so that it loses its extreme chill. Soon you are going to fold in some gelatin, which will set instantly if the cream is too cold. Into a tiny saucepan or metal measuring cup put:

3 Tbs. cold water

Sprinkle over:

1½ tsp. plain gelatin

Let soften for 1 minute, then heat almost to boiling, stirring now and then until the gelatin is more or less dissolved. Let cool for 2 or 3 minutes. Add the still-warm gelatin in a stream to the cream, whisking in circles to mix quickly before the gelatin has a chance to set. Assemble the cake right away.

TO ASSEMBLE THE CAKE Stir the *ganache* over ice water until it is spreadable, the consistency of peanut butter. If lumpy, beat with a whisk. Set aside. Build the cake on the removable bottom from a quiche tin. Place one cake layer on the metal disk. Spread on evenly one-third of the whipped-cream filling. Add another layer of cake, matching the notches to make it level. On this layer spread half of the chocolate filling. Continue building the cake, lining up the notches and alternating the cream and chocolate fillings. Add the top layer, which will not be coated at this time. You will have six cake layers and five layers of filling.

Refrigerate the cake for 2 or 3 hours or until it is chilled thoroughly and the fillings have set, then wrap in plastic. This cake keeps well three days or even longer. It also freezes very well at this point.

TO DECORATE AND SERVE Three or 4 hours before serving, whip:

1 cup whipping cream (¼ L)

until starting to thicken. Add:

2 Tbs. powdered sugar

Beat until stiff enough to spread well, but don't overbeat or you will dry out the cream and it will not spread to a smooth finish. I don't add vanilla because it ruins the beautiful color of the cream, but you could add:

1 tsp. vanilla (optional)

if the color doesn't bother you.

The next instruction may seem a little strange, but there is a problem in slicing this cake. To get perfectly clean slices with no chocolate cake crumbs

marring the whipped-cream filling, you must cut
this cake sideways. Therefore, before you frost the
cake, you cut it in half. (To understand better, read
about the final slicing of the cake below.) Place the
firm, set cake on its side and, using a sharp knife,
cut the cake vertically into two equal halves.
Reassemble the cake on an attractive serving dish,
then ice the top and sides with the whipped cream.
On the top only, in the center, add a scraping of:

    Semisweet chocolate

I prepare this with a vegetable peeler. If you like,
over the chocolate scrapings sprinkle:

    Powdered sugar (through a very fine strainer)

Reserve in the refrigerator until serving time. Bring
out a half hour before serving so that it is not quite
so cold. If you like, place fresh flowers on the cake
plate around the base of the cake. Serve.

TO SLICE After you have presented the cake and
everyone has had a chance to ''ooh'' and ''aah,''
take it out to the kitchen to slice. Lift up one of the
cake halves and place it on a clean chopping board,
turning it so that the cut side is down. All the
chocolate scrapings fall off, but *c'est la vie, n'est-ce
pas?* Slice the cake to the desired thickness (½ to ¾
inch?), cutting down toward the board. The slices
will vary in size, but they will be clean, perfect, and
beautiful. Serve the larger center slices to the big
eaters. Don't eat the flowers.

MARIE SUMMERS'S COFFEE-CRUNCH CAKE

8 to 12 servings

*This is a truly great dessert cake with a breathtakingly spectacular appearance. Known to
some people as the Fiesta Cake, it has been around San Francisco for a long time; the now
defunct Blum's shops featured it for years. The cake is a yellow angel food split and filled
with a flavored whipped cream and decorated with a crunchy coffee-caramel candy. The
concoction is sweet, moist, light, and divine. I have not found a good version of this cake
sold anywhere in the San Francisco Bay area, and the recipe is not in any book that I am
aware of.*

Marie Summers is a friend who, with her husband, Bill, runs Chef's Enterprises, an excellent cookware and restaurant-supply house in Redwood City, California. Marie had this recipe from the old days and gave it to me because she's a nice lady.

1¼ cups sifted cake flour (125 grams)

1½ cups sugar (300 grams)

6 egg yolks

¼ cup cold water (½ dL)

Grated zest of 1 lemon

1 Tbs. lemon juice

1 tsp. vanilla

1 tsp. salt

1 cup egg whites (7 or 8), with absolutely no yolk

1 tsp. cream of tartar (optional; I never use it)

1½ cups sugar (300 grams)

¼ cup strong coffee (½ dL) (not instant)

¼ cup light corn syrup (½ dL)

1 Tbs. baking soda (sifted to remove lumps)

4 cups whipping cream (1 L)

2 tsp. vanilla

2 tsp. instant coffee powder

THE CAKE Preheat the oven to 350°F/180°C. You will need a removable-bottom angel food (center tube) tin with a diameter of 10 inches (25 cm) at the top and with sides approximately 4⅜ inches (11 cm) high. Do not grease. Later, when you turn the baked cake upside down to "hang" while it cools, it is critical that the cake stick to the tin and not fall out. (You hang it on a bottle. Find a bottle with a neck that fits in the hole of the tin's center tube. My favorite is a Grand Marnier bottle, but a Coke bottle will also fit.) I drape a wet paper towel over the bottle, which helps anchor the cake tin and keeps it from tilting.

Sift together in the bowl of an electric mixer:
  1¼ cups sifted cake flour (125 grams)
  ¾ cup sugar (150 grams)
Make a well in the flour-sugar mixture and put in it:
  6 egg yolks
  ¼ cup cold water (½ dL)
  Grated zest of 1 lemon
  1 Tbs. lemon juice
  1 tsp. vanilla
  1 tsp. salt
Mix, then beat to the ribbon stage. I use a Kitchen Aid mixer with the balloon whip and set the speed at low/moderate (speed 4 out of 10 positions). Beating will take 8 to 10 minutes. Do not overbeat and don't let the mixture sit. Keep moving along. Transfer the batter to a large bowl, wash the mixer bowl well and dry, then put in it:
  1 cup egg whites (7 or 8), with absolutely no yolk
  1 tsp. cream of tartar (optional; I never use it)
Using the balloon whip at low/moderate speed, beat to soft peaks. Sprinkle in, 1 tablespoon at a time:
  ¾ cup sugar (150 grams)
Continue beating to stiff peaks. It is important that the whites be beaten to the proper stiffness, but it

is perhaps more important not to overbeat to where they look dry. In other words, be watchful. Fold one-third of the whites into the yolk mixture, then fold in the balance. This is one of the most beautiful things in the world to fold, and this moment is surely one of the greatest pleasures in all cake making.

Tear yourself away from it and pour the batter into the tube pan. With a thin knife, cut through the batter with a quick spiral motion to break any air bubbles, then level the cake with a rubber spatula.

Bake in the preheated 350°F/180°C oven 45 to 50 minutes or until a cake tester comes out clean. (The cake should rise an inch or two above the rim. Sometimes it cracks and develops furrows—that's OK.) Turn the bottle for "hanging" the pan upside down and poke it into the hole in the center tube. Invert the pan and the bottle; let the cake cool while suspended. The cake is supposed to stick to the pan, remember? Isn't it great for once to bake a cake that *should* stick to the pan?

When the cake is cool, carefully cut around the sides and the center tube of the pan. Remove the cake, then cut it away from the removable bottom. Wrap and freeze until the day it is to be served.

THE COFFEE CRUNCH I like to use a heavy 4½-quart (4-L) saucepan, although a smaller one will do. You also need a jelly-roll pan or some other type of baking sheet with sides; grease very lightly with oil. Put into the saucepan:

    1½ cups sugar (300 grams)
    ¼ cup strong coffee (½ dL) (not instant)
    ¼ cup light corn syrup (½ dL)

Bring to a boil slowly, stirring now and then to help the sugar dissolve. After the boil has been reached and the sugar has dissolved, don't stir anymore. Turn the heat to high and boil until the mixture reaches 290°F/145°C on a candy thermometer or the hard-crack stage. This means that a little ball of syrup dropped into a cup of cold water and then removed will crack when you bite on it and won't stick to your teeth. If you're using a candy thermometer, you may have to put on oven mitts and tilt the pan to get a reading. Remove from the heat and let the boiling subside for just a few seconds, then add:

1 Tbs. baking soda (sifted to remove lumps)
Stir quickly with a wire whisk, just long enough for the soda to be mixed in. Don't beat so hard that you get rid of all the air bubbles, which you want. Dump the caramel onto the oiled jelly-roll pan. It will start to swell like a weird blob. Don't attempt to spread it out, just let it swell into one great lump. It will shrink later. When cool, in approximately ½ hour, remove from the pan. Crack into three or four pieces and right away put in a plastic bag or it will get sticky. The coffee crunch keeps well for many weeks if wrapped airtight.

TO ASSEMBLE THE CAKE You can assemble this cake in mid-afternoon to be eaten at nine or ten o'clock that evening, but you must save most of the exterior crunch to add just before serving. If you put it on sooner, it weeps and dissolves and there will be no crunch left by the time you eat the cake.

Slice the cake into three layers using a saw-bladed (serrated) knife. Whip:

4 cups whipping cream (1 L)
until very stiff, but not so stiff as for piping with a pastry bag. (You can use 3 cups [¾ L], but the cake won't be so fabulous.) Fold in:

2 tsp. vanilla
Sprinkle over:

2 tsp. instant coffee powder
Fold in well. Crack the crunch, saving some rather large, quarter-size pieces to cover the top of the cake. Crush the rest into a combination of fine and ¼-inch (¾-cm) coarse crumbs.

Place the bottom (largest) layer on an attractive cake plate. Spread with whipped cream in a generous layer about ½ inch (1½ cm) thick. Sprinkle with some of the crunch crumbs. Add the second cake layer, then repeat the cream and crunch crumbs. Place the top layer on. Cover the top and sides with the remaining cream. Sprinkle some crunch over the top and sides to melt and to flavor the cream, but save most of it to be added at the last minute. Refrigerate uncovered until serving time.

TO FINISH AND SERVE Just before serving, place crunch all over the outside of the cake, using the largest pieces on the top. It looks nice to put a little bouquet of flowers in a glass placed in the center hole. Serve.

Use a saw-bladed knife to cut the cake and serve great big pieces, in spite of all the gasps and protests. The cake is so light and airy and delicious that everyone will eat every bite.

PASTRY DESSERTS FOR BUFFETS

Chocolate Squares with Chocolate Cream

"Le Gorri" Raspberry Slices

Tangerine Cheesecake Squares

Pecan Spice Cake Squares

This section contains some beautiful little desserts I have saved for the very end. Buffets need desserts, just as a good dinner does, but if you must, you can get away with a bowl of truly fine fruits, or some figs, dates, and dried apple slices, depending upon the season. It is always nice and takes no work to put out a dish of good-quality, European-style chocolates. However, if you want to make your buffet truly special, if you are not afraid of making cakes, and if you have a little bit of time, here are four tiny treasures that will add real excitement to any buffet table, particularly around the winter holidays. Present one of them, or two, or all four if you really like to work. They can all be done almost completely ahead and frozen.

If your time is limited and you love chocolate, you will be happy to learn that the easiest of the little cakes is the Chocolate Squares with Chocolate Cream. Next in order of difficulty is probably the Pecan Squares, if you leave off the glazed pecan decorations. Without question, the "Le Gorri" Raspberry Slices are the most complex and time-consuming to make. You know already, don't you, life being the way it is, that they are the best-tasting of the lot? It is really difficult, however, to say which one tastes the best because each of these little squares is a gem.

CHOCOLATE SQUARES WITH CHOCOLATE CREAM

Makes 25 squares

That chocolate desserts are terribly well liked is a grand understatement. Grown men and women behave like children when you serve them anything chocolate. I must confess that I too have an awful time confining myself to just one serving of anything that's chocolate.

These chocolate squares are really elegant brownies. They are spread with smooth chocolate whipped cream and finished with a lovely white whipped-cream rosette. They are terribly good, so if you would like to allow more than one per person, you might want to double the recipe. To do this, simply do two times everything and bake it in two separate tins.

To create the brownie base, I started with the recipe printed on the chocolate box and made a few changes. I rounded out the butter to one stick, and eliminated the salt and baking powder. Then I changed the chopped nuts (presumably walnuts or pecans) to ground almonds. The batter is cooked 10 minutes longer so that the brownies are cakey rather than fudgey. And the whole thing is prepared in the food processor.

For that reason, it is impossible to mess up this recipe. Yes, impossible. Everything is dumped into the machine. If you can read and if you have learned how to turn the thing on and off, you just can't miss. You don't have to melt the chocolate. You can use frozen butter right out of the freezer. The eggs can be added chilled. There is no folding. You can even forget to preheat the oven and let the batter wait in the pan until the oven is hot.

There is only one way to fail with this recipe and I almost did it. I prepared the batter and dumped it out of the food processor into the baking pan, thinking how strangely thin it was. I put it into the oven and turned around to clean up. Then I saw the flour and ground nuts still sitting on their little sheet of waxed paper. I zipped the pan out of the oven, folded the flour and nuts in, and rushed everything back into the oven. In spite of this, it turned out fine.

½ cup blanched or unblanched almonds (2 oz. or 60 grams)
⅔ cup flour (80 grams)
2 oz. baking chocolate (60 grams), cut into pieces
1 cup sugar (200 grams)
1 stick butter (4 oz. or 115 grams)
1 Tbs. rum
1 tsp. vanilla
2 eggs
3 oz. semisweet chocolate (85 grams)
1 cup whipping cream (1¾ dL)
2 Tbs. powdered sugar
½ cup whipping cream (1 dL) plus the remaining ¼ cup (½ dL) from the recipe
1½ Tbs. powdered sugar (optional)

THE BROWNIES Preheat the oven to 350°F/180°C. Butter an 8- or 9-inch (20- or 23-cm) square baking pan. Put a square of parchment or brown paper in the bottom, then butter the paper. Into the container of a food processor fitted with the steel blade put:

> ½ cup blanched or unblanched almonds (2 oz. or 60 grams)
> ⅔ cup flour (80 grams)

Process for 1 or 2 minutes or until the nuts are ground fairly fine. Dump out on a sheet of waxed paper. Reserve. Into the food processor put:

> 2 oz. baking chocolate (60 grams), cut into pieces
> 1 cup sugar (200 grams)

Process 1 or 2 minutes or until the chocolate is fairly well chopped up. Add:

> 1 stick butter (4 oz. or 115 grams), cut into ½-inch (1½-cm) pieces (you can use cold or frozen butter)

Process for about 1 minutes or until the mixture comes together as dough. Add:

> 1 Tbs. rum (or water or milk)
> 1 tsp. vanilla

Process until the liquids are absorbed and the batter makes a ball that goes round and round. You may have to stop and stir. Add:

> 1 egg

Process 10 seconds, then add:

> Another egg

Process 10 seconds. Add the ground nuts with flour and process 1 or 2 seconds. Stir to help mix, and process for 1 second more. Dump the batter into a prepared baking pan. Level with a spatula.

Bake in a preheated 350°F/180°C oven for 35 minutes. Let cool completely in the pan on a rack. Loosen around the edge with a knife, then unmold the brownie square in one piece. Hold your hand under to catch it while banging the edge of the pan against the countertop. Peel off the paper, then turn the baking pan upside down and place the brownie on the pan bottom. Trim off the edges of the cake so that it is approximately level on top. Rip off a 3-foot-long (90-cm) strip of waxed paper; fold lengthwise in half and in half again to make a 3-inch-wide (8-cm) band. Wrap all around the cake (fit as a stand-up collar to hold the chocolate whipped cream) and fasten with tape. Set aside.

THE CHOCOLATE WHIPPED CREAM Have:

3 oz. semisweet chocolate (85 grams)

Cut the chocolate into smaller pieces and put in a pan to melt. You can do this over hot (not boiling) water in a double boiler or, if you are extremely careful, directly over low heat. Be careful—chocolate turns grainy if it gets too hot. Stir until melted and smooth, then remove from the heat and let cool a little. If the chocolate is too hot, it will melt the cream that is to be added, but it should still be warm. Beat:

¾ cup whipping cream (1¾ dL)

(You will use the remaining ¼ cup at the end.) Beat until starting to set. Add:

2 Tbs. powdered sugar

Beat until stiff, but do not overbeat. Don't take it as far as you would for piping out of a pastry bag. (The cream gets dry and doesn't taste as nice.) The cream, however, must be fairly stiff or the dessert will not cut well. Use an electric mixer, but as soon as the cream is set, switch to a wire whisk so you finish a little slower.

Dump the whipped cream all at once on top of the warm chocolate. Beat frantically into the chocolate, taking the wire whisk round and round and in all directions so that you blend the chocolate into the cream before it has time to set. You should get a smooth brown cream. Whatever you get, dump it on top of the brownie layer inside the waxed-paper collar. Spread with a spatula to make even and level.

Transfer to the refrigerator and chill several hours or until the cream sets. Remove the paper collar and fix the edges if they need it.

You may freeze the dessert and serve it a week or two later. Freeze uncovered until firm, then wrap well in plastic.

THE FINAL DECORATION Defrost the dessert in the refrigerator for half a day (even though the cake tastes good frozen). Cut into twenty-five squares, then place on an attractive serving platter. Beat:

> ½ cup whipping cream (1 dL) plus the
> remaining ¼ cup (½ dL) from the recipe

When the cream is starting to thicken, add:

> 1½ Tbs. powdered sugar (optional)

Beat until stiff. Reserve in the refrigerator. One or 2 hours before serving, beat the cream to bring it back together if necessary. Using a pastry bag with a decorative tip (I like a large, odd tip—Ateco 8-B), pipe a nice rosette of cream onto the center of each square. Keep chilled until serving time.

"LE GORRI" RASPBERRY SLICES

Makes 100 slices

For Christmas dinner the year I was finishing this book, I served four of the cakes that I was practicing for this buffet section. I was able to serve all four because all had been made ahead and frozen. I arranged the cake slices and squares each in a paper case, in pretty rows on a platter, and held a cake tasting. Each person sampled all and rated them. The Raspberry Slices were the overwhelming and unanimous choice for first place. They are indeed marvelous-tasting and elegant little cakes.

The combination of ingredients comes from the Andrieu family, with whom I spent a month at their pastry shop in Bayonne. They called this cake Le Gorri, the Basque word for red. It was their big specialty, often made into large wedding cakes.

Wedding cakes are something I rarely do, but many years later I too made this cake for a wedding reception, for actor Henry Winkler. When close to the peak of his fame for the role of the Fonz in the television series "Happy Days," he married a Los Angeles lady named Stacy. Her charming parents, Ed and Belvy Furstman, engaged me to make the cake for the wedding reception. Why did they ask me, in San Francisco, to make the cake for a Los Angeles reception? Well, they had tasted my raspberry cake at a reception for the daughter of Sally Bace, a long-time, faithful student of mine from Palo Alto. I had done the cake for Sally (my first wedding cake, I believe) because she is a great lady who has been very nice to me over the years.

Now we will depart from this not-very-exciting tale, leaving you with the vision of me, a not-very-experienced large-cake maker, climbing on a plane for Los Angeles, lugging two suitcases filled with frozen cake layers, rolls of marzipan, tools, pastry bags, a bottle of framboise, and a 5-gallon tub of raspberry buttercream. I assembled the cake down there.

3 cups cake flour (300 grams)

8 large eggs (1 lb. or 450 grams in shell)

2½ sticks of butter (285 grams or 10 oz.) at room temperature

1½ cups sugar (300 grams)

1 can (16 oz. or 450 grams) red raspberries in heavy syrup

4 Tbs. powdered sugar

2 to 3 Tbs. framboise (raspberry brandy), kirsch, or Grand Marnier (optional)

3 sticks butter (12 oz. or 340 grams) at body temperature

1 can (16 oz. or 450 grams) red raspberries in heavy syrup

¾ cup powdered sugar (75 grams)

3 to 4 Tbs. framboise, kirsch, or Grand Marnier (optional)

7 oz. marzipan or almond paste (200 grams) (optional)

THE CAKE This is similar to pound cake but contains ⅓ more eggs, which make the texture a shade lighter and a little spongier.

Preheat the oven to 350°F/180°C. Arrange an oven shelf so the cake will bake in the center. Liberally butter a baking tin about 9 × 13 × 2 inches (23 × 33 × 5 cm) measured at the top rim. Flour well, dump out the excess, and bang the pan upside down to knock out more. Sift, then measure:

   3 cups cake flour (300 grams)

Put the flour back in the sifter for use later. Take:

   8 large eggs (1 lb. or 450 grams in shell)

Put in a bowl, cover with very hot tap water, and let warm for 5 minutes or so. In another bowl place:

   2½ sticks butter (285 grams or 10 oz.) at room temperature

Beat with an electric mixer for 5 minutes or until fluffy, warming the butter now and then if necessary by putting the bowl over direct heat if it's metal or over hot water for just a few seconds. Just a trace of butter may melt, but be careful not to let more melt or you will have to start over with new butter. Add:

   1 cup sugar (200 grams)

Beat for 5 minutes.

Separate the warmed eggs, putting the whites in a clean bowl while adding the yolks, one at a time, to the butter-sugar mixture. Keep beating as you add the yolks.

With clean beaters, beat the 8 egg whites for a minute or until they form soft peaks. Add, 1 tablespoon at a time:

   ½ cup more sugar (100 grams)

Sprinkle each tablespoon of sugar over the whites and beat for 3 or 4 seconds before adding more. Move along fairly quickly, not taking too long to get all the sugar in. Continue to beat the whites for another 2 minutes or until they stay in the bowl when it is turned upside down. Do not overbeat.

You are now ready to fold the whites into the butter-yolk mixture. You must move along quickly.

Have a large rubber spatula for folding and a wire whisk for fluffing up the whites.

First sift one-third of the reserved cake flour over the butter mixture. Then beat the whites for 1 or 2 seconds or until creamy again and put one-third of them on top of the flour over the batter. Turning the bowl with your left hand, fold quickly but carefully, by cutting down into the center of the mixture with the spatula, drawing it across the bottom of the bowl, and coming up the side with a kind of twist of the wrist.

Sift over half of the remaining flour; give the whites a 2-second beat to make sure they are still creamy, add half of them, and fold again. Finally, sift over the last of the flour and fluff up and add the last of the whites. Fold thoroughly, but not one stroke more than you need to. Dump the batter into the prepared tin, push out to the corners, and level as best you can.

Bake in the preheated 350°F/180°C oven for 35 minutes or until nicely browned but not too dark. When done, there will be a faint bit of shrinkage from the sides of the pan. Let cool in the pan on a rack for 5 minutes. Then turn out onto a rack and invert onto another rack so the cake is right side up. Allow to cool completely. The cake will be about 2 inches (5 cm) high.

Cut in half to make two pieces about 6 × 8 inches (15 × 20 cm), then wrap in plastic. The cake will keep well in the room for three or four days. Freeze it for keeping longer. I generally assemble the cake the day after baking and freeze it ready to cut and serve.

THE RASPBERRIES Raspberries are used in this recipe three ways: in a soaking syrup that moistens the cake layers, in a buttercream used for the filling and topping, and whole between the bottom layers.

My recipe uses canned berries because they are the most convenient, the most readily available all year, and the most economical unless you happen to have a raspberry patch in your backyard. The canned berries may not be the closest thing to the fresh product that old Mother Nature gave us, but they work perfectly well and make a delicious cake. You will need two 16-oz. (450-gram) cans for the whole cake.

If you prefer frozen berries or are lucky enough to be able to get fresh ones, see the notes at the end of the recipe for quantities and adjustments in the techniques that have to be made.

THE SOAKING SYRUP Use:

> 1 can (16 oz. or 450 grams) red raspberries in heavy syrup

Drain the juices into a small bowl; you should have about 1 cup (¼ L). Reserve whole berries to fill the cake later. The juices will be somewhat tart, so add:

> 4 Tbs. powdered sugar
> 2 to 3 Tbs. framboise (raspberry brandy), kirsch, or Grand Marnier (optional)

Stir or whisk well to dissolve the sugar. Reserve.

THE BUTTERCREAM This is very quick and easy. A complicated buttercream would not make this cake taste any better. Have:

> 3 sticks butter (12 oz. or 340 grams) at body temperature

Beat with an electric mixer for 5 minutes or until very creamy. If necessary to soften the butter, heat the bowl for a few seconds over direct heat if the bowl is metal or over warm water. Be careful. Don't let the bowl get any hotter than your hand can stand or too much butter will melt and you'll have to start all over. It is all right if a tiny bit melts. Have:

> 1 can (16 oz. or 450 grams) red raspberries in heavy syrup

Pour into a strainer over a bowl. Work the berries with a rubber spatula so the fruit puree is extracted and just the seeds remain. Get as much of the good stuff separated as possible and scrape all the puree from the bottom of the strainer.

Both the juice and the puree should be at body temperature so they will not stiffen the butter when added to it. So, if necessary, warm them just enough to remove the chill.

Slowly add the juices mixed with puree to the beaten butter, beating in to incorporate while keeping the buttercream soft and fluffy. Then beat in:

> ¾ cup powdered sugar (75 grams)
> 3 to 4 Tbs. framboise, kirsch, or Grand Marnier (optional)

Reserve.

TO ASSEMBLE THE CAKE If you have not already cut the cake into two pieces, do so now. Each piece will be assembled as a separate cake because two smaller cakes are easier to cut and to handle.

Therefore, divide the buttercream, soaking syrup, and reserved drained whole raspberries in half. Also have:

> 7 oz. marzipan or almond paste (200 grams) (optional)

You will barely taste this, but it does make the cake more interesting. Also divide the marzipan in half. Push each half onto a sheet of waxed paper to form a rectangle. Cover with another sheet of waxed paper and roll into a 6 × 8-inch (15 × 20-cm) sheet. Reserve.

If necessary to make level, cut off the top center of the cake halves. Cut each half sideways into three layers, keeping them as even as possible. You may find it easier to stand the cake up on edge to do this. (On the other hand, you may not.) To assemble the cake, proceed as follows:

For easier transferring later, place the bottom layer on a baking sheet. Brush it with some of the soaking syrup, enough to cover it well. Poke all over with a toothpick if necessary to make the syrup soak in. Spread a ⅛-inch (½-cm) layer of buttercream over this bottom layer. If necessary, warm and beat the buttercream with a wooden spoon until smooth and spreadable. Place half the reserved whole raspberries on the buttercream. Use a fork to spread evenly, then mash a bit to flatten and to push into the buttercream.

Add the middle cake layer. Brush the soaking syrup over and poke with a toothpick to make it soak in. Cover the middle layer with a ⅛-inch layer of buttercream. Peel the waxed paper from the marzipan and lay on the buttercream. Then spread a thin layer of buttercream over the marzipan.

Turn the top layer of cake upside down so the cut side is up. Brush the cut side with soaking syrup and poke with a toothpick. Place the soaked side down on top of the assembled layers by inverting.

Push down on the cake with a cutting board or other firm, even object. Use straight pressure downward to level the cake. Don't worry about the messy sides, which will be trimmed off later.

Warm and beat the remaining buttercream for this cake half to make sure that it is very soft and smooth. Spread over the top of the cake and smooth with a knife or spatula until level. Don't fuss too much because neatness barely shows after the slices are cut.

Assemble the other cake half by the same procedures. Refrigerate both cakes until firm, wrap well in plastic, and freeze.

TO CUT AND SERVE The slices look most attractive in white paper candy cases, which often can be found in cake-decorating shops. Try to find crinkle cups with flat bottoms measuring 1½ inches (4 cm) in diameter. Before you put a cake slice in, you will flatten two opposite sides a bit with your fingers so the slice will fit in very neatly.

You can cut the cakes while still frozen if you like. First trim off the sides so they are neat. Next cut strips 1¼ inches (3 cm) wide. Cut these crosswise at ½-inch (1½-cm) intervals. Since the cake is about 2 inches (5 cm) thick, you should be able to cut about 100 slices ½ × 1¼ × 2 inches (1½ × 3 × 5 cm).

Lay the slices in the paper cases or arrange slightly overlapping on a cake plate or platter. They will stay neat enough to be handled with fingers if they don't get too warm. So cover with plastic and refrigerate until the last possible minute. I think they taste better slightly chilled. They can sit on a buffet table and stay nice if it is not the middle of summer or if the room is not hot as blazes.

These Raspberry Slices may be a little bit of work, but they will be well worth it when you start reaping the compliments.

TO USE FROZEN BERRIES Buy three packages or bags, 10 to 12 ounces (285 to 340 grams) *each*, of raspberries in syrup or simply sugared—in syrup preferred. Thaw, then drain off and save any juices. Combine the berries from the three packages, then divide in half. Now you can proceed the same way as if you were using canned berries.

If you do not get a total of 2 cups (½ L) juice (1 cup to use for the soaking syrup and 1 cup for the buttercream), make up the lack with a syrup of half sugar and half water. For example, if you are short

1 cup (¼ L) of juice, take ½ cup (100 grams) sugar and ½ cup (1 dL) water, bring to a boil while stirring to dissolve the sugar, let cool, and add to the juices. If there is not enough raspberry flavor or color, steal 1 to 2 tablespoons raspberry puree after you make it by following the regular recipe and add to the juices. Taste and sweeten with powdered sugar if necessary.

TO USE FRESH RASPBERRIES Buy 1½ pints berries (probably three boxes). Use one box, or about 1¼ cups whole, on the bottom layer. Push the remaining berries through a strainer. Make a syrup by heating 1 cup (200 grams) sugar and 1 cup (¼ L) water, stirring until the sugar is dissolved; cool. Measure 1 cup of syrup and add 2 to 3 tablespoons of strained puree to give good flavor and color; this will be the soaking syrup.

Add the balance of the syrup to the raspberry puree to make the mixture that goes into the buttercream. You may have to make adjustments for sweetness by adding powdered sugar. Neither the soaking syrup nor the buttercream should be too sweet, but just a tangy balance of sweet and sour.

Now that you have the three raspberry variations, proceed with the regular recipe.

TANGERINE CHEESECAKE SQUARES

Makes 48 squares

These are elegant, classy cheesecake squares with an unusual, refreshing, and colorful tangerine topping. The little squares are especially nice around Christmastime when tangerines make their seasonal appearance. If you make this dessert at another time of the year, substitute oranges, but cut the orange sections out of their membranes, which are tougher than those on tangerines.

You will be happy to learn that the pastry base for this cheesecake is not the ubiquitous graham cracker crust. You can use that crust if you insist. Frankly, I am not too crazy about it. In the first place, it has been done to death, and in the second, it tastes too much like graham crackers and therefore terribly store-bought.

The crust in this recipe is a conservative and good one. It is called pâte brisée *by the French,* mürbteig *by the Germans, and sugar cookie dough by us Americans. The classic weight proportion of sugar to butter to flour is 1:2:3. However, in this recipe, the butter has been increased to the same weight as that of the flour; so the proportion is 1:3:3. The dough is easily made in the food processor, then rolled between waxed paper or just pressed into the bottom of the tin. Dough with this much butter is difficult to work any other way.*

The cake is made of cream cheese instead of a curd-type cheese such as cottage cheese or farmer's cheese. Cheesecake snobs tend to look down their noses at cheesecakes made with cream cheese, even though this is a perfectly respectable cheese. I think the cream cheese hucksters, by adding vegetable gum and by enclosing the stuff in tidy silver wrappings, have made this lovely cheese far too popular. Elegant folks won't touch anything so popular and easy to find. However, judge for yourself how significant the difference is between the easy-to-find type and what you can buy in a cheese store. The latter is so soft, lovely, and fresh that it must deserve just as much consideration as the curd types when it comes to making cheesecake.

1½ cups flour (180 grams)
1½ sticks chilled butter (6 oz. or 180 grams) cut into ½-inch (1½-cm) cubes
⅓ cup sugar (65 grams)
2 egg yolks
2 lbs. cream cheese (900 grams)
4 eggs, slightly warmed
1¾ cups sugar (350 grams)
Zest of 1 lemon
2 Tbs. lemon juice
1 tsp. vanilla
2 lbs. tangerines (900 grams)
2 Tbs. reserved tangerine juice
1 envelope plain gelatin (2 rounded tsp.)
Sugar (1 to 4 Tbs. or none)
Lemon juice (1 tsp. to 1 Tbs. or none)

THE PASTRY BASE Preheat the oven to 350°F/180°C and arrange a shelf so the crust will bake in the center of the oven. Butter a 9 × 13 × 2-inch (23 × 33 × 5-cm) baking pan. The butter will hold down the paper pan liner. Cut out a piece of baking parchment or brown paper about 12 × 15 inches (30 × 38½ cm). Push the paper down into the pan so that the bottom is covered and the paper goes up two of the sides, leaving a couple of flaps hanging out. You will use these flaps to remove the cheesecake later.

To make the dough, place in the container of a food processor:

  1½ cups flour (180 grams)
  1½ sticks chilled butter (6 oz. or 180 grams), cut into ½-inch (1½-cm) cubes
  ⅓ cup sugar (65 grams)

Process for 10 to 15 seconds or until the butter lumps are more or less gone. Add:

  2 egg yolks

Process for 30 seconds or until the dough comes together in at least three or four pieces. Take clumps of the dough and flatten out in your hands to ¼-inch (¾-cm)-thick sheets. Lay in the bottom of the pan and continue until all the dough, arranged patchwork style, more or less covers the bottom. Using a floured thumb, work the pieces to make them come together to cover the bottom completely. Next place a sheet of waxed paper over the bottom and smooth out the dough using some flat, smooth object. I use the bottom of a metal measuring cup. When dough is nicely smoothed, peel off the waxed paper.

Chill the dough in the pan for 20 minutes (optional). Bake in the preheated 350°F/180°C oven for 25 to 30 minutes or until lightly colored. Cool in the pan on a rack.

ABOUT THE CHEESE FILLING The ingredients for this filling and their proportions are based on a cheesecake made popular by Craig Claiborne a few years ago. For a cream-cheese cheesecake filling, I have finally given up trying to improve on this combination.

MAKING THE CHEESE FILLING If the cream cheese and the eggs are refrigerated and cold, leave the cream cheese in its foil wrapping and the eggs in their shells, place in bowls, and cover with very hot tap water. If you are using fresh cream cheese, wrap it airtight (watertight, actually) in foil, then cover with hot tap water. Let warm for 5 to 10 minutes. Preheat the oven to 325°F/165°C.

Into the container of a food processor, put the slightly warm:

2 lbs. cream cheese (900 grams)

Process for 4 or 5 seconds or until smooth and lump free. Add:

4 eggs, slightly warmed
1¾ cups sugar (350 grams)

Process, using four or five pulsing on-and-off motions, then add:

Zest of 1 lemon
2 Tbs. lemon juice
1 tsp. vanilla

Process for 1 or 2 seconds or until blended and smooth. Do not overmix. Pour the batter onto the cool baked crust.

Bake the cheesecake in the preheated 325°F/165°C oven for 40 minutes or until it has puffed up in an area 1 or 2 inches (2½ to 5 cm) around the edges. Turn off the heat and let the cake sit 20 minutes in the oven.

Remove and allow to cool on a rack for 2 to 3 hours. Refrigerate uncovered until chilled through, then proceed with the tangerine topping; or, cover cake, refrigerate overnight, and add the topping the following day.

THE TANGERINE TOPPING Have:

2 lbs. tangerines (900 grams)

Choose the larger ones so you don't have so many to deal with. Peel, separate into segments, and pull or scrape off the white strings. I use a knife for this, and it's a boring job. Using a sharp knife, cut off a ⅛-inch (½-cm) strip of the membrane at the center of each segment; removing this gets rid of the part that is too tough to be eaten. It also opens the segments so you can push any seeds out. Cut the sections across into ⅛-inch slices, then chop the pulp finer if you like. Save the juices that accumulate. For the topping you need 2 cups (½ L) of tangerine pulp.

Into a saucer put:

2 Tbs. reserved tangerine juice

1 envelope plain gelatin (2 rounded tsp.)

Wet the gelatin in the juice and let soften for 1 minute. Pour any more juice accumulated from cutting the tangerines into a ½-cup (1-dL) measuring cup and add enough tangerine pulp from the prepared 2 cups to fill the cup. Pour this ½ cup pulp and juice in a small saucepan. Add to it the softened gelatin plus:

Sugar (1 to 4 Tbs. or none)

Lemon juice (1 tsp. to 1 Tbs. or none)

You are on your own for deciding the amounts of sugar and lemon juice to add. Taste the tangerine pulp and decide. If the pulp is vibrant with quality and character, don't add either. If it is a little tart, add a little sugar. If it is dull, add both sugar and lemon juice. (At least the flavor of lemonade is better than no flavor at all.)

Heat the tangerine-gelatin mixture, stirring to dissolve the gelatin and any sugar added. Get it hot enough so you see steam start to rise, but do not allow to boil. Add to the rest of the tangerine pulp. Stir to mix.

Place the bowl of warm pulp over a bowl of ice with a little water in it. Stir with a rubber spatula until the pulp is very cold and the liquid has thickened somewhat. Dump the pulp onto the top of the chilled cheesecake. Spread even with a fork.

Refrigerate for 1 to 2 hours or until the topping has set. Slip a knife around the sides of the cake to free it from the pan, then lift out by the paper flaps. Cut the cake in half, into two 6×8-inch

(15 × 20-cm) pieces, for easier handling and wrap each in plastic. Refrigerate or freeze.

TO CUT AND SERVE If the cheesecake is frozen, cut into squares while still frozen. (The cake cuts easily, however, when simply chilled.) You should get forty-eight squares. To divide evenly, cut the 6-inch side of each cake half into four strips; then cut the 8-inch side into six strips; this gives you twenty-four not-quite-square pieces from each half.

Arrange on a serving platter with some space between the squares. Cover with plastic. Allow about 2 hours at room temperature for frozen cake to defrost. Keep unfrozen cake refrigerated if not serving for a while. *Note:* These are nice served in fluted square paper bakery cups if you can find them.

PECAN SPICE CAKE SQUARES

Makes 40 to 50 squares

These little squares of a Viennese-type nut torte are unusually good. The dense and moist cake, made mostly of ground pecans and eggs, contains almost no flour and is flavored with cinnamon. As it bakes and cools, it fills the air with one of the all-time great kitchen aromas.

Although this cake can be made at almost any time of year, it is especially nice in the fall when the new crop of pecans appears. It is especially appropriate for winter holiday buffets.

The cake itself is so good that you can simply sprinkle it with powdered sugar and serve as is or with some sweetened whipped cream on the side. If you want to take more time to make elegant petits fours, finish the little squares with brown-sugar buttercream and the caramelized pecan halves suggested at the end of this recipe.

---

10 oz. pecans (about 2½ cups or 285 grams)
¼ cup flour (30 grams)
½ tsp. cinnamon
Grated zest of 1 lemon (optional)
8 eggs

THE CAKE Preheat the oven to 350°F/180°C and arrange a shelf so the cake will bake in the center of the oven. Liberally butter a baking pan approximately 9 × 13 × 2 inches (23 × 33 × 5 cm). Flour well, then dump out the excess and bang tin upside down to get rid of a little more flour. Into the container of a food processor put:

10 oz. pecans (about 2½ cups or 285 grams)

1 cup sugar (200 grams)
1 tsp. vanilla
Powdered sugar
3 cups (¾ L) whipping cream (3 half-pint cartons)
¾ cup sifted powdered sugar (75 grams)
1 Tbs. vanilla
1 tsp. cinnamon (optional)
½ cup packed-down dark brown sugar (100 grams)
3 Tbs. water
4 Tbs. whipping cream or milk
2 sticks butter (½ lb. or 225 grams) at room temperature
1 tsp. vanilla
½ tsp. cinnamon
½ cup pecans, chopped into ⅛-inch dice (2 oz. or 60 grams)
¼ cup (50 grams) and 1 tsp. sugar
50 perfect (or almost perfect) pecan halves (about 3 oz. or 85 grams)
2 Tbs. water

¼ cup flour (30 grams)
½ tsp. cinnamon
Grated zest of 1 lemon (optional)

Process for about 25 seconds or until the nuts are ground fairly fine. Reserve. Use:

8 eggs

If they are cold, warm for a few minutes by pouring very hot tap water over them (still in their shells, of course) in a bowl and letting them sit for 3 or 4 minutes. Separate the eggs, putting the yolks in a fairly large bowl where you will assemble the cake batter and the whites in a smaller bowl. To the large bowl with the yolks add:

½ cup sugar (100 grams)
1 tsp. vanilla

Beat right away with an electric mixer for 1 or 2 minutes or until pale and thick. (Use the top speed on a small hand mixer but medium speed on one of the large, powerful mixers on a stand.) Do not overbeat. With clean beaters, beat the egg whites at the same speed you beat the yolks for about 30 seconds or until they increase in volume and just barely make soft peaks. Sprinkle over, 1 tablespoon at a time:

½ cup sugar (100 grams)

Add the sugar rather quickly and beat only 3 or 4 seconds between additions. When all the sugar is in, beat another 2 minutes or until fairly stiff, but don't overbeat. The whites should be stiff enough to stay in the bowl if it were turned upside down.

Have ready a large rubber spatula for folding. Add one-third of the reserved nut mixture to the yolks and over that put about one-third of the beaten whites. Fold quickly but carefully; turn the bowl with one hand and with the other cut down into the center of the mixture, drawing the spatula across the bottom of the bowl and coming up the side with a twist of the wrist and forearm.

Give the whites a 1- or 2-second beat, then add another third of the nut mixture and one-third of the whites to the yolk batter; fold again. Repeat the process for the last of the nuts and whites.

Dump the batter into the prepared pan and level as best you can. Bake in the preheated 350°F/180°C oven for 30 minutes or until nicely browned and just barely beginning to shrink away from the sides of the pan. Remove the cake and cool, still in the pan, on a rack for about 10 minutes. The cake will settle and shrink to about 1½ inches (4 cm) high—just what you want.

Turn the cake out onto a rack, then turn over onto another rack so it is right side up. Let finish cooling. Five or 6 hours later, cut the cake into halves about 5½ × 7½ inches (14 × 19 cm) to make it easier to handle. Put in plastic bags and leave in the room overnight, even two or three days. The cake will stay moist because of all the nuts it contains. For keeping even longer, it can be frozen.

TO SERVE PLAIN OR WITH SWEETENED WHIPPED CREAM Sprinkle or sift:

Powdered sugar

over the cake halves, using a strainer or sifter. Cut each half into twenty squares by cutting five strips the 7½-inch (19-cm) way, then making four strips the 5½-inch (14-cm) way. You'll get a total of forty squares about 1¼ × 1½ inches (3½ × 4 cm) each. Arrange on a serving platter, in baker's fluted paper cases if you can find any.

On the side it is nice to serve a bowl of whipped cream. It's impossible to guess how much cream people are going to take, so the following amount may be more than you need. It's a safe amount, however. You don't want to run out. Beat:

3 cups (¾ L) whipping cream (3 half-pint cartons)

until starting to set. Add:

¾ cup sifted powdered sugar (75 grams)

1 Tbs. vanilla

1 tsp. cinnamon (optional)

Beat just 20 to 30 seconds more or until the cream is softly set. It should be stiff enough to stay put on the cake but still soft and wet enough to sort of flow and taste good. Pile the cream in a pretty bowl and place near the cake. You may have to tell people how it's meant to be used.

The cream can be whipped in the morning and refrigerated. If at serving time it has drooped a bit, give it another beating and it will rise again.

BROWN-SUGAR BUTTERCREAM For a prettier, more professional look, try this fairly easy icing. (You will spread it on the two cake halves *before* cutting into squares.)

Into a small saucepan put:

½ cup packed-down dark brown sugar (100 grams)

3 Tbs. water

Bring to a boil, stirring to dissolve the sugar. Allow to come to a full boil, remove from the heat, and stir until the sugar is completely dissolved. Return to the heat and bring back to a full boil. Boil for 1 minute. Remove from the heat, then add:

2 Tbs. whipping cream or milk

Cool to room temperature, hurrying this along by stirring over ice water if you like. Meanwhile have:

2 sticks butter (½ lb. or 225 grams) at room temperature

Beat the butter with an electric mixer until really fluffy. If necessary, warm slightly with some 5-second shots over direct heat or over hot water, but be careful not to heat so much that the whole thing melts. When nice and fluffy, beat in the cooled brown-sugar syrup plus:

1 tsp. vanilla

2 Tbs. whipping cream or milk

½ tsp. cinnamon

Beat. If the buttercream looks curdled and is not beautifully smooth, heat slightly and beat again. It will smooth out. Set aside ¼ cup (½ dL) of the buttercream to be used as "glue" for attaching the caramelized pecans. Divide the balance into two equal portions. Into one portion mix:

½ cup pecans, chopped into ⅛-inch dice (2 oz. or 60 grams)

Slice each of the two cake pieces in half to make two layers of each. Spread half the buttercream with pecans on each bottom layer, then place the top layers back on. Ice the tops with the smooth buttercream, keeping the sides plain. They will be left as is. Using a knife or spatula, smooth the tops as well as you can.

Using the non-cutting edge of a knife, make guidelines on the iced tops of the cakes where you are going to cut them later. You should mark off twenty-four squares (about 1¼-inch [3½ cm] square) on each cake piece—a total of forty-eight on both pieces.

Put the reserved ¼ cup buttercream in a pastry bag fitted with a small star tip. (Ateco 1-B is fine, or a small plain round tip will do.) Don't get all nervous about the pastry-bag business. The buttercream isn't going to show. Just squeeze a small blob or rosette of it in the center of each of the forty-eight cake squares. On the day you serve these, you will press a caramelized pecan half onto each little blob so the nut will stay in place.

Refrigerate the cakes until the buttercream is firm, then place in plastic. If you plan to serve them in a day or two, refrigerate the cakes. Otherwise, freeze them.

CARAMELIZED PECANS If you are the type who flies into a panic when cooking gets a little tricky, don't make these. They are a little tricky. I don't want to discourage you, though, because they are quick to make and not that difficult if you will just keep your cool while working with the hot syrup.

Get everything ready and organized. Lightly oil a baking sheet. Oil the tines of two dinner forks. Have on the side, ready to use:

1 tsp. sugar

You may want to put on a pair of rubber gloves to help keep from caramelizing your fingers. Look around for a heavy aluminum pot with a 7- or 8-inch (18- or 20-cm)-diameter bottom. I have an old pressure cooker that works perfectly. A larger or smaller pan will do, but don't use a black-iron frying pan because you won't be able to see the color of the caramel. Also get ready:

50 perfect (or almost perfect) pecan halves
    (about 3 oz. or 85 grams)

This is more than you will need, but some will break and others will get sampled by the cook.

Into the heavy pot put:

¼ cup sugar (50 grams)
2 Tbs. water

Stir to wet all the sugar. Bring to a good boil, remove from the heat, and stir to help dissolve the sugar. From this point on, do not stir anymore until the nuts are added. Cook the sugar syrup over high heat until you begin to see it turn yellow. It will develop spots of yellow color. You can tilt the pan to mix the syrup.

Sprinkle in half the pecans, then change the heat to low. Let the nuts warm 10 to 15 seconds, then stir them into the syrup. This is the point where you are likely to panic because the nuts will have cooled off the syrup and now will want to clump together. Don't worry about this for the moment. Just move the nuts to the side of the pan and sprinkle in the rest of the pecans. Let them warm for 10 to 15 seconds on low heat. Then stir a bit, trying to spread all the nuts out and to flatten out the clumps. As everything warms up, the nuts will begin to unstick. At this point sprinkle with half of the teaspoon of sugar you prepared ahead. Try to distribute the sugar over all the nuts. Stir again.

Now move quickly. The syrup will be getting darker, and you don't want it to burn. The nuts should be separating better, so you can stir them around and get each coated with syrup. Sprinkle with the remaining sugar (½ teaspoon) and stir again.

Quickly scrape the nuts out onto the oiled baking sheet. Pick up the two oiled forks and use them to separate the nuts on the sheet. When you have them pretty well separated and they have cooled a bit, you can finish the separating process by hand. This is where the rubber gloves come in handy. Work quickly. Don't hold the hot nuts too long or they may burn you, even through the rubber gloves. When all are separated, let cool completely.

TO STORE THE CARAMELIZED PECANS Put in plastic bags. Even though the nuts are a little sticky, they will hold up pretty well without the caramel turning wet, even out in the air. The undissolved sugar that you sprinkle on at the end of the cooking makes the caramel more stable.

TO CUT AND DECORATE THE ICED CAKE SQUARES Cut the two iced cakes into twenty squares each, for a total of forty squares, using the guidelines you marked in the buttercream on top. (Frozen cakes are easier to cut while still frozen.) Press a caramelized pecan onto each blob of buttercream to "glue" the nuts firmly in their decorative places.

Index